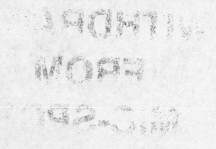

The Boss

THE LIFE AND TIMES OF THE
BRITISH BUSINESS MAN

BY ROY LEWIS AND ANGUS MAUDE

The English Middle Classes
Professional People

The Boss

THE LIFE AND TIMES OF THE
BRITISH BUSINESS MAN

Roy Lewis

AND

Rosemary Stewart

REVISED (1961) EDITION

PHOENIX HOUSE
LONDON

© ROY LEWIS AND ROSEMARY STEWART 1958

Printed by Lowe & Brydone (Printers) Ltd
London
for Phoenix House Ltd, 10-13 Bedford Street
Strand, London

FIRST PUBLISHED 1958
REVISED AND ENLARGED EDITION 1961

CONTENTS

The Boss

'*This is the true philanthropy. He who makes a colossal fortune in the hosiery trade, and by his energy has succeeded in reducing the price of woollen goods by the thousandth part of a penny in the pound—this man is worth ten professional philanthropists. So strongly are the Erewhonians impressed with this, that if a man has made a fortune of over £20,000 a year they exempt him from all taxation, considering him as a work of art, and too precious to be meddled with; they say, "How very much he must have done for society before society could have been prevailed upon to give him so much money"; so magnificent an organization overawes them; they regard it as a thing dropped from heaven. "Money," they say "is the symbol of duty; it is the sacrament of having done for mankind that which mankind wanted. Mankind may not be a very good judge, but there is no better."*'

CHAPTER I
Under the Top Hat

'So shall they be sorely pained at the report of Tyre . . . whose merchants are princes, whose traffickers are the honourable of the earth.'

ISAIAH, xxiii, 5, 8

'Studies of boss-mentality are still more meagre. We tend to think of him in terms of popular opposites. At one moment he is a pantomime ogre in the wings, at another a philanthropic eccentric in the manner of Robert Owen and Jan Bata. As a harassed official whose play has turned sour on him, torn between the implementation of a government policy designed to procure disinflation, the wage claims of workers whom, so far, inflation has suited very well, the rights of shareholders and his professional conscience as the exponent of organisational holders and his professional conscience as the exponent of organisational technique, he is lost sight of at the point where he disappears into hospital with a duodenal ulcer!'

THE EARL OF HALSBURY*

THE RESULT of the British General Election of October 1959 was profoundly satisfactory to British business men. It was the third successive defeat of the Labour Party, and, on this occasion, it was a rebuff to the socialist doctrines of that party in particular. For the future of big business was an issue in the campaign. The steel companies had carried out a poll which showed that the public was not interested in renationalisation. The Labour Party in its manifesto attacked:

> 'The business man with a tax free expense account, the speculator with tax free capital gains, and the retiring company director with a tax free redundancy payment due to a take-over bid—these people never had it so good.'[1]

Implicit in the Labour programme was some form of social control over, or state shareholdings in, 520 of the largest enterprises in the country. Labour speakers assailed the Institute of Directors for bringing out a counter-attack on these proposals entitled 'Mind Your Own

* 'Integrating Social with Technological Change', *Impact*, March, 1957.

11

Business'. The Conservatives, on the other hand, extolled private enterprise. And the country voted firmly for business.

But did it? Certainly Conservatives won an increased majority, but for many reasons. One of them was the general prosperity of the country, another was the disarray of the Labour Party over so many other issues. In fact, the particular issue of business had been settled over a far longer period than one election. Since 1945, the question of how much freedom business men are to have had been hammered out by the nation. Business men are not to be abolished, as at one time seemed possible. After experimenting with nationalisation, the Labour Party and most trade unions have agreed that it has strict limits in its classical form.[2] Even in 1959, it was made quite clear that in the socialist, egalitarian Britain which Labour stood for, there would be an important role for private enterprise; there would be a 'private sector' reserved for the activities of business men, even for the capitalists and financiers who used to be conventionally portrayed by left-wing cartoonists with distended stomachs and elongated toppers. The only question was whether the more radical wing in the Labour Party would win the day. It did not, and the election sparked off, for the unfortunate Labour Party, the acrimonious internal debate on the amendment of the basic canon in its constitution which calls for the nationalization of the means of production, distribution and exchange. Only the fundamentalists of the Party take it seriously; the sole question is whether, like the first passages of the Book of Genesis, it should be regarded as pure myth, or of symbolic significance.

The defeats of the Labour Party, and still more important, the growing public indifference to the literal interpretation of the socialist bible, has not meant that business men or methods have been taken out of politics. Even the Conservatives have made it clear that business men must turn over a new leaf if they are to be defended. Young Tories are not content to draw up 'industrial charters'[3] when in opposition and to forget them when in power. They showed their determination to enforce reform by passing, in the teeth of considerable opposition from the Federation of British Industries and the National Union of Manufacturers, the Monopolies and Restrictive Practices Act, 1956. But this was by no means an isolated example of the way in which the Tories are capable of snatching the garments of their Socialist opponents. The great election argument about expense accounts and business men's perks did not end with the Tory victory. At the very next Tory budget, the Chancellor of the Exchequer introduced regulations to tax the very 'golden handshakes' which Labour politicians had attacked on the hustings, to stop the offsetting of genuine profits by fictitious losses on farms, and to give the Inland Revenue (in the words of *The Director*) 'arbitrary power over any stock and share transaction which has a tax consequence'—such as 'bondwashing' and 'dividend stripping'. Immediately after the election, the business men had rejoiced that 'Labour must now accept ungrudgingly the basis of society that the nation has now endorsed'[4] (i.e. one with steel and road transport in the hands of private firms), but these provisions in the 1960 budget produced a strong protest and a campaign to defeat them in the Finance Bill stage;[5] the new government's vigorous inter-ference in the affairs of the aircraft industry came as another shock.[6]

Both political parties are committed to raising the British standard of living rapidly: it is this, however achieved, which decides elections. The Tories have decided that even if this policy of enriching the country could be most easily achieved by allowing business men to combine or compete as seemed to them best, it is not practical policy; nor is it practicable to let business men enlarge their incentives in ways not approved by the Treasury or countenanced by a society which is in-dulgent to the lucky pools winner but is easily roused against a moneyed class. The Tories took a good, shrewd, hard look at the business classes, after their defeat in 1945, and decided that private enterprise as it used to be cannot be preserved by the Big Business Party.

The Socialists on the other hand, after wrestling with their strong distaste for the acquisitive instinct in mankind, have finally decided that there is something in private enterprise which, even in the process of putting over socialist policies, they cannot do without. Some Social-ists have indeed conceded the point that if the State owned everything, and was everybody's employer, personal freedom would be endangered and that to give at any rate a proportion of the population a minimum of opportunity to change employers, some sort of 'private sector' ought to be preserved; and they have admitted that the right to set up on one's own to make a living by trade should be retained (though with ever increasing requirements of training and licensing) even if that means retaining some capitalism too.

It looks as if an informal bargain has been struck. Provided the busi-ness man becomes more efficient and more enterprising, provided he accepts greater accountability for his actions (or omissions) to the government, and submits to further curtailments of his privileges and perquisites; provided, too, full (if not always brimfull) employment

13

continues, he is to be allowed a certain if as yet not fully defined field of endeavour and—though this is vaguer on the left—a measure of security for his achievements. Where the lines will be drawn, in what proportions this mixed economy will be mixed, is still unsettled.

It is true that the Tories hope to stamp out socialism completely, and the Labour Party in the year that followed the 1959 election has revealed a notable death wish; but one party rule is not yet assured in Britain, still less that business men will run that party. For some years, perhaps, the business man can expect to go on much as at present; though he faces a world in which he is not allowed to operate rings or build up monopolies, in which he will be expected to keep the country safe for Tory Chancellors of the Exchequer by building up a huge export trade, and in which he may have to survive without imperial preferences in a European free trade area (or, worse still, as some business men were feeling in spring 1960, he may have to live off the vestiges of imperial preference without being in on the expansion and mergers and prosperity of the European common market). He has no certainty that, if he fails to keep Britain on top in a world of commercial giants, he may not face an incoming political opposition party ultimately—whether (by some miracle) socialist, labour, liberal or (quite possibly) neo-lib-lab—determined to make his days and nights still more strenuous, and quite capable of evolving new variants of 'guided capitalism' which he will not like at all. He will certainly be kept in reserve as a scapegoat if there is a slump, even if this is the responsibility of American capitalism.

The British business man has, in fact, been on trial; and he has been reprieved. Yet can he truly be said to have left the court without a stain on his character? He may think so; but would he not do better to regard himself as on probation a little longer? Now, in any case, is a good time for the judge—the British public—and the accused—the business man—to reflect on the implications of the prosecution by the Socialists; it has not ended in a gaol sentence yet, but the man who leaves the dock is very different from he who entered it some—perhaps 50—years ago. The public should now take a more objective look at the business man, consider what he is really like, and really for, in the context of Britain in the second half of the twentieth century, and should consider what are the implications of keeping him at liberty or on a loose rein. The business man ought to ask himself (over a glass of champagne) what led to the prosecution, and what changes in conduct and public deportment are necessary to keep him out of court in future.

This book is intended to make a small contribution to such a stock-taking—small because it attempts to do only one thing, to throw some light on what the business man is really like. He is the mainspring of the economic mechanism; his decisions make the wheels go round even if other people control the brake and accelerator. But business men not only make business decisions; they also form a class with great influence and considerable power, a class made up of members who possess particular traits of personality—particular interests, ideas, ambitions, drives and attitudes which differ, at least to some extent, from the rest of us. What are these ambitions and attitudes? How are they formed, and how are they satisfied? The business man influences the life of almost everybody, and the culture of the country at large. This he does not only by organizing the production of the things which make up the standard of life and pay the wages, salaries, dividends—and taxes; he also presides over the environment in which the majority of the nation spends its working hours; he largely creates the environment in which it spends its leisure too. The boss is of interest whether you are working for him, angling for promotion under him, aiming to become a boss like him or bigger than him, or wondering if there will be anything left on the bone when you get his office chair.

The business man, on the other hand, might be expected to be interested in what the public thinks of him. Is it enough to be efficient—filling the shop windows and the pay packets and being frightfully polite to the shop stewards? If not, why isn't it? What else is expected? If business men think there is no point in bothering with such questions, that their public relations are satisfactory, and that they have nothing to learn, then they are remarkably self-confident or else have espoused the view 'let us eat, drink and be merry on expense accounts, for tomorrow we shall be nationalized'. Either spiritual condition at this delicate moment in British national fortunes would be worth some attention.

1. BUSINESS MEN AND MANAGERS

There has never, of course, been any question about the future of *managers and management*. They are as necessary to nationalized industry and State-controlled corporations as to private businesses, other than the most primitive. The manager's functions do not change when the State buys a firm outright (like Cable & Wireless Ltd) or when it obtains a controlling interest in it (as the British government obtained a controlling interest in the British Petroleum Co., by acquiring just over 50 per cent of its voting shares). The manager's salary, promotion prospects and conditions of work might change under State ownership. Managers could conceivably become a wholly State-paid profession like the doctors; colliery managers already are one.[7] But under any industrial system, organizers are necessary; the managerial revolution is complete. Managerial prestige, too, is high and rising. Politically, it is thoroughly respectable to be a manager. Some workpeople thought that nationalization meant the end of *all* bosses—but they have now discovered how wrong they were. Nor have their socialist mentors any sympathy for them.

Criticisms of *managements* are like criticisms of regional hospital boards: they concern efficiency, which includes humanity: they do not suggest abolition. The public may often read complaints in the newspapers to the effect that British management is not good enough. But it cannot fail to read that efforts are being made to improve management, like any other profession such as medicine, architecture, or teaching. This gives a general impression which is reassuring and vaguely scientific. The Labour government first gave State support to training for management, and sought to increase the supply of managers for industry. It thought of managers as substitutes for business men; as tamed and civilized business men, whose acquisitive instincts had been sublimated. Professional management is now solidly established;[8] it has problems —technical ones as well as those of status, training, organization and pay—analogous to some other professions; it has, however, no past to live down, no apology to make. Its role in society, whether capitalistic, socialistic or mixed, is as settled as that of the civil service.

Business men are something different. They direct, they control, they decide policy, and they have power. They found, inherit, own, buy, sell, and expand businesses—and they may bankrupt them. They are the employers of the managers, as much as they are the employers of workpeople. They constitute the commercial oligarchy 'in possession' of the great industrial and commercial empires; just as they are the owners or part-owners of the smaller firms. They are the men at the top, the bosses in the proper sense, and the heirs to the masters of nineteenth-century industry. They are the bosses who are liquidated by nationalization, though they may become members of the new nationalized boards—sharing these top management posts with former managers and with trade unions (out of 47 full-time members of nationalized industry boards in 1951, 13 had been company directors against 10 who were managers by training, 4 civil servants and 9 trade union bosses).[9] Socialists like to think that the interests of business men as such and of professional managers often clash; certainly this may happen. They also sometimes contend that as management becomes professional and scientific in large business bureaucracies the business men on the board become like the shareholders useless excrescences, vestigial organs, at best useless, but when inflamed dangerous to health unless excised.[10] Recently a senior manager in a firm in a basic industry said to one of the authors, 'We are not concerned with the directors, as we are in the full flood of the managerial revolution.'

This distinction between the business man and manager is of central importance to this book and one to which, from different angles, we shall at intervals return; but we do not pretend that it is an easy one to make in practice. The difference between the salaried manager and the individual capitalist who owns the company of which he is chairman and managing director is clear enough. This type of business man still lingers with us; he would be readily recognized by Karl Marx as his beloved enemy, and by Professor Alfred Marshall, the great classical economist, as *his* beloved entrepreneur. But the men on the boards of the five hundred-odd firms in Britain which, according to the socialists, 'control' 50 per cent of the country's economy, hardly fall into this category at all. They may live by salary and a fair proportion have no capital worth mentioning—certainly the merest nest-egg compared with the capital of the companies they control. Yet if the small capitalist is a business man, they must be called business men too; there is no clear dividing line between big business, medium-sized business and small business; there is every grade of 'ownership' between the man who owns 100 per cent of the shares of the firm he directs, and the man who owns not even one per cent of the shares of the firm which pays him to direct it.[11] If it comes to a showdown, a man is not master of a firm unless he has 50½ per cent of the voting stock; but security of tenure can be very complete for the directors of a firm in which they have barely a share apiece. It takes a cataclysm—that is, a shareholders' revolt organized on a formidable scale—to unseat them. This can happen. When shareholders must be consulted, as the legal owners of a firm, about mergers or the selling of their property to a take-over bidder, they may show their legal power, which is almost invariably exercised in favour of their pockets. In lesser issues concerning their profits, shareholders are powerless to interfere. It did not, for example, avail Mrs Gladys Harvey to demand a higher dividend from Sir Ellis Hunter of Dorman Long when Sir Ellis was determined to plough back the profits. 'In whose interest is this blessed company being run?' she protested. 'We are the proprietors—and the Cinderellas, too.'[12] On a card vote, that is, using the proxies of the shareholders who did not attend, the directors had their way with 'their' company. Twenty per cent of a company's equity is sufficient in practice to ensure control, but much less often suffices.

This distinction between 'managers' and 'business men' will not appeal to those who say that 'policy' and 'execution' cannot be so rigidly separated in business life; that there can be no such functional division as that which finds expression in the separation of the civil service into an administrative or first-division (or heaven-born) grade, and an executive grade. It was a distinction made by Alfred Mond who 'employed men of intelligence and intellect to govern his companies, able to carry on once he had outlined the policy. . . . With regard to the policies of the companies, however, this he held was a matter which could only be dealt with by those responsible to the shareholders'.[13] It depends what one means by policy; the board has its legal responsibilities, but many company directors will argue that the 'direction' of the company in reality is diffused inextricably through all the upper reaches of what is ambiguously called 'top management'; they may even agree with the managing director of the engineering firm which is the *mise en scène* of one of Mr Priestley's novels, an executive who

> did not feel outside the different jobs they were doing there was any great difference between himself and any other man in the factory . . . unlike several elderly members of his board of directors, who felt entitled to live an altogether different life from that of all the people who worked for them.[14]

This is only to say that the dividing line between professional management and the business men in control of the firm's destinies does not necessarily coincide with the boardroom door. It may lie quite distinctly between the managing director's chair and the rest of the boardroom table. Even today in some firms of enormous size there is only one boss, who is even more an autocrat of the board table than ever Lord Melchett was; and everybody in the business world knows who these great dictators are, though it would be unwise to attempt to give any instances. Other firms seem to be run by a whole series of committees of directors and senior managers from whose confabulations policy emerges. The director in such a company, whether large or small, will testify that profits and strategy play a smaller part in his daily life than production or marketing. He will warmly insist that his affinities are with the managers 'below' him and who, he may aver, 'are just as good business men as I am, and just as much a part of the brains of the business'. This attitude is consciously struck by some managing directors. Thus Mr W. J. Aris of Burroughs:

> 'We don't give a hoot for titles. All the titles we hold at Burroughs are honorary titles to enable us to perform our work. . . . Someone has to occupy the managing director's chair, and it happens to be me. But the judgement on me is how I carry out my work, my title is of no importance at all.'[15]

Yet, even if top men like Mr Aris choose to minimize it, the distinction is there, though it may be one of attitudes rather than of titles. The distinction is between men who understand the strategy of business and those who are only concerned with their own functions. The salaried company official in middle management, whose highest ambition is to be head of his department—even if it is the sales department —and retire on the firm's contributory pension scheme in a manner perfectly analogous to that of his suburban neighbour, a civil servant, will not think of himself as a business man as he thinks of one of his directors as a business man, or the tough owners of firms to whom he 'sells' his firm's output, or the proprietors of the garage that services his car. It is this sort of business functionary who caused a hard-faced director to remark, in one of Mr Nigel Balchin's novels, 'These production manager types who started at the bottom never really understand the *strategy* of business.'[16] Plenty of men in middle management, have, of course, business strategy in the blood, and are determined to rise, whether in their own company or another, to a position where they will have scope to make business decisions. These are, in our sense, business

19

men *in potentia*, and their attitudes, careers and ideas will be discussed later.

It is significant that some people would like to drop the word 'business men' altogether, or relegate it to the small firms.* Young men who do not care to admit that they are going into business can nowadays primly say that they are going into management. This tendency to euphemism extends to some directors who like to speak of their companies as 'organizations' serving the public rather than as businesses making profits, and refer to themselves, like Mr Aris, as simply senior members of the management team. 'I'm a business man, sir!' was a remark which carried a precise and unashamed definition of personal status when uttered in 1858, and indeed in 1908. Today, it is not a remark that is called for in big business; in 1955 it might even have been described as non-U. It might be employed facetiously in the same way that a high Treasury official may say, 'I'm a bureaucrat,' or for emphasis, when a Roman Catholic of infinite lineage and terrific patriotism says, 'I'm a papist.' The late Mr R. R. Stokes began an attack on the extravagance of the Government's aircraft programme from the socialist front bench by referring to himself as a 'hardheaded business man'.[17] It is a useful word at certain moments in the game of being one up. The nuances of language are significant. It is part of the camouflage being adopted by business men who prefer to be described as directors, industrialists, executives, merchant bankers, etc. But directors do not, as a rule, like to be called managers. On the contrary, there are directors of small firms who have refused better-paid jobs in larger firms because they would there lose the status and title of 'director'.

The frontier between business men and managers is thus for many reasons hard to define. Nevertheless, it is a real frontier, dividing one class and one set of functions and values from another. Many men who cross it, if not all, know when they do and have a conscious feeling of having 'arrived'. At the same time they are often conscious of entering a new moral atmosphere. In management, a man's personal standards of conduct and those required in his day-to-day work are often, and indeed usually are, the same: those of fair dealing between equals. On the board, the moral atmosphere of action, we have been assured, is likely to be much lower than a man's personal standards. He has entered the jungle.

---

* 'Me a business man,' an oil company director said to one of the authors, 'why, I couldn't be trusted with a corner shop.'

2. THE BUSINESS CLASSES

The business community is, therefore, a large and miscellaneous one. As we have defined it, it includes all those concerned with the strategy of business, the directors and the moving spirits (however entitled) of large and small public companies, owned in strictly legal terms by thousands of small capitalists ranging from orphanages, trust funds, aged pensioners, small and large nest-egg savers, speculators, and even workpeople, to the Prudential Insurance Company. It includes the directors and top managers of the subsidiaries owned by these big businesses. It includes, too, the ruling dynasties (not always exclusively male) of thousands of old-established family firms: the business squire-archy in fact. Some of these firms are still entirely under the control of one family; in others, 'the family', under stress of death duties and the need for new capital, shares control with outsiders. The business community includes, further, the directors or partners, who are also very much the managers, of small firms which may well be financed by other business men, bankers or financiers, who are the legal owners. It includes the founders of countless small firms which were started on one man's capital and ideas, and which are expanding out of ploughed-back profits. It includes, in contrast with all these, the finance grandees whose activities were analysed by the Report of the Bank Rate Tribunal which 'showed that a small charmed circle of men 10 ft tall, who are the heads of the merchant banks and who have the ear of the Bank of England before anyone else, run the City much as their fathers did'.[18]

The type of industry in which these men operate varies in every conceivable way—far more widely, for example, than do the headings of the national census of production. This not only varies their attitudes and outlook, it causes them to see each other almost as different breeds of men. Many of those in manufacture, for example, have an ingrained suspicion of those in finance.* Shipbuilders, shipowners, textile mill-

* Thus Samuel Courtauld in an address to the Society of Friends in 1942, on industrial relationships: 'We [industrialists] are suspicious of banking, because we think that it is often overpaid for its services, and also because we doubt its efficiency. Historical development has given it a privileged position on which it is apt to trade. We are suspicious of company promoters and gamblers in stocks and shares, because they want something for nothing, and do far more harm than good.' A Birmingham manufacturer showed the same distaste two generations earlier: 'If we compare the manufacturers with the smart brokers and gamblers of Liverpool or the smug and self-sufficient traders of the City, we may fairly say that, judged by their actions in the last generation, the manufacturing towns have the advantage.' William Sargant, *Essays of a Birmingham Manufacturer*, 1869.

owners, steelmakers, are terms that carry a cultural connotation in English and Scottish life. There are cultural contrasts in everyday experiences and associations between those in charge of engineering factories which make machinery for other business men at home and abroad, and those who run or own firms making consumer goods—things sold over the counter by competitive advertising: branded goods, patent foods and medicines, detergents, household appliances, clothing, and so on. There are the august morning-suited rulers of department stores; the directors of shops and multiples; the purveyors of mass meals or mass pleasures whose eyes are fixed on very different markets than, for example, are the large and small contractors who tender for dams or bridges at home or abroad, or for sub-contracts to supply the equipment needed for them. There are men of business whose pre-occupation is the creation of an organization exquisitely sensitive to the tastes of the English floosie and her boy-friend; there are men of business whose aim is to be no less responsive in the supply of 'muck and truck' to millions of Asian customers; there are men of business who direct the operations of plantations, mines, railways or other undertakings in which those customers draw their pay packets (and some of them are listed in Foreign Office handbooks). There are business men who preside only over the making of things; those who preside over the moving of things; those who see nothing made and nothing moved, but buy, sell, finance and insure everything made or moved. There are those who could only direct their firms' affairs from a knowledge of science or of technology; others whose supremacy is based on a life-study of a single trade such as the 'rag trade'. The mastery of finance and accountancy is the foundation of other panjandrums' control over squads of scientists, engineers, salesmen and office managers.

Though the breed shows a rich variation, the species is the same and recognizes itself (as dogs recognize themselves as dog for all the differences of size, shape and coat), as *homo mercator* or *homo pecuniarius*. It may seem easy to divide the big business man from the rest and regard that as an adequate classification. This distinction we shall firmly refuse to make, first because of the gradations of size already referred to; second because, in terms of reward, the director of a quite small firm not infrequently does better in terms of take-home pay than the 'economic statesman' in charge of a large combine; third because the business man in the small firm often becomes the industrialist in the large one by growth or purchase or transfer; fourth because there is not even a hard-and-fast distinction between the functions of the salaried director and the proprietor of the one-man business.

We propose to draw an arbitrary line much lower down—one that divides business men, not only from managers and professional people, but also from the *lumpenkapitalismus* of self-employed shopkeepers, barrow-boys and jobbing contractors. It is true that from this stratum some of the biggest industrialists of our day have sprung—from bicycle shop and backyard business. But the vast majority of such enterprises remain tiny, and the life of a fair proportion is solitary, nasty, brutish and short. The distinction is arbitrary and is one of imponderables rather than capital employed, scale, turnover, or type of entrepreneur. Big business begins at that indefinable critical point where small business becomes promising—potent for growth or for status and the reward it will bring its owner.

3. THE ECONOMIST'S BUSINESS MAN

To the economist any difficulties in classification seem to arise from failure to identify the business man once and for all with the entrepreneur of the textbooks, the man whose function

> is to reform or revolutionize the pattern of production by exploiting an invention or, more generally, an untried technological possibility for producing a new commodity or producing an old one in a new way, by opening up a new source of supply of materials or a new outlet for products, by reorganizing an industry and so on.[19]

It is precisely the element of enterprise, of entrepreneurial ability in the business system which conservatives are so keen to conserve; but which socialists are so sure that they can, to a considerable degree, socialize. The plain fact is that the economist's definition of a business man is equally well fitted to committees of business men; in large firms, 'enterprise' rarely emerges from the mind and commands of one man, but coagulates slowly from the arguments and conflicts of many flesh-and-blood business men, all of whom have private lives, ambitions, loves, hates, virtues, vices and immortal souls—but some of whom may have no entrepreneurial ability whatsoever. Nor has the name entrepreneur caught on in business circles or in the management movement, although the word 'enterprise' is often used to describe business, and quite often entirely falsely. Modern economists recognize this, and the Americans are even distinguishing 'entrepreneurial drones'

23

among firms or business men.[20] Such subtleties are all very well, but they leave the nature of the business man no longer purely entre-preneurial, and hence play havoc with the neat rationalism of business behaviour, based solely on the profit motive, which is the starting-point of almost all economic analysis. Bagehot clearly saw the difficulties when he wrote:

> Men of business have a solid judgement, a wonderful guessing power of what is going to happen, each in his own trade, but they have never practised themselves in reasoning out their judgements and in sup-porting their guesses by argument; probably if they did so some of the finer and correcter parts of their anticipations would vanish. . . . And so the 'theory of business' leads a life of obstruction, because theorists do not see the business and the men of business will not reason out the theories: far from wondering that such a science is not completely perfect, we should rather wonder that it exists at all.[21]

This has not deterred economists from elaborate theories of how an economic system works when all business men are like Charles Clore or Themistokles Onassis, and in which unenterprise quickly leads from underpayment of dividends to swift and condign obliteration of business men at the hands of alert and greedy shareholders. Marshall believed firmly, even neurotically and irrationally in the rationality of the market place. He thought that 'he who with small ability is in command of a large capital speedily loses it'—to a better business man. A fool and his money are soon parted. But the most mediocre men on the board of a large combine speedily do nothing of the sort; the combine makes money for a long time in spite of them. Mr Wiles has now frankly admit-ted that the business man will never fulfil Bagehot's hopes of him:

> Business men do not in fact maximise their profit because they cannot do so, because they are too stupid, and because even if they were not stupid there would generally be many practical difficulties in the way. They are unable to understand marginal costs, and use the idea of total cost. But when they are down, they do minimise losses. . . .[22]

Business, in fact, is not a purely competitive game in which business men only keep on top by making larger profits or smaller losses than other business men. It is a system of power, a hierarchy of positions, an important part of 'the Establishment', a constellation of—more than five hundred*—social institutions which are so firmly established

---

* A recent study by the National Institute of Social and Economic Research, listed 512 large companies, each with assets in excess of £2.5 million. These com-panies account for just under 50 per cent of total profits earned by private industry.

that almost no competition can break them, however stupid their directors are about the theory of marginal costs or anything else. 'In the long run' such business men would have to file their petition; but 'in the meantime' there may be half a business lifetime of personal pickings for the men at the top. Their limitations are somewhat corrected by the existence of competition. But the real guarantee that moderately able men rise to the top in big and even in middle-sized business, is that the job is well worth having and there is intense *internal* competition for it, which means that only men of some drive and intelligence are likely to get it. Such men need not be entrepreneurs in any economist's sense; and that is precisely why their motives, conditioning and social origin as individuals, as well as the influences which play on them as a social class, are worth examination, since this will be reflected in the community at large. Of course, as our description of the business community indicates, entrepreneurs on the economist's model exist, and competition plays its part, so that the over-simplification of the business man's psychology is by no means fatal to the superstructure of economic theory. But today it is only in the arena of rather small business that Marshall's law of business success has much meaning:

> two sets of forces, the one increasing the capital at the command of able men, and the other destroying the capital that is in the hands of weaker men bring about the result that there is a far more close correspondence between the ability of business men and the size of the businesses which they own than at first sight would appear probable.[23]

The economist's business world is thus not one that is readily recognizable to the ordinary top manager, who will rarely peruse the latest copy of the *Economic Journal* with quite the feeling of the doctor who reads *The Lancet* that he will find something professionally useful in it. Perhaps the modern economist will retort, 'Why should he? He is the disease—or the patient; not the doctor.'

The relation between economists and business men is a curious one. It was cordial in the nineteenth century. The business men felt that the economists were defending them against sentimentality and socialism, and the economists (with the exception of Bagehot) thought the business men pursued profit single-mindedly and scientifically. Gradually relations have grown cooler, as the economist has proved unable to make accurate forecasts of the economic weather, and the business man has taken to monopolistic practices and indeed behaviour of such downright irrationality as to make higher economic theory almost an exercise in scholasticism.* The economists are now often frankly hostile to their erstwhile heroes, while the big business men only employ economists in a menial capacity, to work out marketing trends in back rooms.†[24] Few economists take their rightful place on the boards of large firms—the banks have a few‡—while business men are but rarely invited to economic seminars to explain how they make profits without understanding marginal costs. It was Keynes who said 'the most substantial joys I get are from the perception of logical arguments'. The wonder to business men is that such a man made so much money; the average business man is a good deal less intellectual.

In fact, one of the major outlets for business ability is not building a business but capturing command of a business which has already been built, and which, by its size and momentum and its firm grip on its own specialities, may be virtually indestructible in one autocrat's lifetime. The enterprise devoted to becoming a director, for the power, security, pay and perquisites it confers, certainly produces a pattern of materialistic behaviour—but it is one for the political scientists rather than for the economists to analyse. Yet besides being the influential social figure in our midst that we have described, the business man also remains the central figure in economic science. It is not enough to be told that he is the entrepreneur; he is obviously much more than entrepreneur, and we want to know if he is sufficiently an entrepreneur. The business man himself knows that it is not enough to insist that he is

* Cf. Mr Gordon Newton, in the *Director*, November, 1954: 'One board of directors will meet a particular problem by spending even more money than it normally does on new plant, while another board in exactly the same circumstances will meet the same problem by retrenchment everywhere. But we do not know why the two reacted in totally different ways. In a free economy, in other words, the degree of investment depends on the state of mind.'

† They are also witty at each other's expense. The economists tell the story of an economic don who came into hall one evening looking white and shaken, and when asked by a colleague in the faculty what was wrong, said, 'I've lost my faith.' The other said he had never realized he was a religious man in that sense. 'Oh' no,' the first replied. 'It's not that. But I've been teaching economics for twenty years and I've just realized that I don't know how business men make a profit at all.' 'Oh,' said his colleague, 'surely you see that they have only to compete against other business men?' The retort to this is the story of the large firm which advertised for a one-armed economist. This proved hard to come by, and when the managing director was asked by the university appointments board why an unmutilated specimen would not do, replied, 'We must have a one-armed one to advise us. All the others keep saying, "On the one hand you could do *this*, but on the other hand you could do *that*."'

‡ Lord Stamp's career provided an example of an economist who became a leading industrialist.

enterprise in person, or even 'the dynamic life-giving element in every business', as his most vigorous American spokesman put it.[25] What else is he? To defend himself he must explain himself.

4. THE MAN NOBODY KNOWS

The economists evolve their theories endlessly round the entrepreneur and his activities—but they leave him a faceless, bloodless, anonymous automaton; the most they can do is to make the mechanism work faultily. But though the economists provide no more than an outline, it is far from clear whence the materials to fill it in are to be drawn. The British business man is the man nobody knows; and to study him outside the covers of economic textbooks is to launch oneself on an exercise in anthropology with the scantiest facts to go on.

So far the psychologists' interests in business have been utilitarian and in the service of organization—the study of physical working conditions, the raising of efficiency, emotional attitudes to work, the state of relations between management and workpeople. 'Industrial psychology' has been almost confined to the mind and muscles of the operative. Very recently in Britain, however, the psychologists have raised their sights and begun to take an interest in the managers, in, that is, the mental health, the efficiency and the 'job satisfaction' of the professional organizers of factory production. But they have hardly penetrated the boardroom. There have been 'attitude surveys' which are intended to elucidate if the managers and directors are liked, if there is real and acknowledged leadership; and one factory—Glacier Metals Ltd—has actually been put through a form of group psychoanalysis.[26] But the psychologists have not been concerned with top management as a group, even in factories; they have taken no interest in the business man in all his variety, merchant and financier as well as manufacturer.

Libraries of management technique exist setting forth the whole art of leadership and organization; it is not difficult to teach yourself how to run a bassoon factory, or to read how they are run; but almost nothing is said about the lives, origins and inner thoughts of the men who own or control such a factory. There are not only books on how to succeed as a manager, there are also books on how to make money as an entrepreneur; but they do not hint at the possibility that in climbing to the top, a man may have to use other means than working hard and avoiding—as Andrew Carnegie implored him to do—speculation gambling and endorsement. They do not suggest that at the top a man's own interests could ever conflict with his firm's; they do not deal with man as a political animal at all. If they suggest anything to the reader it is that life in business is quite extraordinarily dull, and that advancement in business is simply a matter of plodding merit. There are also many studies of industries and some of individual firms, even in detail; but there are almost no studies of industrialists.

The biographer's art has hardly been practised on the business man. This is surely remarkable. Few business men would admit that the country owes nothing to its business leaders in the past; yet they have done almost nothing to make anyone want to write about their achievements. Politicians, statesmen, soldiers, explorers, divines, jurists, doctors, artists and literati, savants, sportsmen and actors and actresses, even minor figures in the arts, sciences and professions, are written up and every scrap of evidence that bears on their motives and thoughts is collected. Many of them write autobiographies; some write more than one, so much happens to them. But good biographies of British business men can be almost counted on one hand, and even bad biographies are scarce. The lives of the engineers and inventors are written; but the fact that some of them were business men (like the Oldknows, Watt or Ludwig Mond) is incidental to the main theme. Unless a business man has other claims to fame—for instance has been prominent in politics (like Cobden or Rhodes) and particularly if he has controlled newspapers (like Beaverbrook or Northcliffe), the mere creation of a business, small or big, rarely makes him an attraction to a biographer.

Business men are accounted even less interesting than civil servants; even less heroic. Scandal, however, may make a business man a subject for a full-length portrait; he may then, as a failure, rank in interest with criminals and racketeers. The lives of Hudson and Bottomley have been written more than once. An honest man must do business in a spectacular way to rival the interest of a big swindler in the dock. This perhaps provides the key to the problem. In the dock the business man must give answers to the real questions which reveal his character and motives; in a trial, his business decisions are examined mercilessly. Only then does the material for the appraisal of the man become available; in other walks of life—except, in general, the civil service— the deeds and words of men and women speak for them. Business men work in silence and in secret. It is remarkable how few of them leave diaries, documents or letters of any interest; though there is quite a scavenging for those of Victorian bankers.

Such lack of interest suggests that business life is flat and dull; but in fact it does not necessarily mean this. It means rather that most business men are men of action, and generally have no need to write dispatches about their campaigns; however, when they do, they edit the record with extreme care, and censorship is fatal either to literature or science. Business men, in many eminent cases, have plenty to cover up, or to forget; and this should at least dispose of the economists' conception of them as consisting of a set of reflexes conditioned to the stimulus of profit-making. It is that in their lives it is almost always to their advantage to keep their mouths shut, to preserve their counsel, and to put out only what is creditable to themselves. Advertisement is another matter. Business *names* are to be found in every newspaper—occasionally backed by a character like Mr Barratt, the subtopian shoe manufacturer—but mainly in the advertisement columns. When they speak, it is usually strictly business, in the section devoted to company meetings. The proportion of business men thought worthy of mention in the obituary column is tiny;* so are the entries in the *Dictionary of National Biography*. American business biography is in better shape—partly because the period of the finance moguls—the Goulds, Vanderbilts and Morgans—was more spectacular; partly because there has always been more publicity and less secrecy in America; partly because American economic historians are more interested in the American capitalist.

Because the business man has always been the leading figure in American society, at least since the mid-nineteenth century, business life and business figures have also received far more attention from American novelists, including those of the first rank. They are interested in business, though they have found in the study of business behaviour the best weapon for criticizing American values. They have, in consequence, studied the American business man, whether top manager, tycoon or Main Street Babbitt, with an insight and technical knowledge unknown to the British novelist. The anthropologist of the British business man, therefore, gets even less help from the novelists than he does from the biographers or the economic historians.[27] In general, business men are minor characters in Victorian fiction and are rarely made the subject of full-length portraits. The English novelist does not

* The authors studied the obituaries in *The Times* for three months in 1957 and found that out of 203 male obituaries only 12 referred to business men compared with 34 for the armed services. Further, even when there was an obituary of a business man it was more often short.

know the life of business, and a business man, even an English one, cannot be portrayed without estimating the influence of his work upon him, since so much of him is his work. The novelist has been attracted, moreover, by business men of the flamboyant type rather than the men of sterling worth who in forty years create from a paintshop the Universal Floral Wallpaper Corporation. The lead given in *John Halifax, Gentleman*, was not very energetically followed up. Dickens dissected the crude Bounderbys, philistine Gradgrinds and Scrooges, the cold, practical, moneybound Dombey, whose inability to understand the principles of modern management succession provides the plot of the novel. Wells created Uncle Ponderevo, and though he admired great industrialists, stuck on the whole to advertising tycoons; Arnold Bennett's weakness for hoteliers was no less typical; basic industry was left to Shaw, who produced Undershaft, the armaments' king.

The English novel in the nineteenth century studied, usually with distaste, business and the business man in the context of its general preoccupation with social class and snobbery; and on this it provides a valid commentary on the struggles of the business man to rise in society. The school of later sociological novelists have in the twentieth century studied business mainly in relation to its failure—failure to meet technical and social change, and impotence in the face of disaster, such as unemployment. These are the themes of Armstrong's *Crowthers of Bankdam* and Cronin's *The Stars Look Down*; and in these settings the novelist has been able to make the business man small enough in the nutcrackers of social forces to treat him with imaginative sympathy.

Though the English novelists generally find little of interest in the business scene, when they do they go at once to the heart of the big business situation—ambition, conflict and the struggle for power. Arnold Bennett alone has made the pure entrepreneur interesting and indeed irresistible (in *The Card*). Control of the board is the issue in a high proportion of the others. The relation of men and management is the other point at which the novelist seeks the business point of view— John Halifax's fight with the Luddites, the master's determination to crush the men in Galsworthy's *Strife*, and, in the modern vein, the frustrations that lead to the pure 'wildcat strike' in Mr Clewes' *Men at Work*. Such dissections of business mentality may not be very flattering; they may perhaps justify the business men's dislike of artists and intellectuals; but they reflect the public's flat refusal to believe that the business man is either a noble Captain of Industry in shining (protection of industry duties) armour or just a desiccated calculating machine.

They again hold up the mirror to the business man who wonders why he has no friends and why his essentially creative work and life is so wantonly resented and denigrated by the community he serves. Both in what they pick on and what they ignore, English novels on business men and their role in the community must be given due weight in any estimate of the business man.

The proper study of the board is, of course, the members of the board. The only sound basis for estimating the power, wisdom, efficiency, philanthropy, use and abuse of the British top business man is to have on one's regular visiting list names like Bowater, Currie, Cadbury, Drayton, Earle, Fleck, Gluckstein, Heyworth, Hennessy, Jacobson, Lord, Rank, Sinclair and Wolfson—to start with some of the biggest in terms of money. But though access to the heart of the business man is a privilege to be prized, it is supremely hard to win. Business men are often happy enough to talk economics, politics or ultimate values; some will talk about management; some will even discuss their own careers; but few if any will be frank with the student of social institutions about the strategy of business life. They preserve the secrecy which so hampers the economist, the biographer, the historian, the novelist and the social research worker. 'They love the secrecy of *private* enterprise', Professor Sargant Florence has said,[28] and privacy is the keynote of British business character; any invasion of it is intensely resented, and instantly attacked, as injurious to the national interest.

> Any mishandling of the vast mass of confidential matter so thoroughly sifted by the Monopolies Commission might damage in a twinkling the prestige of this great industry . . . Such a report would no doubt be a best-seller among our foreign competitors, but could scarcely replace the foreign currency so hardly earned by our continuous efforts.[29]

This is a typical business reaction to any study of business method that goes beyond the general and harmless management principles expounded by Elbourne or Brech. Anything that tends to bring top managers into discredit is now increasingly resented by the business community with which this book deals. The publicity and ostentation of Sir Bernard and Lady Docker, and the washing of dirty linen in the publicity of the B.S.A. annual general meeting would have bothered nobody in 1880, when Sir Georgias Midas and his kind paraded a degree of conspicuous spending which led Veblen to work up the 'theory of the leisure class'; but the *Director* voiced the feelings of modern business men when it commented bitterly:

> The heart of the matter is the damage to the reputation of directors generally which has been wrought in the minds of the general public . . . The man who deserves sympathy is the ordinary director going about his daily business who now finds himself the target of ill-informed and mischievous abuse. [30]

A feeling of horror spread through the business community when, in the critical second week of the general election of 1959, the Stock Exchange suspended dealings in the shares of the Jasper group of companies and charges were brought against Mr Harry Jasper and Mr Frederick Grunwald: the State Building Society had to close its doors, and it appeared that speculation of the very kind so attacked by socialist critics had led to this. The stock exchange reacted sharply for a week, and the *Financial Times* deplored ' a blow to the City's reputation and one which comes at a significant time. '[31] In the event, the incident did not swing the floating vote, but it might be unwise to assume that the public brushed Mr Grunwald aside as a necessary risk in capitalism. The politicians did not: the abuses of the Building Society movement by financiers are to be halted: and some highpowered business figures were appointed to make amends by rescuing investors in the State Building Society.

The Report of the Bank Rate Leak Tribunal, which appeared in January 1958, gave great satisfaction because it so emphatically testified to the integrity of the great merchant bankers and other financial magnates which it brought to the witness-stand; but, similarly, the raising of the veil upon the way City men lived—their grouse-moor parties, their lunches, their little notes to each other to sell this and that, their difficulty in quite remembering just how many directorships they held, their references to £5 million as a small sum—all this was strongly disliked. It engendered a suspicion that, probity apart, it would rouse improper emotions—envy, malice and uncharitableness—in the uninstructed public at large.[32]

Not letting the side down is now becoming second nature to British top management in all its dealings. But the greatest difficulty about being frank with shy business men is that they find it so hard to be frank with themselves; and even when they want to be frank, they often remain inarticulate. A well-chosen circle of business acquaintances is one of the most stimulating anyone—even a novelist—could have; but to get at the inner thoughts of what is called a 'representative sample' of business men in Britain is a formidable undertaking. Any industrial anthropologist who claims to have done so is making a big claim. No such claim is made here; although in our attempt to understand the business man we have used all available sources, including the American which are by far the richest and fullest.

5. PUBLIC RELATIONS

This anonymity, deliberate or accidental, has not done the business man any good. On the contrary, it has meant that, failing any better analysis, he has suffered the more from the Marxian caricature of him. It is true that the American big business tycoon and small-town Babbitt have suffered at the hands of the American novelist; but this great and continuing if critical interest in him testifies that he is the accepted leader of the American way of life. Despite his good showing in the past ten years, the British business man can feel no such sense of acceptance or security.

Many of them do not care; many are hardly aware that they have a public relations problem at all; many consider that business men as well as managers are so necessary that it does not matter; many again retain the faith of their Victorian forebears that business is natural in the sense that it is a law of human nature, and that therefore all the fulminations of theorists, the envy of intellectuals and the ignorant prejudice of the public cannot change the inevitability of their being bosses, knowing what has to be done, and being properly paid—if iniquitously taxed—for doing it. Others more sensitive to their position, are becoming conscious of themselves as a group with interests to defend, reputations to uphold. This group consciousness was recently, if perhaps exaggeratedly, remarked by the magazine *Industrial Welfare*:

> Each century discovers its own significant group. During the nineteenth century it was undoubtedly the Worker. During the twentieth it is equally undoubtedly the Director. Journals are named after him ... societies are formed where he may congregate, discuss his problems and protect his interests. Conferences are held in which he turns up in his thousands, as witness the recent conference at the Royal Festival Hall, with its 4,000 registrations.[33]

Some directors feel the force of Bertrand de Jouvenal's observation that 'judged by its social fruits, by its mores, by its spirit, capitalism today is immeasurably more praiseworthy than in previous days when it was far less bitterly denounced',[34] and wonder what can be done to cure such perversity. Most place their hopes in talking less about 'business' and more about 'management', in having management professionalized in institutes and taught in universities, and in describing themselves merely as 'top management' so that they will persuade the public to look on them in a new, and perhaps even American way. They wish to get over to the public an echo of the modesty of the Elizabethan statesman who said ,'We are but the upper servants in a great house.' They want to know how they fit respectably into the scheme of things; they want their role recognized. Others wonder why the reward for all that they do, in money and in public esteem, is so low, and ask how quality in 'business leadership' can be kept up, let alone improved, if the reward should be eroded further. The man who is building up a business, 'a great national asset', against all odds in the time-honoured capitalist, Marshallian manner, wonders why he must be so throttled and what is going to happen to all his work and plans. Even the 'professional director' of the mammoth public company hates to think that its future and its ownership is in question; and wonders why the public cannot somehow be got at and convinced that the trinity of management, workers and shareholders is a perfectly evolved form which ensures a sense of public responsibility that would never be achieved in any government department. Sometimes the boards of such companies devise friendly little basic-Englishspeaking manikins like Mr Cube to explain all this, or subscribe generously to poster campaigns to announce the remarkable fact that 'private enterprise delivers the goods'.

How much of such sensitivity to change there may be among top British business men is hard to guess. It is so much easier to talk to the small stage army of progressives among them. There are certainly signs of a growing feeling among many of them that business ought to be made more popular, and many would agree with Drucker[35] that the ignorance of the 'citizen without direct management experience' of the function of management and 'of its standards and of its responsibilities is one of the most serious weaknesses of an industrial society— and it is almost universal'.

NOTES

1. The Labour Party Manifesto, *Britain Belongs to You*, issued by the Labour Party, September 1959.
2. Cf. Socialist Union, *Twentieth Century Socialism*, Penguin Books, 1956, pp. 15, 146 *et seq.*; Crosland, C.A.R., *The Future of Socialism*, Cape, 1956, pp. 462 *et seq.*; The Labour Party, *Industry and Society*, 1957, p. 47.
3. Conservative Political Centre, *The Industrial Charter*, 1950, pp. 23, 33.
4. *The Director*, November 1959.
5. *The Director*, May 1960.
6. *The Director*, March 1960.
7. Lewis, Roy and Maude, Angus, *Professional People*, Phoenix House, 1952, pp. 126–7.
8. The reader is referred to the Bibliographical Appendix and especially to Urwick, L. and Brech, E. F. L., *The Making of Scientific Management*, Vol. II, London, Management Publications Trust, 1946.
9. Acton Society Trust, Monograph No. 4, *The Men on the Boards*, London, The Trust, 1951, p. 6.
10. Albu, Austen and Hewett, Norman, *Anatomy of Private Industry*, 1951. Fabian Research Series, No. 145, Gollancz.
11. Parkinson, H., *Ownership of Industry*, London, Eyre & Spottiswoode, 1948, pp. 5, 35, 97.
12. *The Times*, 27 January, 1956.
13. Bolitho, H., *Alfred Mond*, London, Martin Secker, 1932, p. 102.
14. Priestley, J. B., *Daylight on Saturday*, Oxford, Heinemann, 1944.
15. 'Man of the Month: W. J. Aris', *Scope*, June 1954.
16. Balchin, N., *Sundry Creditors*, London, Collins, 1953.
17. Hansard, vol. 549, Col. 1037, 28 February, 1956.
18. *Manchester Guardian*, 22 January, 1958.
19. Schumpeter, J. A., *Capitalism, Socialism and Democracy*, 4th edition, London, Allen & Unwin, 1954, pp. 132 *et seq.*
20. Alderson, W., 'Determinants of Entrepreneurial Ability', *Social Research*, Autumn 1954.
21. Bagehot, W., 'Postulates of English Political Economy', in *Works*, ed. F. Morgan, Century Insurance Co., pp. 245–6.
22. Wiles, P. J. D., *Price, Cost and Output*, Oxford, Blackwell, 1956, Chapter XI.
23. Marshall, A., *Principles of Economics*, London, Macmillan, Vol. I, 5th ed., 1907, Chapter XII, Sec. 12, p. 312.
24. Cf. Dalton, C. P., 'The Economist in Industry', The *Financial Times*, 23 September, 1954.
25. Drucker, Peter, *The Practice of Management*, London, Heinemann, 1955, p. 1.
26. Jaques, E., *The Changing Culture of a Factory*, London, Tavistock Publication, 1951.
27. For reference to English business novels see Appendix, Sec. 7.
28. Florence, P. Sargant, *The Logic of British and American Industry*, London, Routledge and Kegan Paul, 1953, p. 301.

29. Statement of Policy by the British Electrical and Allied Manufacturers' Association reported in *The Times* of 9 May, 1955.

30. *The Director*, September 1956.

31. *Financial Times*, 22 September, 1959.

32. Cf. *The Economist*, 25 January, 1958; letter to *The Times* 3 February, *et seq.*

33. 'Directors—A Significant Twentieth Century Group', *Industrial Welfare*, January/February 1956.

34. Cf. de Jouvenal, B.,'The Treatment of Capitalism by Continental Intellectuals' in *Capitalism and the Historians*, ed. Hayek, F. A., London, Routledge & Kegan Paul, 1954, p. 122.

35. Drucker, Peter, *The Practice of Management*, op. cit, p. vii.

CHAPTER II

'Under Entirely New Management'

> '*The Fathers have eaten a sour grape, and the children's teeth are set on edge.*'
>
> EZEKIEL, xviii, 2

> '*England is the last home of the aristocracy, and the art of protecting the aristocracy from the encroachments of commerce has been raised to quite an art.*
> '*Because in America a rich butter-and-egg man is only a rich butter-and-egg man or at most an honorary Ll.D. of some hungry university, but in England he is Sir Benjamin Buttery, Bart.*'
>
> OGDEN NASH

BUSINESS MEN HAVE THE AUTHORITY of the greatest name among them for disposing of history over the tip as 'bunk'. They know enough history to know that capitalism has changed out of recognition in the past hundred and fifty years; so much so that the capitalist as Marx, G. B. Shaw or Professor Alfred Marshall knew him has almost disappeared. Robustly concerned with forecasting the technical and social change of the immediate future, busy with the immediate situation revealed by their order books and cost sheets, they may ask of what use to them is even the most cursory glance backwards at Grandfather's way of doing things. To the practical man Henry Ford was right; history is irrelevant.

Yet everybody lives more in the past than he realizes; even business men cannot live for very long in the future, important as forethought may be for estimating the course of demand. Foresight is based on hindsight. The optimism which distinguishes business mentality, the sense of progress and the belief in continuous expansion which most business men possess, has been implanted in them by education and by technical development over the past century or so. Business men read more history than they realize—if not from books, then from the layers of social, technical and economic change which are built into the machines they make or the businesses they run, and which are often as decipherable as the rings of a tree. The mental climate of the top leader-

37

ship group is deeply influenced by the experiences of the top leaders, in all their variety, in their own and their families' lifetimes. This is sometimes the 'dead weight of tradition' against which the young up-and-coming boss must fight; sometimes the sheer know-how of the business. Personal memories stretch quite a long way back into British business history.

Business men do not retire until they have to; whatever the strains of modern organization, modern medicine and the sense of their own importance keeps many of them in a good state of preservation once they have reached the top. Unless they have the superannuation provisions of the Companies Act 1948 enforced rigidly against them, they can stay at the helm well past seventy,* and in family businesses much longer. Not so long ago, Mr Theodore Taylor died at the age of 102, chairman of Messrs J. T. and J. Taylor Ltd, woollen manufacturers. He was only a salient example of many senior business men who started their business life over half a century ago, which means that many of their memories and first impressions are those of the end of the nineteenth century. A few go back still further. A large number knew the world of 1914; there no doubt survive some of the original 'hard-faced men' who did well out of World War I; the memories of others is of the long inter-war period of revolt against Victorian elders and of mingled 'normalcy' and stagnation. Now, in the 1950s, a contingent of managing directors who started in business just before the war, men who were progressives revolted by the waste of unemployment and depression which formed the memories of their youth, have begun to arrive. Finally, though mostly in the smaller firms, dealing mainly in the most modern technology, or in new companies, the first of the war and post-war generation are possessing themselves of the power they need to try out their ideas. This background of experience across the years is the collective unconscious of business men of all kinds—manufacturers, merchants, financiers, contractors, administrators.

History lives, moreover, on the shop floor as well as in the boardroom. The Irish are quizzed by the English for keeping Oliver Cromwell alive; but the English sometimes seem just as determined to go on living in the early years of the industrial revolution. Every firm has its roots in the past, every factory, every industrial town is somehow invisibly but potently scarred by that revolution; its ghosts can take up

* At seventy, directors of public companies must declare their age and vacate their office unless reappointed by the company in general meeting, which in practice usually happens.

residence in the most modern glass-and-aluminium, welfare and works-council-ridden plant. The sins of the gaffer (real or imaginary) are visited on the board—even the nationalized board—generations later. 'Sometimes,' wrote Dr Zweig of the British working-man, 'the managers would like to start afresh and establish friendly relations between themselves and the workers, but they often find the atmosphere of the place is stronger than their good will.'[1] He tells this story:

> 'I remember talking to an old taxi-driver, who took me to a firm in the Midlands. He warned me, "It's a bad place, you know." "Why?" I asked. "Is it the management or the conditions?" "It has always been bad," he said. "It has a bad reputation."'

Every firm, Zweig said, has its own history and is conditioned by that history; though whether it is a history which is fully narrated in the sumptuously got-up official histories of centenary or bi-centenary history-proud firms may sometimes be doubted. Since all firms are conditioned by industrial history, it is no use the board crying, 'But we weren't started till 1937!' In the eyes of a generation which learnt its economic history from the Hammonds, every business man is the grandson, or great-grandson, of Mr Gradgrind.

1. MERCHANT AND MANUFACTURER

The British business man knows that over the last hundred years or so his function in society was interwoven with two dominant themes—technical progress on the one hand and social change and class conflict on the other. He can see his forebears transforming the social scene in various ways. He can see the rising commercial class gradually destroying the power of the old ruling caste in Britain; supplanting it; outstripping it; intermarrying with it; dispossessing it of its acres and rents and rural consequence; emerging with its titles and dignities to adorn his own office or factory, his sons ensconced in its schools, his daughters accepted in what remains of 'Society', its shrines and sinecures in his hands.

He can see too how the vast changes which have taken the English labourer off a diet of oatmeal, bread, potatoes and little beef or mutton, under leaky thatch, and put him, as a Brylcreemed artisan, on to a diet of tinned and frozen foods in a modern council flat piped with electricity, gas and television, have been achieved by the business man's ceaseless pursuit of the maxim 'the customer is always right'. It is *this* which has helped to convert the smartly turned-out trade unionist of today into a type which his ancestor of 1800 would find even harder to recognize as a workman than the business man of 1800 would find it to recognize the top executive of today as a 'master'. To the business man such a transformation cannot help looking like service. He will genuflect to the illustrious roll of innovators who did the actual inventing; but he will point out that it was the business men (some of whom were inventors too) who made the prototypes practicable, tooled up, produced, marketed and got the things into the hands of the masses. In the eyes of a practical man, Gladstone and Disraeli did not change Britain as much as men like the Stephensons, Bessemer, Cunliffe-Lister, Josiah Mason, Joseph Whitworth, Thomas Bazley, Royce, Mond, and scores of other 'eminent manufacturers' to be found listed in Victorian books of industry and invention.

He will concede, because he has had it dinned into his ears by his adversaries, that the industrial revolution had its abuses: sweated labour, children in factories, slumdom, exploitation—and will handsomely admit that trade unionism was right and proper and the former masters' denunciation of it misplaced. He will point to the rise of modern management, large-scale organization, industrial psychology, the idea of service as opposed to shareholders' interests, in order to distinguish sharply the former ideals of business men from those of today. He will say everything has changed in the last thirty years, adding impatiently that it is only trade unions that live in the past.

All this is to see the history of the business man in terms of the manufacturer. This is natural enough, since his rise has transformed the scene, and altered the attitude and activities of every other sort of business man. Yet the business man's lineage goes a long way further back than the sons of Boulton and Watt who, according to Erich Roll, pioneered planned machine layout, standardized parts, unit costings and market research in the early years of the nineteenth century.[2] The merchant and occasionally the banker often operated on a large scale at a time when manufacture was confined to craft workshops, to petty factories equipped with wooden machines, to mines whose headworks were a monument of the wheelwright's art. Large-scale organization existed in international banking, in contracting and in the great joint-stock trading, colonizing and plantation companies before steam-power made factories of any size possible. The organization of domestic craftworkers was of course occasionally a considerable business—some clothiers employed up to 5,000 craftworkers—and even in the time of water-power there were a few largish factories (for example, the silk factory of Thomas Lombe in Derwent). But the point is that the germ of business goes back long before the days of the factory-owner, and this should not be forgotten; socialism and communism are concerned to change types of organization related to patterns of motivation, which originated, not with the invention of steam-power, but hundreds and indeed thousands of years ago.

Thus business philosophy and the business way of life, not only in England but throughout Europe, was created by a mercantile and commercial, not a production-centred community. In the oft-told tale, this community built upon the middle-class virtues of thrift, diligence, sobriety, prudence, trustworthiness and respectability.[3] Protestantism was its religion, puritanism its regimen and liberalism eventually its political philosophy. These virtues and these values helped to create a wealth upon which merchants, clothiers and bankers prospered and began to become influential before manufacturers became important as a class—as distinct from their wares, which, together with agricultural produce, was the stuff of the country's seaborne trade. Their dealings in trade—which involved them in political controversy—and in money brought many of them into close touch with the aristocracy and landed classes; which in time they joined. The greatest business enterprise of the time was, of course, the East India Company; though not popular with the free traders, its prestige and public relations were such that it perhaps inspired Rob Roy's encomium: 'It is impossible, sir, for me to have higher respect for character than I have for the commercial. . . . It connects nation with nation, relieves the wants and contributes to the wealth of all.'

If it was on a large enough scale, business was respectable in the eyes of the English aristocracy. When trade was as magnificent as when conducted by a great adventuring or plantation company, younger sons could be put into it, as they could later into the Colonial service. The London bankers, because of their close connection with trade, and the financing of land transactions, early entered good society. Tradesmen they might be called; but they were awarded knighthoods and (especially if they served as Lord Mayor) baronetcies. To Sir Reginald Hoare in 1702 'the honour the Queen was pleased to confer on me was as unexpected as undeserving', but by the time the Glyns were given handles to their name it was quite the usual thing.[4] But ennoblement and trade did not in the eighteenth century go together. When the banker Smith was ennobled by Pitt he had to undertake to leave trade: 'to take his quill from behind his ear'. But throughout the nineteenth century, the status of the City bankers continued to improve with their wealth, as Britain emerged as the financial centre of the world, as it became respectable to deal in an ever-wider variety of stocks and shares, and as it became possible to invest a greater and greater surplus from the balance of payments overseas. Very great wealth made in the City eventually made the top rank of financiers and bankers acceptable to most ranks of the nobility, if not to the Duke of Omnium himself. The family trees of the merchant bankers began to intertwine with the pedigrees of the nobility in the middle of the century (though they began with the newer creations first), and presently with the great immigrating Jewish and Levantine families.

The manufacturers, in the sense of factory-owners, started some way behind. The division between finance and manufacture is not merely a temperamental but a social one, which persists in vague and vestigial form to this day. The social origins of the manufacturers were often humble;[5] but though some were artisans, others came from the professions. For a considerable time—almost to the end of the nineteenth century—in many industries manufacturers operated on a very small scale; much of the machinery was still simple, manned by craftsmen, turning out goods in batches under the proprietorial and paternal eye of the master. In comparison with the cottage crafts of earlier days, their operations seemed mass-production, whether of pins, cloth or steel pen-nibs; but it was still mostly small-scale, confined to the provinces and grimier and less gentlemanly than mercantile operations. There were, however, shipyards and iron and chemical plants which were fairly large-scale even by present standards, and manufacturers on this level were accorded corresponding respect. Further, both in the eighteenth and nineteenth century there was as much respect for and interest in the inventor and the maker of new and beautiful things as there is now. Thomason of Birmingham, to take but one example, was knighted and published his memoirs—not because he wished to describe his business but because he had met so many crowned and coroneted heads.[6] Men like Boulton, Wedgwood, Oldknow, and Garbett were recognized as men of culture and learning and moved in correspondingly cultured circles; George Stephenson's broad accent in no way prevented him from being taken up by London society—whose accents were highly non-U by modern standards anyway.

It seems as if there were, from the first, two streams in business society; the smaller, which included the more cultured manufacturers and some of the richer, that rose rapidly like the Strutts; the broader, more ordinary majority of masters and millowners who started from the bottom, and who though they made money fast made no important innovations to catch the imagination of a progress-minded cultural élite.

> They were rough men, men of the people . . . they knew most of their men by name, and would always speak to each man as he passed. Those old leaders lived and worked in the works amongst their work-people. The office was a very small show and their overhead charges, and in particular their non-productive ratios, were the lowest the world has ever seen.[7]

It was their descendants who, in the main, rose into the middle class.

Once successful, whether in the first or the second generation, the ordinary manufacturers and their families joined the provincial suburban middle class, for they worked in the provinces, in the industrial towns, while the financiers worked in London. Their meeting ground with High Finance, which was operating on a big scale was through the local bankers, often the great Quaker provincial banking families; they banked their profits, and ploughed them back into the business. A Birmingham portrait of the mid-sixties found that:

> The ordinary manufacturer is intelligent rather than narrow: that he is favourable to school instruction but justly estimates still more highly that industrial education which gives skill, steadiness, and a pride in independence: that his mind is not overstrained with speculations because he knows that in the long run he is secure of success through his good and careful management: that he is temperate and domestic, being too intent on his affairs to lose time and health in excesses and too busy to be driven by ennui into vice: that he is inelegant and careless of aesthetical considerations, but free from those pretences which are the worst of vulgarities: that he is firm and self-reliant: a little dogmatical and impatient of contradiction, and when very successful apt to run into purse pride: puritanical in his belief but with a singular tolerance . . . radical in his politics but possessed with a horror of revolution . . . industrious, greedy of success, enterprising . . .[8]

As wealth flowed to the manufacturers, many of them sent their sons, or grandsons, to public schools and universities; and they came back united to the emerging British middle-class culture. Many of them went into the office and lost touch with manufacturing and production techniques, or with manufacture altogether; but the ranks were continually being refreshed with new men starting up from nothing, doing things by rule of thumb, on the capital supplied by their own savings in the time-honoured way of Samuel Smiles; and by recruits from overseas. On the manufacturing side, men like Brunner, Mond and Hans Renold came to Britain; from the Jewish international world came great financiers, while from the Levant came men like Gulbenkian.

Whatever exceptions intelligent circles made, the established hierarchy of noble, landed professional and suburban classes resisted the business invasion, thus providing Victorian novelists with rich material for their studies in snobbery and sterling worth, in prejudice and pride. Thus does one of Mrs Gaskell's heroines cast business into outer darkness:

> 'Are those the Gormans who made their fortunes at trade in Southampton? Oh! I'm glad we don't visit them. I don't like shoppy people. I like all people whose occupations have to do with land; I like soldiers and sailors, and the three learned professions, as they call them. I'm sure you don't want me to admire butchers and bakers and candlestick-makers, do you, Mama?'[9]

The business community endured the slights put upon them as best they could, working steadily to the precept that in the end he who pays the piper calls the tune; and in the end money, progress and development won, though often not without some hard fighting.

> 'I'm new and ye're an old family. Ye don't like me, ye think I'm a pushing man. I go to chapel, and ye don't like that. I buy land, and ye don't like that. It threatens the view from your windies. Well, I don't like you and I'm not going to put up with your attitude. Ye've had things your own way too long, and now ye're not going to have them any longer.'[10]

The view from the windows got worse and worse, but money talked, and everyone, as Anthony Trollope pointed out, began to go to 'Mr Melmotte's' so long as his money talked.

The established merchants faced competition welling up from the industrial provinces and were often pushed out, as Bagehot noted with pleasure 'by the dirty crowd of little men. . . . The rough and vulgar structure of English commerce is the secret of its life'.[11] But it did not remain vulgar or rough; by the early 1900s the great manufacturers, helped to greatness by free trade and limited liability, were big enough to join the company of millionaire bankers and gold magnates. At Edward VII's accession the first rank of business men got to Court—Maple and Lipton as well as Ernest Cassel, the Sassoons and Albert de Rothschild.

Lower down, finance and manufacture came together as the promoters helped to float off family firms as limited companies and took a stake in expansion, in mergers and in amalgamations. Bankers like Charles Geach went into iron as iron ships came in, and from the coal areas emerged great names like Vickers. Through limited liability and the proliferation of company directorships, gradually the aristocracy became the guinea-pigs of those seasoned City men 'of strong lungs and brazen countenances' who blew bubble companies in such a way that in the last third of the nineteenth century investors lost their money in one of every three. If some of the manufacturers had earlier 'exploited' the workers, limited liability enabled the City gentlemen to even some of the score by fleecing the middle classes.[12] Both manufacturers and financiers followed the time-honoured practice, when they had made their money, of buying estates, becoming gentry and duly acquiring titles. Thus providing, incidentally, the contrast between America and Britain referred to by Ogden Nash.

The business man did not come into his inheritance without paying a price. It was not just his vulgarity which repelled the squirearchy, gentry and professional classes; it was also his inhumanity to the labouring stock from which he sprang. Declaring that he knew the working class quite well, he denied that there was any inhumanity at all —that, on the contrary, workpeople were better off than they had ever been, even if the drains *were* a little smelly. In this, the economists of the time overwhelmingly supported the business men. Indeed the economists were almost their only friends among the learned or well-to-do although some doctors also testified that conditions in the mines and factories were comparatively healthy.[13] The business men were often held up to opprobrium for stunting the children's bodies in the mills, and for squeezing their 'hands', worked to the limit of human endurance, for the last ha'penny. Noblemen might even keep cripples on their pay-roll to demonstrate the vileness of manufacturing, which destroyed not only the countryside but the countryman; the evangelicals were against them because of the vice and irreligion in the slums; the aesthetes were against them for having no souls; the angry young men, from Disraeli to Dickens, were implacably against them for having no consciences. Royal Commissions, an invention of middle-class Victorian reformers, laid bare the condition of their workpeople, who forfeited sympathy only when they combined to help themselves. The extraordinary story of a manufacturing country, a world power, built upon the suffering of little children, took hold—and all the efforts of economists and historians will now never release its grip. It is mythology, not history; but it sits firmly and permanently on the neck of the British business man—who, indeed, even believes it himself, and can only bleat despairingly, 'But it's all quite different now!' or even, 'I wasn't there myself!'

He wasn't there. But many of those who were there, firm by firm and industry by industry, fought State interference in business every inch of the way. Many fought their men every inch of the way too—and not all of them considered that, in accordance with the law of marginal utility of labour, this was as much in the interests of the men as of the masters. They fought simply to be masters in their own houses, for the right to employ men and machines, in the way that seemed best to them. They provided the material for Carlyle's saying: 'it is almost trite to remark that there was never yet an age of the world in which one part of mankind did not prey upon the rest . . .; the only difference is that in the nineteenth century cunning takes the place of strength'. This was business, which was progress, which was the newly discovered law of life; and State interference was treachery. The literary people, living in suburban factory-made comfort, yet not entirely without insight, summed up the state of labour relations:

> I have had to do with 'men' for fifty years; I've always stood up to them; I have never been beaten yet. I have fought the men of this company four times and four times I have beaten them. . . . It has been said that times have changed; if they have I have not changed with them. It has been said that master and men are equal. Cant! There can be only one master in a house. It has been said that Capital and Labour have the same interests. Cant! Their interests are as wide asunder as the poles. It has been said that the Board is only part of a machine. Cant! We *are* the machine; its brain and sinews; it is for us to lead and to determine what is to be done. . . . There is only one way of treating men—with the iron hand. . . . Yield one demand, and they will make it six. . . . Mark my words: one fine morning, when you have given way here and given way there—you will find you have parted with the ground beneath your feet. . . . I have been accused of being a domineering tyrant thinking only of my own pride—I am thinking of the future of this country, threatened with the black waters of confusion, threatened with mob government, threatened with what I cannot see.[14]

Not many industrialists were as explicit as Galsworthy's mine-owner, or as prescient. In the end the unions won. Many progressive business men were glad that they did. They had put in welfare and works councils and they wanted to turn over a new leaf and get on with the job. But the two sides of industry remained—and still remain.

2. GROWTH IN SCALE

The first world war brought many new influences to the shaping of the British business man. Social change now ensured him in many industries a growing mass market at home. The general standard of living had risen for all classes after being stationary for some time after the turn of the century; some redistribution between rich and poor was adding to the purchasing power of the lower classes. The war itself had given an insight on what was the meaning, costwise, of long runs; Lloyd George's ceaseless cry for shells and more shells had made conveyor-belt production a reality. Where British business men fell down on delivery, the Americans had stepped in and shown that they, equipped with a know-how entirely new to most British manufacturers, could mass-produce. Finally, though the markets were there after the war, they were not the old markets, but new ones; they had to be located, tooled up for, and supplied in the teeth of keen competition. Sombart even before the 1914–18 war considered that British business had lost its forcefulness compared with German and American. Now he seemed to be right.

One set of business men were, in fact, being elbowed out of the way in the twenties and thirties, and another set were making the most of new opportunities—and making fortunes. There were several groups: the wartime millionaires, who had made their pile, and were able to expand in heavy and light industry; the business men and families who were on the down grade in certain traditional industries, of which cotton was the salient one; and the men who, though they had to scrape up capital and start small, or elbow their way into an old firm and revitalize it, saw where the new opportunities lay. In the decaying industries, sound firms survived and prospered, adapting to change, making, for instance, quality cottons in a single integrated organization like Hendy, or, like Bullmeir, making a go of the apparently hopeless state of shipping. Some, on the other hand, failed even in the industries which were on the verge of a consumer boom—the men who continued to believe that a motor-car was a custom-built job for the upper-class fancier, and not, as William Morris did, a standard piece of furniture for the middle and lower-middle classes.

Taxation was of course far heavier than before the war. By the end of the thirties the head of a medium-sized prosperous business paid as much as half his income in tax. Yet even this left room for saving and as he accumulated capital and drew dividends his fortune could still grow rapidly. A public company was only liable to tax at between 5s and 6s in the pound and could build up large reserves out of taxed profits.

Nor was there any Capital Issues Committee to decide whether the company could raise public money in this way above a limit of a mere £10,000. Not only was it possible even in the stagnant and depression years of the twenties and thirties to make a fortune in business, it was easier than ever for a fortune to buy a man into the nobility and gentry. The gap between the aristocracy and the middle classes disappeared as death duties ground away at fortunes in land, and as 'Big Business' grew bigger.

Big business arrived in full panoply before the Great War with men like Melchett; though James Baird was described in the 1880s as the wealthiest commoner in England. Such men built great firms by sheer organising skill. After the war, when American big business had already become subject to anti-Trust legislation, British big business was helped by official policy to form amalgamations, and associations for the restriction of 'wasteful' competition. Attempts made at the end of the nineteenth century to set up trade or employers' associations were poorly supported; and the call by some declining industries for tariff protection failed. But the movement grew and by 1914 over 1,000 employers' associations existed. The Federation of British Industries was formed in 1916. The collapse of the 1920 post-war boom left many industries with surplus capacity, faced with cut-throat competition at home and in overseas markets. Associations were formed to close down redundant plants, to limit output and to institute 'fair trading codes' among manufacturers. At the same time, concentration of production units by means of amalgamations was part of the process of 'rationalization', which for a time became a magic word.[15] The Government led the way by merging the railway companies into four quasi-monopolies. The banks were being steadily swallowed up into the Big Five; the process of cutting down the national and provincial press into a few huge commercial groups had begun. Great combines like Lever, I.C.I., Vickers, J. and P. Coats, were building quasi-monopolies in their own lines and were praised for it. Governments got together to restrict production of raw materials by various control schemes. The Macmillan

report recommended amalgamation; the new management experts
called for it; and progressive thinkers favoured it. Keynes, for example,
wrote in 1926 that:

> Progress lies in the growth and the recognition of semi-autonomous
> bodies within the State—a return, it may be said, towards the medi-
> aeval conceptions of separate autonomies,

and in 1939 still more confidently that an

> amalgam of private capitalism and State Socialism . . . is the only
> practical recipe for present conditions. . . .[16]

Accordingly, many top business men were essentially concerned
with problems of control and scale; of creating bigger units either by
buying up rivals and enlarging one sovereign concern, or by creating
co-operative or federal business bodies which made marketing, technical
and production policies for whole industries. As the new firms were
created by men like Morris, Dowty, Forte or Fison, they either joined
the rings or competed according to their strength.

Management had grown steadily with the growth in scale permitted
by technological progress and limited liability since 1856. As early as
the 1860s, the economist Henry Fawcett noted dubiously that 'in a joint
stock company all depends on the manager or agent'.[17] The twenties and
thirties were the era in which functional management spread rapidly.
Before 1914, only a few industrialists in Britain, such as Hans Renold,
had heard of American experts like F. W. Taylor; but thereafter
American ideas and indeed American 'systems' of better management
began to spread through British industry. To some extent these were
made known by the activities of a devoted band of experts who con-
stituted the 'management movement', and spread the ideas of men like
Taylor, Gantt and Gilbreth.

Business bureaucracy spread and proliferated of itself, modelled in
part on the army system of delegation, in part on the civil service. In
the inter-war years, the taking of entrepreneurial decisions began
extensively to be made in committee and in conference. Mary Follett,
the business philosopher, went so far as to say:

> As a business is organized today, with its many experts, its planning
> department, its industrial psychologist, its economic adviser, and its
> trained managers, the illusion of final responsibility is disappearing.[18]

This gave rise to a new sensation in big business—as opposed to
smaller firms, which continued to prosper even on nineteenth-century

lines—the sensation that 'the enterprise assumes an independent life as if it belonged to no one'. The words were Walter Rathenau's. He began to speculate on the possibility of businesses which could own themselves by buying up all their own equity shares. The actual appearance of a firm which nobody owned—Volkswagen—awaited, however, Hitler's régime and Germany's defeat in World War II. Yet the loss of a sense of ultimate authority in fact made most British top managers and directors increasingly feel themselves to be controllers. Some, as the Kylsant scandal showed, did not consider that there was any particular need to worry if material facts were concealed from the legal owners, the shareholders.

3. BUSINESS MEN AND SELF-ESTEEM, 1850–1939

By 1939 almost all the skeins of present-day business experience had been woven together: the big business man had emerged as the richest and most prominent member of society while the social gulf between the small manufacturer and the princely banker had almost vanished. Though every stratum of business life continued to exist, the business man as controller rather than founder and owner, as a man of power rather than a man of profits, had become the figure of the man under the top hat.[19] The top business man was becoming strategist, administrator, politician and financier all in one. At the same time the man with a winning idea, or a revolutionary invention, backed by an entrepreneurial flair, could still create from smallish beginnings a great productive enterprise in a working lifetime or less. Business, in terms of social change and a rising standard of living, had delivered the goods. Yet there was a depression to account for, stagnation, lost markets, unemployment, spectacular failures; and the challenge of socialism was never so strong. It is now necessary to trace the climate of business opinion, the business man's relations with national life and thought, in this period when technical and social change had so transformed the scope of his activities.

The history of British business thought, so far as there is such a thing, can be described as a loss of certitude, a search for a philosophy. In the nineteenth century, the business man had to reconcile his own philosophy of low costs and production with the spectacle of poverty and suffering. He found that justification in the teachings of the classical economists, many of whom, in upholding their ideal of *laisser-faire*, were willing to fight on the employers' side against shorter hours or restrictions on factory conditions. They readily gave evidence to royal commissions, campaigning against so-called 'reform', and inveighed against trade unionism. The automatic, self-adjusting machinery of a freely working competitive system, in which everybody, master or servant, by working in his own interest served the utmost possible interest of all, provided the business man with his case.

This case seemed to be strengthened when the Darwinian theory began to gain acceptance, for it was used to provide authority for the equation of economic law with natural law—that of the competitive struggle of species for survival. Business men, even the most intellectual among them, rarely studied political economy, or realized how the professors disagreed amongst themselves over many of their theories. They took in a simplified picture which suggested that to try to legislate socialism into existence was to make water run uphill. 'A law of political economy is a law in no other sense than the law of gravitation, and . . . is *not* an act of Parliament,' wrote Platt in the 1870s in his book *Business*, and observed, 'If you could establish absolute equality tomorrow, the inequality of men's minds and characters would necessarily re-establish an aristocracy in twenty years.'* It was accordingly a shock to business men when other social scientists, under the leadership of Karl Marx, used Darwinism to proclaim that the strife of social classes, also working according to the inexorable laws of nature, was bound to destroy capitalism itself.

Robert Owen tried in his New Lanark mills to set up a type of benevolent paternalism based on sound personnel management which he intended should take the conflict out of the relations between employer and employed; but though his experiment was one of the wonders of the age, other business men were so convinced that immutable laws settled the wages they paid and the conditions of their hands that they did not imitate him; though often in the family firm a kindly if authoritarian human touch produced in workpeople in humble circumstances with simple religious beliefs and limited worldly ambitions a sense of security and personal worth which big firms now try to induce in much more synthetic ways. But Owen's more elaborate ideas of organization, instead of founding a 'management movement' went into the foundation of ethical socialism, and when men like Cadbury in Bournville and Lever in Port Sunlight tried to set up ideal communities, successful as

* Was he the first literary business man to reiterate this hoary tautology?

51 *i.e. the second to utter it?*
who was first.

these may have been in themselves, they were too late to change the psychology of industrial life; such paternalism no longer convinced working men elsewhere or trade unions of the basic benevolence of the British business system, but often seemed showpieces which were the whim of individual rich men. Late in the nineteenth century other business men began to seek a bridge between the 'two sides' of industry in profit-sharing and co-partnership schemes; but again that was too late. Nine in ten business men were talking economic and human verities in the words of Mr Platt well on into the twentieth century. By then the Labour Party had come into existence specifically pledged utterly to destroy them. Casson, the efficiency expert, echoed the business men's horror: 'Socialism is the wiping out of all business. It is the destruction of the whole profit system. It is the inauguration of universal and compulsory civil service.'[20] By the 1920s two generations of Fabian intellectuals had turned the sacred word *profits* into an obscenity. The long road of re-educating the public into thinking of it as a mere integer in accounting lay before the business men.

After World War I rescue seemed possible from other sources. The politicians were in deep disrepute. American ideas were taken up, and a stream of American management know-how and business philosophy poured in. The idea took hold in many business and professional circles that a new generation of business men, devoted to efficiency, to the eradication of the faults of the old-fashioned and 'wasteful' competitive system, might rescue the world from the crazy state in which, by 1923 or 1924 it seemed to have fallen. Mary Follett said: 'Among business men (not all, but a few) I find the greatest vitality of thinking today and I like to do my thinking where it is most alive.'[21] The problem, of course, was not merely to think out better systems of management or marketing or amalgamation; but to think out ways of selling business itself to the community.

H. G. Wells, who had before the war ridiculed business, advertising and high finance in *Tono Bungay*, put into the mouth of his new big business man, William Clissold, in 1926, the words: 'Big business in its increasing quest for efficiency will work steadily and purposefully to eradicate all the faults of our economic organizations which mar the smooth running of the industrial machine.' To this end, the ideas of F. W. Taylor were taken up, though when reduced to the terms of the Bedaux system[22] they had a poor reception from trade unionists. But 'rationalization'—time and motion study, plant reorganization, wage incentive schemes, industrial psychology—at least showed the business man to the public in a new light. The slogan 'Captains of Industry', originally invented by Carlyle in 1843, was given new vogue.

Advertising, the creation of a mass market depending on high wages, was one American idea; efficiency based on scientific management and standard costing was another; the third—perhaps the most hopeful propaganda of all—was the idea of service. Seebohm Rowntree defined the new business philosphy in the words, 'Whatever may be the motives which induce any given individual to engage in industry, its true basic purpose must be the service of the community.'[23] Selfridge had already dedicated his store to the 'service of women'. Mooney and Riley, in America, expanded the idea in *Onward Industry*: 'The objectives of industrial organization have . . . been defined as profit through service —profit in this sense meaning the compensatory material gain obtained through service.'[24] Filene, the American department-store owner turned into business philosopher, became quite widespread reading among the more intellectual British business men, who nodded approvingly when he pontificated that 'not only is industry approaching an exact science, a real profession, but it has itself become a social force, perhaps the leading social force.'

Unfortunately, the impression of the competent business man, organizing and rebuilding the world which the politicians had led into a blood bath in 1914, received a bad shock in 1929. 'Rationalization' had been Hatry's work; but he crashed hopelessly and dishonestly in his efforts to buy up large chunks of the steel industry to rationalize it.[25] The great men too often proved to have feet of clay; Kreuger, engaged on the beneficent work of creating an international match monopoly, was found to have been printing bogus bonds. In his book *Recovery*, Sir Arthur Salter, surveying the mess as it stood in 1932, took pains to disabuse his readers of the idea that there were mighty men of business somewhere who could clear it up. He spoke enthusiastically, it was true, of the international credits which Mr Kreuger was busy making available, but he insisted that 'to imagine that at the centre of the intricate web of man's economic activities stand a few constructive and controlling intelligences is to entertain a romantic illusion. There are no such Olympians'. Stresemann had never been in any doubt of the limitations of industrialists:

> These gentlemen who conduct their concerns so impeccably, often fail when they have been asked to deal with larger policies. Europe's future depends on industrial reconstruction, but the reconstructing will have to be carried out by politicians and not by leaders of industry.[26]

In the end the world had to struggle through the depression until the semi-automatic machine of which Salter spoke so enthusiastically put itself partly to rights. Nobody understood quite what had happened; it was the politicians, however, who scrambled together the system of protection and imperial preference and stumbled into currency devaluation and gave the undercut British industrialists a new chance to compete, despite their antiquated equipment and limited managerial efficiency. It was reserved to the economist Keynes to have a vision of a new regulated private enterprise system which would not run into periodic crises because it would bring into relation the two basic qualities of the business sp.rit, thrift and enterprise, saving and investment. He could be described as the saviour of private enterprise as he showed how limited government planning could maintain a reasonable equilibrium in the economic system and thus remove some of the revealed defects of private enterprise without destroying it. Though many business men disliked him, Keynes alone could claim to have produced the only usable philosophy of business since *laisser-faire* ceased to be an all-conquering battle-cry.

What impressed many humane big-business men was that unrestricted competition seemed to be at the root of the trouble—they wanted control. They feared the 'self-regulating and automatic quality of *laisser-faire*' as much as the small business men of fifty years previously had made it their light. Professor Jewkes (who thought the smaller humbler men of the 1890s were right) wrote:

> It appeared by 1939 that the case for competition had been completely and finally rejected; certainly those few writers who were bold enough to defend it were regarded either as well-meaning but hopelessly archaic in outlook or as blindly and savagely reactionary in their social attitude.[27]

As he noted, business men thought 'restrictive practices' were not only good for their industry but good for the nation, responsible for stability and regular employment at higher wages for workpeople, and facilitating investment in scientific research. But in taking this line they opened the way for socialists to argue that public monopoly was better than private monopoly; that profits coming from monopoly rather than private enterprise in a competitive world ought to be public profits. To this there was, during and after the war years, no very easy reply; though the more thoughtful business men were in fact insisting that even with monopoly and bigness there was quite a lot of incidental and especially quality competition and inter-product competition which would finally disappear in a State monopoly. *The Economist* in 1940 tilted at

> an orderly organization of industries, each ruled feudally from above by the business firms already established in it linked in associations and federations and at the top meeting on terms of sovereign equality such other Estates of the Realm as the Bank of England and the Government. Each British industry . . . has spent the past decade in delimiting its fief, in organizing its baronial courts, in securing and entrenching its holdings and in administering the legal powers of self-government conferred on it by a tolerant state. This is the order of ideas that has transformed the trade association from a body of doubtful legality, a conspiring in restra nt of trade, into a favoured instrumentality of the state, until membership in such a body has become as necessary to the business man who wishes to be successful as the old school tie has been to ambitious Conservative politicians.[28]

The war simply made plain what had been hidden; the trade associations became a vital part of wartime planning—and, later, of post-war Socialist controls and rationing in the interest of fair shares. The Federation of British Industries worked out in some detail plans for 'self-government in industry' which it had been toying with since the thirties, plans which amounted to creating various bodies to enable trade associations to regulate industry from top to bottom, in accordance with the wishes of the majority at every level, a scheme which the Labour Party approved, only modifying it to include certain schemes of outright nationalization to 'own and operate the essential instruments of production: their power over our lives is too great for them to be left in private hands'.[29]

The business man, his functions, activities, ambitions and ideals, were thus transformed as he entered the first full Socialist era. Yet he remained, in these new dimensions, in the most vital respect, still what he had been in the days of Gradgrind and Bounderby, in the heyday of merchant banking families who despised Cobden and Bright for their ignorance of the classics and of the Cunliffe-Listers and Levers who rose by manufacture to equality with merchant princes and noblemen of any degree. He remained controller and boss, in the seat of creative power, even when that power was circumscribed by other Estates of the Realm —such as a Socialist government or the Trade Unions. Those business men who dealt with the political end of things found, however, that they had to go back to the ideals of the earlier era and dig up words like 'efficiency', 'enterprise' and above all 'competition'. The radical, younger generation of smaller business men were beginning again, by

1945, to talk about profit, as distinct from cost-plus, as its own justification.

Other young men, furthermore, were simply studying business as a system of power and authority like any other, estimating its rewards, planning to get into it, and considering how to get to the top of it.

NOTES

1. Zweig, F., *The British Worker*, London, Penguin Books, 1952, p. 87 ff.
2. Roll, E., *An Early Experiment in Industrial Organization*, Longmans, 1930.
3. Cf. Sombart, W., *The Quintessence of Capitalism*, London, Fisher Unwin, 1915.
4. *Hoare's Bank, A Record 1672–1955*, Collins, 1955, p. 32; Fulford, R., *Glyn, Mills*, 1955, p. 22 *et seq.*; Robinson, R. M., *Coutts: The History of a Banking House*, London, John Murray, 1928, p. 28 ff.
5. Mantoux, P., *The Industrial Revolution in the Eighteenth Century*, London, Cape, 1928, p. 60; cf. Ashton, T. S., *Economic History of England in the Eighteenth Century*, Methuen, 1955.
6. Cf. Gill, C., *History of Birmingham*, Vol. I, O.U.P., 1952, p. 109.
7. Ord, Lewis C., *Secrets of Industry*, London, Allen & Unwin, 1944, p. 79.
8. Sargant, W. L., *Essays of a Birmingham Manufacturer*, London, Williams & Norgate, 1869, p. 59.
9. Gaskell, Mrs, *North and South*, 1855.
10. Galsworthy, John, *The Skin Game*, Duckworth, 1920.
11. Bagehot, Walter, *Lombard Street*, London, Kegan Paul, 1896, pp. 11, 12.
12. Shannon, H. A., 'The Limited Companies of 1866–83', in *Essays in Economic History*, ed. Carus Wilson, Arnold, 1954.
13. Hutt, W. H. 'The Factory System in the Early Nineteenth Century', in *Capitalism and the Historians*, ed. F. A. Hayek, London, Routledge, 1954, p. 163 ff.
14. Galsworthy, J., *Strife*, Duckworth, 1909.
15. Meakin, W., *The New Industrial Revolution*, London, Gollancz, 1928, p. 19 ff.
16. Keynes, J. M., speech at University of Berlin, 1926, and article in *The New Statesman and Nation*, 28 January 1939, quoted in Brady, R. A., *Business as a System of Power*, Columbia University Press, 1944, p. 181.
17. Fawcett, H. A., *Manual of Political Economy*, Macmillan, 1863, Vol. I, Sec. II, pp. 77–8.
18. Quoted in Urwick, L., *The Making of Scientific Management*, London, Management Publications Trust, 1949, Vol. I, p. 54.
19. Mond, Alfred, *Industry and Politics*, London, Macmillan, 1927, p. 12.
20. Casson, H. N., *The Axioms of Business*, Efficiency House, 1925.
21. Follett, Mary P., Freedom and Co-ordination: *Lectures in Business Organization*, London Management Publications Trust, 1949, p. xii.

22. There is no reference to Bedaux, C., in the *Golden Book of Management*, Newman Neame, London, 1956; see *Everyman's Encyclopaedia*, 1958, art. 'Bedaux System'.

23. Rowntree, B. Seebohm, quoted in *The Making of Scientific Management*, op. cit, p. 68.

24. Mooney, J. D. and Riley, A. C., *Onward Industry*, New York, 1931.

25. Vallance, A., *Very Private Enterprise*, London, Thames & Hudson, 1955, p. 11.

26. Quoted by Beard, M., *A History of the Business Man*, New York, Macmillan, 1938, p. 733.

27. Jewkes, John, 'The Control of Industrial Monopoly', in *The Three Banks Review*, December, 1955.

28. *The Economist*, 15 June, 1940.

29. Madge, C., *Industry After the War*, London, Pilot Press, 1943, p. 34.

CHAPTER III

The Way In

'Ask, and it shall be given you; seek, and ye shall find; knock and it shall be opened unto you.'

MATTHEW, vi, 7

'The things we make . . . are in growing demand all over the world. . . . All of which means, to the man who joins Westinghouse, a future of unbounded opportunity, in a job of great and growing importance.'

Manchester Guardian, 28 January 1958, page ad.

'I had four young children and I was out of a job and I can think of no better reason for starting a company than that.'

MR FRANK PERKINS *of Perkins Diesel Engines*

IN THE PAST THE CONTROLLERS of British business have in the main been recruited from three social levels: first, the ranks of the business families organized in a network of private firms; second, from the successful among the possessors of the entrepreneurial spirit in all walks of life, high and low, but mostly fairly lowly; and third, from the outsiders who began without capital or even ideas on which capital could be raised but with the ability and stamina to rise to the top from a long and often dreary apprenticeship from the bench, counter or counting-house. All these gateways to the top involved 'goin' through t'mill'—but in a family firm this was a training course which carried the certainty of a partnership or directorship in comparative youth when money, power and position are most enjoyable and, in intelligent and creative men, most usable.

These traditional sources of recruitment meant that it was hard for the children of professional families, and especially for the young university graduate, to get into business. Business men who had come up from the bottom with little education were opposed to formal education; if they wanted a likely lad to train up, they thought he should start straight from school at an early age. Educated men did of course get into industry in the past, in growing numbers from the

1880s onwards—as engineers and technicians at first and later as managers, though in nothing approaching the numbers in America where, as early as 1910, 41 per cent of senior business men had been through college.[1]

Even when graduates went into British industry, they were at a disadvantage with the scions of the family firms which employed them. The latter were often educated and indeed university men, and while they were 'up' they sometimes collected young 'brains' which might prove useful to the family; but they made the distinction between their wealth and position of power on the one hand, and the position of the graduate hired for his brains—even if he had been at Magdalen with Mr Jack—very, though friendlily, plain. Thus business for the most part offered a way of life and a type of associate uncongenial to the professional classes—uncultured, limited in outlook and materialistic. Even where it was relatively cultured it was dynastic—and, it should be added, the culture was often the puritan culture of dissent. As Sir Frederic Hooper has pointed out:

> ... the distaste of the professional classes for their stereotyped picture of a business man is equalled by the business man's distrust of the intellectual. The two worlds seldom meet in the flesh. When they do, the university product, more likely than not, appears to the business man as an opinionated coxcomb, ignorant of practical realities, thoroughly *unsound*.[2]

Even today business is sprinkled with men who get angry at the thought of long-haired intellectuals, although the wartime experience of working together sometimes led to a radical reassessment of each other.

1. THE FAMILY BUSINESS

Starting at the bottom in the family business in the early days meant starting very low—usually being apprenticed like any tradesman, and perhaps then going on the road for the product. A typical case is the men who built the Reckitt business, one of whom recorded:

> In 1843 (July) I returned from Essex and was retained in the starch business by father. At this time I was 18 years old and Frank 16. The starch business at this time paid nothing nor had it paid anything from the commencement, and in December 1843, I being 18/2 ... proposed travelling to introduce our patent starch. Both father and mother objected to my travelling as I was so young, but as I felt

competent of my powers I prevailed upon them to let me try. . . .
How I worked at my uphill career no one can ever know fully but
myself, but I am safe in saying I did not have a dinner more than
once a week if so often and I went without food from starting in the
morning until late at night as I seldom came in till 8 or 9. . . . However,
I succeeded in introducing our starch very generally. . . .[3]

Another member of a family business, writing eighty years later,
records a very comparable apprenticeship:

> My own business training began with a year in a German woollen
> mill, followed by nearly four years in a Leeds clothing factory, where I
> worked for five shillings a week. On asking for a rise I was told I was
> not worth what I was already being paid and instead of getting more
> money I found myself out of a job. The Vickers business to which I
> then came in 1906 was small and uncertain, but during the next ten
> years, as attention was turned from merchanting to manufacturing,
> the situation improved. . . .[4]

This type of hard grind was probably more usual than the fairly easy
transition from the university to the boardrooms of the family firms
that had become wealthy.

To realize what it often took even in family businesses to get to the
top in the nineteenth century, it is only necessary to read the diaries of
Walter Leaf, who fought for years to save his father's clothing business;
here was no optimistic hard-headed Victorian boss. A typical entry
reads:

> I hope I shall never forget that for months on end I have begun every
> day with the earnest wish that I were dead. I only lived through last
> year because of father and mother.

In the end the firm was sold to another; but Leaf's personal charm and
culture, and his wide circle of friends, led to his being made a director
of the City and Westminster Bank; he ended up with a vast reputation
as a banker as the respected head of the Westminster Bank.[5]

Jesse Boot, the future Lord Trent, founder of Boots, also records a
hard grind which he only survived with several breakdowns in health:

> It was not easy work. In those days our small shop kept open until
> nine o'clock at night and eleven on Saturdays. I still have a vivid
> recollection of the long monotonous drudgery. I was busy behind the
> counter, but my days did not end with the closing of the shop, for I
> had hours of writing to do. Later on, when there were several branches,
> I would work right through the night for a fortnight at stock-taking.

I had very little capital and could not obtain credit. . . . My health suffered so much and I was so worn out that at 36 anybody could have had my business very cheap. Later on, at 50, my health gave way again, and as I had a competency I was strongly tempted to retire, but I had business ideals, and I remained in harness solely to carry them out.[6]

Our last example is George Paulson, who built railways in every continent in the last quarter of the nineteenth century. He began in a glove factory, went precariously from job to job, served as timekeeper, buttyman, brick tallyman and quantity surveyor on various British lines under Joseph Firbank, and then, having mastered the technique of tunnels, went to South Africa and made his first £15,000 by the time he was twenty-four.[7]

If the position of 'members of the family' was difficult, that of complete outsiders, working their way up, was even harder. Yet a few succeeded. It is recorded that even in the Mond-Melchett business, now I.C.I., Lord McGowan, the chairman, Sir Frederick Bain and Mr John Rogers, the deputy chairman, were all born in the same block of streets in Glasgow as poor boys. Sir John James, former chairman and managing director of the Lancashire Steel Corporation, started as a furnace hand in the melting shop of the firm.

Today, the number of established private family firms is dwindling steadily, as they are turned into public companies in order to raise capital for expansion. But the network of family firms, and the influence that goes with them, remains considerable. The great family dynasties like the W. H. Smiths, the financial Smith clan, Colmans, Albrights and Wilsons, Wedgwoods, Cadburys and Jardines still go on. Even where the family has lost control, it still enjoys advantages in starting its young people in the firms as management trainees, although they may now have to compete on more equal terms with management trainees from other walks of life.

2. STARTING ON A SHOESTRING

What of starting on one's own? Is this, the ideal of the professor of economics, still a possible first step to a fortune rather than merely being one's own boss at a very moderate level? The list of newspaper boys who ended as company chairmen is long and well known; though this type of success story is more common in America. But what of today? In the first place, it should be frankly noted that, even in the past, the number of failures among the would-be followers of Samuel Smiles was enormous—as every economist, anxious that the competitive process should weed out all but the most competitive among entrepreneurs, would wish. Of those that did not fail, the vast majority have always remained small tradesmen, and do not become business men in the sense defined in this book. Not one retail shop in ten thousand burgeons into a chain like W. H. Smith or Boots. It remains small business, essentially and inevitably lower-middle class, either because the talents of its founder are too restricted or the economic opportunity for expansion in that line simply does not exist. It is often said that 90 of every 100 businesses fail in less than twenty years.

Though their importance is declining, entrepreneurs are still 'going into business' in this traditional way, risking their capital, and ploughing back their profits in the hope of creating a large asset even under current conditions in which taxation is high and many of the best positions are already occupied by established companies. As in the most formative periods of capitalism, the same basic virtues are required of the business man who chooses this path: the readiness to live extremely simply, to save and put back his money into the business; regular habits of industry, thrift and application. Such a man could even read with advantage the early tracts of capitalism, such as Defoe's *Compleat Tradesman*, for hints on his way of life, making suitable translations into modern idiom. He can envy the economy of Robert Chalmers, the publisher, who noted 150 years ago that 'as a final achievement in the art of cheap living I was able to make an outlay of one and ninepence suffice for the week'. In a study of post World War II businesses, an economist writes:

> One small family engineering business pays the owners the same salary they would earn as employees, the rest being left to accumulate. One man started with £1,200 after the war, and in six years the company's reserves exceeded £5,000: all net profit after meeting the managing director's salary was left in. Another man started with £500 and now has a capital of £3,000; another went from £800 to over £6,000 in the same way. Six people working together started with £700 plus a large loan from one of the directors. In six years the capital had increased to £15,000 and the loan had been paid off. There have been no extravagant drawings and the directors are content to use small horsepower cars.[8]

The men who have started businesses in this way are not of one social class. They come from all walks of life. In contrast to the entrepreneurs of the Victorian heyday, many of them come from the middle management of medium-sized firms. Some secede from a family business and start on their own from a neurotic desire to prove themselves better than their fathers. Many are men who have not the temperament to rise to the top in modern business in ways to be examined later in this book; some frankly describe themselves as 'unemployable'. Their aim, however, is often not power and fortune, in the sense that most business men desire; it is sheer independence in an increasingly collectivist world. They have, the Americans say, an 'unscratchable itch' to try out their ideas. Some reveal this anarchist motive by their preference to develop their little firms relatively slowly from their own money rather than accept, at the cost of losing control, the large sums which are usually offered to any good going concern by financial institutions or by big companies cruising round for little fish to swallow. Independence is their main reward. The other reward is the pleasure that such men take in the product itself; many of them left the security of big firms because their employers would not themselves exploit the ideas these entrepreneurs had put forward. Many firms of this type have been built out of the gratuities which formed the initial capital from civil applications of wartime weapons and gadgets developed during the war.

3. NEOPHYTE IN THE BUSINESS HIERARCHY

All the traditional ways into business remain, therefore. There is still scope for sheer business instinct. But today even those who feel most strongly the entrepreneurial urge do not necessarily have to start, or start in, a small firm. For those who want to rise into the ranks of management, to graduate to the boss class, a series of ladders via technical education exist, and it is said that modern firms are only too keen to encourage the promotion of anyone who shows, so unusually, the power and desire to take responsibility. The large corporations and many of the medium-sized, now offer terms of entry which are recognized alternatives to the civil service or the professions. As the previous chapter has shown, the prestige of industry has steadily risen with its size and organization; the managements of some of the big firms are filled with professional people who are broadly of the same type, intellectual discipline, and to some degree outlook, as the young graduate would expect to encounter in the civil or foreign service.

The increase in the prestige of industry as a career can to some extent be judged from the growing number of public school boys and graduates going into large and medium firms as trainees under some formal or informal trainee scheme. The returns to the Public School Appointments Board from 170 schools show that 51 per cent went into commerce and industry in 1956 compared with 38 per cent from 125 public schools in 1951–2. This in itself was a great increase on pre-war days, when there were relatively few trainee schemes. A recent study by PEP[9] found that of a sample of those graduating from British universities in 1950 just over 23 per cent went into manufacturing industry and just over 7 per cent into commerce. Industry succeeded, moreover, in attracting a high proportion of the best brains; 24 per cent of those with firsts went into manufacturing industry but only 2 per cent into commerce. Manufacturing industry had suffered a net loss of 12 per cent of its intake by 1954 and commerce a net loss of 11 per cent. A third of the graduates who left industry went into teaching or took a paid appointment at a university which suggests that, after a short time in industry, some graduates yearned to get back to academic surroundings.

These recruitment figures suggest that an industrial or business career now stands high in middle-class favour. But they should not be taken wholly on their face value. More children are now going to school and, above all, more are going to universities and technical colleges—so that it is increasingly difficult for businesses to recruit an intelligent boy at fifteen or sixteen. Further, the important range of official careers overseas open to the professional classes, which have themselves greatly increased in numbers, is declining. In the first half of the twentieth century, for example, Britain was administering the Empire, as well as policing and guarding its shores and sea communications. The Indian civil has disappeared. The colonial service offers diminishing opportunities and the forces have been ruthlessly cut down. The home civil service, of course, has expanded and so has the foreign service; but at existing rates of pay both are finding it hard to get all the men of quality they require. Overseas, what is needed in Britain's interest is now salesmen, contractors, agents and traders, rather than district commissioners. Yet discussions with graduates and the secretaries of university appointments boards suggest that the prestige of business is still not as high as that of the civil service or the professions. According to appointment board secretaries, 'undergraduates still tend to prefer the professions, journalism, the civil service or the B.B.C. or an international organization'. Such jobs are considered 'interesting' while business seems dull and even rather unworthy.

There is still some truth in Sir Frederic Hooper's picture of the way young men are steered away from industry:

> Let us imagine a young man, fresh from grammar school, public school or university, who has done well in his studies, has been head of his house or captain of his team, but is undecided about his career. Perhaps he goes to his teacher or tutor. You can almost hear the advice. 'Business? Good enough for a second-rater; you can do better. You could do research. You could teach. The civil service. Medicine. The Law. I don't think you'd like *business*! My dear boy, you'd get to the top, no doubt, but is it worth it?' And so another young man of promise and parts gives business the go-by and drifts to the chair-borne occupations—to teaching or Whitehall.[10]

Talks with recent graduates both in industry and outside suggest that they mainly enter industry for one of three reasons: family tradition, money, or because, having failed to get the kind of work they want, it is the only alternative to teaching: as one said to one of the authors: 'My first choice was the Foreign Office, my second UNESCO, my third the B.B.C., my fourth *The Times*, then there was nothing left but teaching or business, and as I can't bear little boys it had to be business.' This is very upsetting for some business men, who feel that 'industrial leadership' is a career to be entered for its own sake by the first-rate among British youth, as it is said to be in the United States. As the Anglo-American team on management education complained,

> To be a high industrial executive in America is considered not only eminently 'respectable', but also 'socially desirable'. It is a prevailing opinion that business attracts the best talent from educational institutions, whereas in Britain there is a strong tendency for the best students to find their way into the civil service and professions. . . .

Those who want to marry young find that industry[11] offers several hundred a year more at the start than in the professions and an assurance for middle age with a pension for retirement. Above all, even the young begin to feel that a career in a big business contains built-in hedges against inflation which other middle-class careers do not. Industry is in fact increasing its grip on the nation's youth by the simplest of processes—offering a bigger wage packet plus fringe benefits. As the number of pro-consulships declines, the advantages of top management jobs in oil, steel or chemicals becomes clearer to the middle classes. They are a way to power as well as money. As a top-drawer business man in one of Mr Priestley's novels put it:

> 'Now my class, Angleby, may be stupid about some things—their taste in literature, for example, is appalling—but they're wonderfully quick at allying themselves with any new power. Instead of fighting it, as so many of their kind have tried to do abroad, they get to know it, they dine and wine it, they marry it and finally control it.'[12]

Most young men deciding to go into industry or commerce may be unconscious of the managerial revolution; they simply realize that nowadays the administrative qualities they offer can find their most promising outlet in business. Another post-war business novel puts their motives understandably:

> 'To me,' said Henry, holding up his polished glasses to the light, 'this has always been quite simple. The Lord didn't see fit to make me able to paint, write, compose music, or do anything of that kind. After that, it didn't really matter. I imagine that the problems of creative work are peculiar. But the problems of every other sort of work are exactly the *same* problems. I was born into a position where I could become what is called an "executive" and not just another pair of hands. And all executive problems are the same. Whether you're in business, or the army or the civil service, or what. They only differ in scale or the material you reckon in. Most of the problems are produced by the peculiarities of the people one has to work with . . . and if you work in sheet metal or custard powder it doesn't make any difference.'[13]

Business, in fact, is one form of the executive life, and increasingly as Britain goes out of the Imperial Great Power business, it is the leading and best-rewarded form; and because the leading one, surely one's friends will be there too?

We have suggested that the word 'management' is not only respectable in the Labour Party but is also becoming tolerable in West End clubs. Although business men give the impression that management is a career for which one is trained as much as a doctor or a lawyer, only a small proportion of managers have been, or are being, formally trained. There has been much discussion since the war about training for management; one Anglo-American productivity team devoted itself to the subject; there have been several White Papers and out of them Sir Stafford Cripps, when Labour Chancellor of the Exchequer, conjured the British Institute of Management, whose task was not only to develop a specific set of 'management studies' but also to develop the new profession as such. Yet, despite all this talk about management education, in point of fact the entry is not into a profession but into industry, into business, for those whose full understanding is that they are going in to do a job, to play the game for all it is worth, according to the rules, and to get as much out of it as they can. There is no such network of business schools and technical universities as there is in America, or business degrees or management qualifications and letters designate. The latter do exist, but it is all on a puny scale and constitute no real recommendation for the young graduate having a look for the front door rather than the servants' or tradesmen's entrances into industry.

4. THE IVORY HUNT

The young man thinking of going into big business need look no further than the advertisement pages of the newspapers. Most of the big firms now realize the need to recruit talent for management: though only a few are specifically looking for top business men. They are now increasingly offering a career in the civil service sense rather than merely a try-out to see if a man has any business gumption in him. Large companies are engaged on expensive and intensive ivory hunting. This does not mean, of course, that all, or even most, big companies are actively looking for bright young men.* In recruiting, as in all other aspects of management, a few play a leading part and the others rely simply on what turns up in the way of letters from job-hunters, recommendations from its own staff, and requests and string-pulling from among the director's acquaintances. But for companies who take seriously the quest for a fair share of the nation's young talent, recruitment is now a major worry.

In their drive to attract graduates, especially engineers, scientists and technologists, the leading companies have for some years been taking half or a whole page in such papers as the *Manchester Guardian* or *The Times*, to set forth the advantages to be got by a keen young man

---

* Some firms are even proud of the fact that they have no policy for recruitment; an executive of one remarked to the authors, 'Well, when we feel we ought to take someone on we do and turn him loose to see if he can find a job for himself in the firm. We reckon if he's any good he is sure to find something worth doing in the course of six months or so. The last man we took on because we thought he had something was seventy-two, and he's doing awfully well.'

from joining the company. In the first couple of months of 1957 (when the annual talent hunt season begins) young men were told:

> Men are not turned into managers by magic. We do not use any impersonal formula. Each man who comes to us, not to fill a job but to find a career, comes with individual talents and inclinations.

> For young men who want an exciting and varied career in power engineering The Future Is Here.

> We need you because, in a large organization like ours, we must never stand still.

> *To-day's Outstanding Career Opportunity.*
> A future as big as you are big enough to make it.

> A progressive organization operating in a continually expanding world market, the Company offers opportunities to responsible young people who are seeking a worthwhile career of absorbing interest leading to a substantial future.

> If you feel you would be interested in working with the team that achieved these successes for Great Britain, write to us.

It is noticeable that the companies give no definite indication of salary expectations in their advertisements*—and any young man who is unwise enough to ask will earn a black mark, as he is told 'it all depends on you'; no clue will be offered on what 'all' might amount to in £. s. d. What the companies stress is the prestige of their name and the prospects that their type of firm or industry offers. Those that are expanding can point to this as solid promise. Prestige is more intangible, but it sways the choice of young men. The aircraft industry has lost some of its high prestige, but oil, especially international oil, is almost like going into the civil service. Chemicals rank high; and then, in an interesting but as yet uncharted scale of social gradations, all the capital goods industries. Retailing (even though the departmental stores have led in management training and the recruitment of graduates) is a notch down except for shrewd young people who know they are going to find the climb fairly easy and the pickings good. The

* It is rare to find a company which says as frankly as Geigy did in its page advertisement in the *Manchester Guardian* of 29 January 1958 that 'salary the key to independence—something we believe is uppermost in the minds of most young people today. So forget the polite conventions, and let's talk money first'. However, they too gave no indication of future salaries.

manufacture of consumer goods, especially foodstuffs or cheap jackery, is also lower in prestige. So is contracting, except in matters of international tendering, where members of the Sudan service, for example, found billets.

The difference between sheet metal and custard powder *is* significant, though such meaningless snobbery horrifies Americans. Mr David Brown, the Yorkshire manufacturer, has wryly said:

> As David Brown, manufacturers of gears, ballbearings and machine tools, no one has heard of me but the engineering industry. As David Brown, tractors, a few more hear the name. But as David Brown, maker of racing cars, they grab my hand, offer me drinks and want my autograph.[14]

Advertisements are only one of the many ways which are used to attract able new recruits. Conferences are held for schools' career masters; sixth forms are taken on factory tours, with superb tea; vacation employment is offered to—mostly scientific—undergraduates and career booklets are pressed into the hands of all. Most of the big firms employ talent spotters, whose job it is to cultivate good relations with appointments officers (who sometimes have trouble with their figures nowadays) and with professors, who are delicately invited to indicate their best students, so that these may be offered something better than that research fellowship, and to advise all their students that Messrs X is a respectable and progressive concern for a university man to work for. To graduates unacquainted with industry such advice can be very persuasive. Sometimes the talent spotter will cultivate outstanding students. According to the Acton Society Trust, one young man in 1955 in his second year at the university had already been offered £750 a year by a large company upon his graduation and was being courted by the talent spotter of another, who took him to lunch with the managing director.

Efforts on this scale cost a great deal of money for a numerically small return. One company, for example, sent its talent scout to 20 universities; 130 men were interviewed, but one was finally taken. Another spent £3,000 advertising for qualified engineers; they received 977 applications, interviewed 96, but only appointed 20 from outside and 7 from within, though they needed more of this calibre!

The seller's market for administrative ambition is smaller than that for technical ability, partly because it is more difficult to assess which young man is a potential top manager than to tell who is a good technician. Some companies try to make just such an assessment, but others are only concerned to recruit good men for middle management, assuming that among them will be a few winners. Most companies offer similar starting salaries for graduates, £550 to £800, scientists and technicians will tend to receive the higher figures, but may have less opportunities for promotion. In 1958 the average was about £650. Smaller companies have more chance to offer a good starting salary, as their salary scales are not so rigid; and of course they usually offer more responsibility sooner.

Some companies consider that their management trainee schemes are useful as a bait to catch able recruits. These schemes do give the graduate who is unused to industry a chance to look round before committing himself to a particular job. But such schemes have run into the difficulty that graduates of any worth quickly get bored going from department to department without a job to do, and other employees may resent them as 'crown princes'. Indeed, some of these schemes are of such poor intellectual calibre that they are in danger of producing a new strain of angry young men.

Other companies, large as well as small, are altogether unconvinced by the ballyhoo about graduates,* and some having tried them say they are disillusioned. The graduate—usually the arts graduate is meant here—is accused of being conceited, of expecting too much, of lacking practical experience, of antagonizing other employees, and of having a high wastage rate.

> And still they come, the promising young men with their B.Sc.s, and their honours, very pleased with themselves, and blandly unaware that for the next two years at least they will be a total liability. And their first question is still, 'How much do you pay me? I understand Such & Such offer £500 a year.' After which comes the vexed question of holidays.[15]

Rare apparently is nowadays the boy who can write: 'The question of salary is of course quite secondary to that of the experience involved, and would presumably depend on my services to you.' One who did became assistant managing director to British Glues and Chemicals.[16]

---

* As the P.E.P. study of 'Graduates in Industry' showed, industries varied greatly in the number of graduates they recruited. Of the graduate sample studied by P.E.P., one in four went into chemicals and oil, but only one in a hundred into shipbuilding and a much smaller proportion into railway engineering. *Graduates in Industry*, Political and Economic Planning, London, Allen & Unwin, 1957, p. 225.

University education, say some business men grimly—especially if they own firms in declining industries—spoils young men, destroys their natural verve, their singleness of heart, their simple enthusiasm for, say, the product, and makes them too sophisticated to be loyal to the firm. They say it prolongs adolescence, makes the third-rate man narrower, which may be true, as he has to spend so much time trying to pass exams, yet gives him an inflated idea of his value, and the time taken up is utterly lost to the practical education on the shop floor which he must have. Such criticisms have led to predictions that the floor will drop out of the graduate market in a few years. The later school leaver has certainly become more popular, because business men like to catch him young and make sure that his part-time studies are of an eminently practical kind.* He is, however, helping to make up the shortage of graduates rather than to replace them.

Criticism of the graduate is nothing new. Many business men still cannot understand why Oxford and Cambridge do not teach accounting, while few can see even the sense of the London or Manchester schools of business administration, to which they firmly do not send their young management men. They echo Carnegie, who declared roundly that 'in my experience I can say I have known few young men who were not injured by a collegiate education'. Such criticism is partly jealousy; self-made business men dislike the graduate not coming up as slowly and toilsomely as they did in 1910 or 1925, and some see clearly that there are graduates who outclass them in sheer business acumen.

Talent spotters confine their interest almost entirely to school leavers and graduates. They reflect Platt's dictum that 'a man , if he means to make a business of his own, should be in business before thirty'. In this day and age, promotion from within is becoming a sacred cow, as the unfortunate colonel or naval captain discovers soon enough when he tries to offer his administrative ability for sale to big firms. Promotion from within may be stretched to buying a bright man from a competitor, or buying him with the business he was in; in smaller firms buying out executive talent is the recognized way of trying to do without training —in fact, it works as a kind of cross-fertilization of talent, which is no bad thing. Some firms have a gentlemen's agreement not to poach.

In all this it is notable that finance and commerce, on the whole,

---

* Some firms now prefer the sandwich course, arguing that a man who takes his Dip. Tech, alternating study at the technical college with practical work at the factory does not get fancy ideas.

do not feel much need to go talent spotting or advertising for juniors. The City knows that there is a queue of keen young money-makers knocking at the door. Many, it is true, when they get into an enormously wealthy merchant banking firm, find that they have chosen a drab grind, and that the plums are reserved to the partners or the family; but it is clear that the prospects entice and that salary expectations are more definitely stated than in industry.

5. PICKING THE WINNER

It may be asked what qualities do companies look for in their recruits. They cannot test them in the way that the market tests the entrepreneur. Their degrees mean little or nothing, except in terms of the technologist. Even these do not guarantee the type of mind that the business man wants. Mr Cotes told *Scope*:

> But I do not want the type of scientists turned out to-day, the civil servant type, the clocker-on from 9.30 to 6. So they say to me: What DO you want? Do you want a biochemist, a scientist, a mathematician, or what? And I answer: I want a brain. And they don't know what I mean. Give me a brain and I'll do the training. But it must be an original brain. A brain that can look at a bone and see in it world without end. . . . Bones are my business. . . . This company will be as big as any in the world in A.D. 2000 if I can find a dozen men.[17]

Many heads of companies have very rough-and-ready yardsticks of the qualities they desire. Sir Halford Reddish, for example, is reported to have demanded:

> Above all one hundred per cent loyalty, twenty-four hours a day, inside business and out. Then a capacity for work. And only third I ask for a knowledge of the job.[18]

He hated young men who raise questions about pensions and terms and conditions of employment.

> I never have and I never want, service agreements. I only want people to work with me who prefer to work with me.

Mr Newland of Goodman's Industries wants 'a spark . . . or sparkle . . . a something in a face . . . something that tells me this boy or man is not just another cipher, unit, or whatever it is they turn out nowadays in their thousands'.[19] Mr Colin A. Samuels of C.A.S. (Industrial Developments) Ltd says: 'I ask ice-cold efficiency, coupled with a warmth of humanity in human relations. Never employ a man who slouches, he has no confidence in himself or his work.'[20]

Mr Kenyon Jones, of Ronsons, looked for 'an indefinable quality of ease and understanding, an inborn quality, greatly to be envied, impossible to acquire'. He also 'would rather have a less brilliant man I could trust than the brilliant sort with whom you never know where you are'.[21]

Another company says it wants 'an industrial type'; but what is that? It is easy to think of people who are not industrial types; men who would not have the good-humoured tolerance of fools which is necessary to work in a community, and particularly in one where there is a danger of industrial strife; men too idealistic to adapt to business *mores* (though many idealistic men will be found in business, usually stuck somewhere in middle management where they can do no harm by it). The artistic type, naturally, is not favoured—though management is an art, not a science, and many top business men are not only artists but have all the perfectionism and temperament of artists. It is not hard to make a list of the attributes which an industrial type would *not* have, but it is harder to define the qualities he should have. This will be examined in a future chapter.

Among the traits mentioned as essential for the young man applying for his first job in an industrial empire are: drive; decisiveness; determination; push; 'toughness combined with civilisation'; analytical ability; an inquiring mind; ability to get on with colleagues—this last is highly prized by business men—the 'dependable, combinable type', as Andrew Carnegie put it. Above all they want 'good mixers'; and, of course, drive. These are the alpha and omega of desirable traits for entering management, if not for going into business. There is wide agreement that academic distinction is less important than personality. In some firms this simply means 'public school'. The great and indeed American emphasis on acceptability to colleagues is significant; it shows how British business is changing, and with it the 'type' that goes into business. How many of the old giants would have passed this criterion? —Leverhulme? Lipton? Mond? Braithewaite? Josiah Mason? or Rhodes?

How do companies ensure that they get the men with the qualities they want—whether as committee men or individualists? The directors who are most sure that they know the answer to selection believe in the infallibility of their own judgment. 'I can tell what a man is like when he comes into the door' is an extreme but not an exceptional attitude. Now it is more common to ape the old-time civil service 'Viva' with an interview before a board of managers. A further step towards what the civil service now describes as 'Method II' is to wine and dine the young man on the short list and see what he is like in company and in liquor. The largest companies give short-listed candidates the full treatment with intelligence tests, group selection, and multiple interviews with managers and a psychologist; the group test is a favourite with some, where the candidates discuss a set subject together, often a quasi-business problem, before the selection committee, which watches to see the potential managing director emerge by taking discreet charge of the group. It is certainly not common, as has been suggested,[22] for big firms in this country to submit young men to I.Q., ability and adaptability tests or to probe their unconscious with Rorschach and Thematic Apperception Tests.

The smaller firm usually buys men with experience, who have been in business for at least five or six years, and their method is often to discuss the candidate in extreme detail and frankness with his former employers. 'We don't mind if we spend a fortune taking up references,' said a firm to one of the authors. 'We go and see the chap's previous employers ourselves. We do a complete M.I.5 and we don't miss. It's worth it when you're only taking on an important executive every three years or so.' A firm of immensely wealthy merchant bankers has a simple test. After discussing with the candidate all the usual things, the one really important question is put. 'If you were today given, or inherited, an income which would be completely adequate to permit you to live exactly in the way you wanted, and do just what you wanted, what would you do?' The winning answer is: 'Bring the money into Merchant Banking and make more.' Such a reply, tested for sincerity, makes it clear that the man is not even interested in great wealth as such: what he likes is doing deals, making bargains, enjoying business at the highest level simply for business' sake. At least that is the theory. As a test not for managerial qualities, for administrative prowess or leadership, but for sheer business instinct, it may be a good one. Men who can answer like that ought to be business men. Dealing in everything from film stars to firms and from armaments to government surplus is their nature. They always become rich. Untrained, they make and lose fortunes and sometimes end in jail; trained, they are merchant bankers, brokers and dealers on the grand scale.

What is the young man starting on a business career to think of all this? *Jeunesse dorée*, of course, goes into the family business, but those less well-placed have a harder choice. As a young girl enjoys the court-ship leading to marriage, he can and should enjoy the ivory hunt, not merely for what he can get out of it in material terms: good dinners and trips round the country, but also for what it can teach him of industry and of the kind of firm he would like to work for—or it may convince him that he would prefer to start on his own. The entry door he chooses will depend upon his assessment of his best route to the top. (If he is good the choice of most of the best firms will be his.) What considera-tions should guide him in his choice? To this question we shall turn in the next chapter.

NOTES

1. Miller, Wm., ed. *Men in Business: Essays in the History of Entrepreneurship*, Cambridge, Harvard University Press, 1952, p. 203.
2. Hooper, Sir Frederic, 'The Nation's Attitude to Industry', *The Manager*, January 1953, p. 18.
3. Reckitt, Basil M., *The History of Reckitt & Son Ltd*, London, A. Brown & Sons, 1951, p. 5. Cf. Brookes, C., *Graysons of Liverpool*, Liverpool, Henry Young & Co., 1956, pp. 27, 39.
4. Vickers, B. R., *This Family Business*, privately printed, 1954, p. 45.
5. Leaf, Charlotte M., *Walter Leaf, 1852-1927*, London, Murray, 1932.
6. Quoted in Rees, J. Aubrey, *The English Tradition, The Heritage of the Ven-turers, a Survey of Six Centuries*, London, Muller, 1934, p. 274.
7. Paulson, George, *The Chronicles of a Contractor*, ed. David Buchan, Con-stable, 1926.
8. Quoted by Jerris, F. R., 'Private Company Finance in the Post War Period', The Manchester School of Economic and Social Studies, Vol. XXV, No. 2, May 1957.
9. Political and Economic Planning, *Graduate Employment*, London, George Allen & Unwin, 1956, pp. 59, 73, 180.
10. Hooper, Sir Frederic, 'The Nation's Attitude to Industry, op. cit., pp. 17, 18.
11. Cf. *Quinquennial Survey of Graduate Appointments*, University of Man-chester, 1958.
12. Priestley, J. B., *Daylight on Saturday*, op. cit.
13. Balchin, Nigel, *Sundry Creditors*, op. cit.
14. 'Man of the Month: David Brown', *Scope*, November 1945.
15. Reported quotation of Harold Cotes, *Scope*, March 1955, p. 47.
16. Ibid.
17. Ibid.

18. 'Man of the Month: Halford Reddish', *Scope*, October 1952.
19. Reported quotation of E. S. Newland, *Scope*, March 1955, p. 48.
20. Reported quotation of Colin A. Samuels, *Scope*, January 1955, p. 50.
21. 'Man of the Month: Kenyon Jones', *Scope*, August 1953.
22. Cox, S. J., 'The Priesthood of Industry', *The Twentieth Century*, April 1958, p. 355.

CHAPTER IV

The Way to the Top

'*The race is not to the swift, nor the battle to the strong, neither yet bread to the wise, nor yet riches to men of understanding, nor yet favour to men of skill, but time and chance happeneth to them all.*'

ECCLESIASTES, ix, 11

'*What is called leadership is simply the determination to get to the top . . . if you know where you want to go yourself you will always find hundreds waiting to follow. Do you really think people really like a successful person? I think they hate him. At their kindest, they resent him.*'

MR B. A. WILLIAMS *of Williams and Williams Ltd*

IT FOLLOWS FROM WHAT HAS BEEN SAID that while there are two main routes to the top from the point of entry—by promotion through the business hierarchy in established firms and by creating a sizeable firm of one's own from small beginnings, the former is steadily becoming by far the most important. This chapter will therefore be addressed mainly to the ambitious young man in a hurry in big business. It is, too, far easier to study and generalize about the means by which young men climb upwards in a business bureaucracy than to reduce to any simple pattern the ways in which the contemporary entrepreneur is making money—enough money to put him in the top rank of big business in his lifetime.

1. MAKING A FORTUNE DESPITE SURTAX

It may, however, be convenient to take the traditional method first: that of 'the business man pure and simple' who even in this socialist age 'plunges into and tosses upon the waves of human affairs without a life-preserver in the shape of salary', as Andrew Carnegie described him. It is still possible to make a fortune. It is possible, indeed, to start a business with a small capital and by dint of hard work, producing something for which there is a rising demand, end up in seven or eight years with a substantial capital asset. It may be bottle-washing, export-packing, window-cleaning or making electronic components. The characteristic growth chart of such a firm has been described by the founder of the Crittall metal window firm, who testified how 'for years I put back into the business every penny I earned from it, except for £300 or £400 a year demanded by my growing family', and from long business experience affirmed that:

> A firm is usually born of a new idea, a new method, or by reason of a fresh angle of approach to an old problem. Its very newness and the initial enthusiasm of its sponsors brings it an early measure of success. Then there invariably follows a testing period of slow progress, tremendous effort with little apparent consequence. . . . It is then that an enterprise must prove its quality. At such a time doubts and unbelief pave the high road to disaster. An unwavering certainty that your product is worthy of your effort, an invincible determination to hold on in the face of obstacles and failures, a resolute grappling with the thousand problems that beset a newcomer—only with these qualities can you hope to hold fast against the day when opportunity knocks. And eventually, if the product is good, the development steady . . . almost inevitably will come the tide which sweeps the ready vessel to the shores of fortune.[1]

If the product is good, 'eventually' the ready vessel will be swept to the shore of fortune—but today this will be a more modest fortune than when the late Mr Crittall built up his firm for the fifteen years before the tide gripped him about 1917.

The heads of companies small, newly founded in the post World War II era though they may enjoy almost the same standard of life as the heads of big business, remain small beer in the business world unless they turn from inventing and manufacturing to company promotion and selling—selling not only their business assets but themselves as supremely valuable, up-and-coming men.* They must turn, at some stage, from the design and packaging of goods to the design and packaging of assets, goodwill and personalities. The individualist, who slaves to run his own show because he loathes working with others, is today unlikely to create a business so large that he will find himself on close terms, business or social, with the Flecks, Heyworths, Beavers and Kippings of the modern business world.

---

* An illustration of the value of an able business man was the £200,000 insurance on the life of W. A. de Vigier which the Drayton group took out when they bought a 40 per cent interest in Acrow, the firm he had built up. 'Man of the Month: W. A. de Vigier', *Scope*, January 1950.

Taxation is the barrier; but today as before the war there is still a loophole in the British tax system through which a rising business man, building a big firm from very little, can slip.

> You start a business with your own money or loans on fixed interest, make a success of it, and finance expansion by further fixed interest stock, keeping the equity yourself. Then if your business is well-established you make a public issue of common stock (ordinary shares) of a part of the equity. This may easily bring in as much or more than the whole business is worth, and not only has your company, of which you are now the chairman and managing director and perhaps still the controlling stockholder, suddenly got a lot of money, but if you allotted yourself a fair slice of the stock issue for your services to the company, you may have a big sum in your own pocket without having to pay tax on it at all.[2]

This was indeed the way in which William Morris made a fortune when he floated Morris Motors as a public company just before the war; the stock quickly went to several times its nominal value, and he kept a large part of it (until he endowed charitable institutions with it).

Today variants of this process remain possible, even though rates of tax are higher, and the floating of public companies is subject to official agreement. It has, furthermore, become very much harder to raise fixed interest loans since the credit squeeze was instituted by the Conservative government. Bank accommodation has been cut back and small firms have suffered; the terms on which they can hire-purchase their plant and machinery—normal ways of helping to finance expansion have also become costlier. To make millions by creating an enormous productive asset, or even a moderately sized one, is much harder now than before the war. The moment of inspiration may come when a thing catches on—as, for example, when Frank Smith, the grocer's boy, put a screw of salt in his packets of potato crisps. But taxation cuts the immediate return, which might have been ploughed into expansion, to very little.

The greatest post-war fortunes have not been made out of a productive asset, but out of the buying and selling of businesses on a large scale by means of the 'take-over bid'. Small and medium-size public companies which have been unduly conservative in their dividend policies, either in response to the government's call for wage restraint or perhaps because the management does not care for shareholders, are sitting ducks for this kind of deal. It is possible to offer the shareholders a very much higher price for the assets than the existing stock market price of the shares, which reflects past dividend distributions and current and conservative management polities. Often the break-up assets of a firm exceed the current market valuation of the equity capital. If the shareholders accept the offer—which they normally do—it is sometimes possible to pay them off from the accumulated reserves, and thus acquire the buildings, plant, machinery and goodwill for next to nothing.

Economists praise Messrs Clore, Wolfson, Sunley and Fraser, whose activities, in a perfect economists' world, would simply force boards of directors to give shareholders the proper return on their capital invested at risk, and thus end the possibility of bidding. But the world is not perfect, and so the scope for arranging take-over bids in post-war Britain remains vast, and men with the Clore technique (and the necessary finance) can, for a long time, expect to make untaxed fortunes without driving boards, generally, into preventive action. For the business man of this, the most perfect entrepreneurial type, uncomplicated by creative urges, inventive quirks or political ambitions, 'money, real, exciting money . . . is the money which you venture with to outsmart the other fellow'.[3] This is reputedly such an exciting game that it has inspired a mystery play, *Any Other Business*, which in 1958 was produced in the West End.

There are, however, other if more modest ways of building big business by making good use of the circumstances of the time, as all good business men should do. The man starting on his own who is likely to be successful will do one of two things; either build up a firm in a rapidly expanding industry or produce old products more efficiently by means of new organization or techniques in an old industry which is declining and which by protecting itself against its own inefficiencies has laid itself wide open to the really tough and efficient entrepreneur.

War itself always offers great opportunities to the really tough and efficient; so does a period of hasty rearmament; so does the period of beating swords into ploughshares. Mr George Dawson made millions by selling war department surplus for scrap; his downfall was caused by failure to make provision for high taxation. In a smaller way, some scores of dealers in government surplus have made, but kept, considerable fortunes by dealing in the steady stream of surplus and obsolescent equipment that must flow, in a time of rapid changes in defence policy, from defence spending at the rate of £1,500 million a year. It is only necessary to read the strictures of successive Committees of Public Accounts to know why.[4]

Circumstances may be against the building up of productive assets from very little, and certainly against thinking of founding new family dynasties; the age is too uncertain, too inflationary, too confiscatory, the young in too much of a hurry. But inflation itself,which destroys the rentier, starves the pensioner, and squeezes the life out of the professional classes, puts money into the hands of the well-organized trade unionist—because he demands and gets an annual increment in his wage equal to or larger than the depreciation of his money—and into the hands of the shrewd business man because it raises capital values. The great thing is to have an asset whose value will rise, and preferably one which gives scope for being floated off in a series of subsidiary companies. The virtue of being born into even a small family business is therefore great. Since the war, the floating of family businesses as public companies has not only made fortunes of up to a million pounds for the families concerned[5] who, at the same time, remain in effective control of the firm, but has also made fortunes for the private banks and finance houses which have specialized in the art of introducing manufacturers to the capital market. A. J. Whitehead started in this business with one room and a typist; since the war the rush of business has made it one of the wealthiest of promotion companies.[6]

Here, perhaps, a point should be made about the survival of the family business by these means, and the use of a family business as a nursery of talent and forcing-house of sheer business flair. The outsider who enters a family business, with the idea of working his way on to its board by methods to be dealt with later, as well as the promotor who imagines that the family will lose control once it becomes a public company, should bear this in mind. The man brought up in a family business has a long start, if his upbringing has been of the right kind. As Mr Gluckstein has said:

> Why should we not be all cousins and nephews and uncles and brothers? Who can possibly know more about the business than they do? Their whole lives are wrapped up in it. From an early age you have the experience of your elders around you. Our boys listening to the grown-ups talking don't hear the racing news or cricket scores or football pools. They hear their seniors talking about business and they absorb it. What better training could they have? By the time they come into the firm there is not much left to teach them. I don't think any of us could talk anything BUT business when we get together.[7]

An impressive example of business talent in a family is the clan of

F

financial Smiths, who seem to have a member well placed in almost all the important finance institutions in Britain; the head of the clan, Lord Bicester, is managing director of Morgan Grenfell and a director of the Bank of England; another, Desmond Abel Smith is chairman of Borax Consolidated; Alexander Abel Smith is on the board of J. Henry Schroder and is chairman of Pressed Steel, and John Hugh Smith is on the board of Hambros Bank and Amalgamated Metal.

The man with a small company may do best by selling to a large one provided his becomes a subsidiary, and he continues to direct its destinies as managing director. He will generally obtain a seat on the board of the foster-parent company as part of the deal and, of course, an allotment of shares in the foster-parent which gives him the private means to maintain his position, and enlarge it, with propriety. He thus enters, at a relatively favoured rank, the hierarchy of big business. His job, thereafter, is to work his way into a position of power and control in the purchasing firm and in doing so he has this advantage, that by creating an asset and selling it with tactical skill he has already proved himself to have business acumen of a high order. However, the man who sells the firm that he has created himself to a large corporation probably makes such a deal only once in his lifetime but the firm that buys may well be doing it frequently. The terms of the deal are therefore probably the supreme test of his ability as a business man. Of course, it by no means follows that a man who has the ability to build up a business will have either the qualities needed to sell it shrewdly or still less to tread successfully the labyrinth of power politics in the large corporation.

2. THE MANAGEMENT LADDER

There remains the other, and increasingly important, way to the top; that of the young man who starts in a company as a potential manager and climbs up the management ladder. This is a partly charted route and hence the one on which it is possible to offer a modicum of advice even in competition with the many excellent manuals which have been published for this purpose.* As has been explained, most young men fall for the prestige of the larger firms; and certainly a seat on the board of the I.C.I. is a more glittering prize than a seat on the board of Snooks & Son Ltd, which only employs 150 men. Yet there are advantages

* A short bibliography on how to get on in business is given in the Appendix.

in starting in a small firm if it is carefully selected. It may be better to be boss of a small show in your thirties than to be a member of the ruling junta of a large one in your fifties or sixties. Nor is it necessary to make a final choice. A young man can start in a medium-size company and have the pleasures and experience of general management in his thirties and then move, at a senior level, to a larger company. Indeed, in large companies which do not operate a closed shop for management promotion this may be the best way of getting to the top, since the man from the smaller company can offer something which none of the specialist managers in the large company will have, experience of general management. The chance of rapid promotion in large well-established firms is tending to decline because such firms are becoming afraid of promoting men in their thirties for fear of upsetting too many expectations in the rest of the hierarchy.

A man who is starting his career in a large company must first decide if it is the right one for him. He might ask himself the following questions:*

> Is it the kind of company in which his personality is likely to fit?
>
> Is it full of raw northern engineering types, or is its citadel held by an embattled family or staffed by gentlemen traders who are charming but only susceptible to social origin?
>
> Are its prevailing ethical standards in reasonable harmony with his own?
>
> Is it making something worthwhile or only ballyhoo; does its whole life revolve round whether the housewife buys its product or some almost identical one by its competitors, or is it deep in atomic or entomological or petro-chemical research?
>
> Is it a company which is likely to expand rather than one which spends its life fighting for textile markets from dingy offices of Victorian gothic architecture? (It is obviously an advantage to get into a firm where there are growing points: to be factory manager of a plant that is to be expanded to 2,000.)
>
> Are young men favoured?
>
> What is the retiring age and is it enforced?

A company whose board is elderly may offer chances of promotion; but elderly managers sometimes think young men unfit for responsibilities, for it is human to define as old somebody older than yourself and somebody younger as young and to assume that youth, so defined, is too callow to be entrusted with anything serious.

---

* These questions are based on one of the author's discussions with fifty young graduates in industry, with personnel managers and appointment board secretaries.

The graduate aspiring to top management and power has further things to consider. Should he choose a company which already employs many graduates or one that has hardly seen the like before? If he goes to one accustomed to graduates he may find a fairly well-thought-out training scheme which makes allowances—perhaps too many—for the graduate's ignorance of industry. He will meet there men with similar backgrounds to talk to, which will make his work less of the intellectual desert which most arts men find commercial life, at least for the first few years. It may even be possible for him to discuss John Osborne or world affairs at the staff dining-table, rather than last night's TV. In a company with few or no graduates he may be lonely and meet suspicion and even ridicule; but if he has both the intellectual grasp and the business instinct and does not make too many enemies, he will beat his competitors to the top jobs the more easily.

Even in the civil service or the armed services, merit does not automatically bring a man a senior command in the end. Merit is usually an essential condition of success but, whatever the textbooks on success may say, it is not the only one.* A man's work must not only be distinctly good; but he must also be heard about by his seniors. There is the story of two naval officers who, on leaving Dartmouth as midshipmen, made a brotherly pact that throughout their service careers whenever either of them heard the other's name mentioned in conversation he would chip in with the remark, 'Did I hear you say old So-and-so? He's a marvellous chap, simply marvellous.' Both ended as admirals.

In industry, even in medium-size firms there is some rigidity in promotion, if less than in the services; and there may be less in commerce or distribution. The common remark of top managers 'It's up to you here' or 'You can't keep a good man down' is often a cloak for the fact that promotion is completely chancy and that merit plays a subordinate role simply because no system for assessing performance by men in junior and middle management exists. In others, however, there is a full scheme for what is now called executive development. This idea, though still much more popular in America, is gradually spreading among the progressive firms in this country who tend to go to American companies like Esso for their model.

Executive development means anything from a simple plan for

* Nor is merit always essential for high promotion. In some companies mediocrity may be most acceptable together with a capacity for never putting a foot wrong. But we are not addressing our remarks to those who are interested in such promotion.

recruiting and training a small group of crown princes to an elaborate administrative system. When it is confined to crown princes it often means, as Mr Brech has pointed out,

> little more than a search for the seemingly all-glorious winner, the fine upstanding personality with an intuitive hunch and great allotment of drive—too often representing motive-power without steering and without a regulator.[8]

At its most elaborate, executive development will start with forecasts of future management needs based on graphs of estimated annual wastage and expansion for the next five, ten or twenty years—the young man should beware of companies who tend to overestimate their future management needs. The next step is 'job descriptions' which list the duties and responsibilities of a post, and which may range from one to ten pages, depending upon the meticulousness of the organization specialist employed. They may tell you, for instance, that the twenty-third duty of a purchasing manager is

> Advising and assisting the Clerical Methods Officer in regard to determining specifications and sources of supply for all stationery and administrative supplies.[9]

Job descriptions are followed by job specifications which describe the experience and qualifications which will be necessary for, say, the purchasing manager. It is awkward when these specifications show, as often happens, that none of the present managers, who seemed quite satisfactory, fit the specification. Faced with the choice of dumping the specification or the manager, top management will usually try to do neither by describing the specification as the ideal which should be aimed at when the *next* appointment is made.

Up to this point, executive development procedures will not concern the young man on the make. It is the next stage which is important—that of talent spotting. If his company is being guided by the textbooks on executive development, it will have an appraisal scheme which provides for each employee to be rated by his superior at six-monthly or annual intervals. In American companies this appraisal would be discussed with him, after his boss had been coached in role-playing sessions on 'how to counsel effectively, how to put your subordinate at his ease, start with his strong points, think of something nice to say about them, then discuss his weaknesses constructively.'[10] The young man in a British company is at present likely to be spared this embarrassing discussion although he may suffer torments of anxiety wondering what was in the reports. Even under the most scientifically designed system of rating, the young man who thinks that diligence and good results alone will ensure success is going to be disappointed; for, in addition to merit, promotion in business depends on three p's—personality, pull and push—and on chance.

3. TOP BUSINESSMANSHIP

It is essential for the ambitious young man to be considered to have personality, otherwise he will be classed as a backroom boy. He must be—or appear to be—a natural leader. Some firms attach importance to the recognition of this which is accorded by holding an elected office whether in the company's social activities or outside. What is meant by personality will vary from one company to another, but most require poise, drive, alertness, and a young man would be wise to cultivate a rough charm while remembering that the statement 'what a charming fellow' may not be a commendation. He should take care not to be thought a 'personality' in any eccentric form which might reflect upon his common sense—that quality which business men value so highly. If his personality proves unacceptable in one company he can encourage himself with the thought that the character of companies varies almost as much as that of individuals and that hence a man who is a failure in one company may make good in another. While personality is a valuable asset, exhibitionism is not appreciated in business, however necessary it may be for getting to the top in academic and artistic circles. Indeed, an Oxford don, with business contacts, suggested to one of the authors that exhibitionism was the main difference between his colleagues and the business men he met. 'You see,' he said rather wistfully, 'there are so many bright people at Oxford, that it is hard to get noticed.'

Pull, more often called nepotism, is usually thought of as the main obstacle to promotion by merit. In some companies it plays an important part and it exists in all. In family businesses, from father to son— provided the son is at least willing or pliant—is the usual succession. If the family has no sons, sons-in-law may take their place. Marry into the family is a recognized way of achieving the first push up in a business career; it is of course only possible in family businesses, or in public companies in which family interest remains strong. It is a way families had in the past of keeping the blood fresh while retaining the property in the family. Marrying the daughter of a member of the board—even if he has less than one per cent of the equity—is a very powerful recommendation and many wise men take care to love where promotion lies. However, it should not be forgotten that, depending upon the personalities of both father and daughter, this may prove no easy option—'Either you do what I want or I shall tell daddy' is only one of the many ways by which a son-in-law's life may be made difficult. The life of the son may be difficult too, not merely because of the possible clashes with his father, but also because he may suffer from a lack of self-confidence if he has only worked in the family business and has therefore no means of judging his own competitive ability.

There may today be less tendency to use family business to provide sinecures for inefficient members of the family. The incentive to build a firm round a family is declining. Samuel Courtauld declared:

> Modern employers do not want to found dynasties, they expect their sons to pull their weight and work for a living in a working world . . . They would consider it a betrayal of trust to hand over their jobs lightly to men whom they thought less competent than themselves.[11]

Strictly speaking, nepotism means 'undue favouritism to one's relations', but it may be used to describe any kind of favouritism. It includes the directors' friends who press for the opportunity to have their sons recruited with the golden password, 'Sir John Recommends'. Business men, who go very largely on what they know, are often thankful to take a young man that way rather than select from fifty unknowns (after all, they can complain to the father if the lad is not up to much). Relations and friends are not the only form of pull that can influence promotion. There is the Church or sect—and a large part of British family firms are sectarian in origin; the Quakers help each other. In other companies the proportion of Jews or of Roman Catholics or Christian Scientists is high (somehow the idea of Anglicans log-rolling does not convince; but it may be so).

Push is, however, the most essential quality of all. The meek shall not inherit top management, and those who are to be powerful in the business world cannot afford to hide their lights under a bushel. In fact, their concern must be to find other people's lights under other people's bushels and appropriate them (quoting the parable of the unjust steward). Push is grounded in self-confidence, or at least the appearance of self-confidence, for that is essential to convince others of one's ability.

Another essential is the art of drawing attention to oneself; not blatantly, but just as much as the company's culture permits. A man must be able to attract attention without incurring too much enmity among his colleagues.

The means of drawing attention to oneself as an up-and-coming manager are innumerable; plenty of American success books enumerate them all. Making a good impression is an important beginning; in Britain one must dress right. At the university a man can dress as he likes, but in business, clothes make a lot of the man. This may seem truer in finance or insurance than in manufacturing, but in some engineering works the managing director is also sensitive to dress, and is impressed by a well-groomed, alert appearance, achieved by new, well-kept clothes of a hue and cut he approves and he may, as one eminent industrialist does, expect his lieutenants (earning £3,000 to £5,000 a year) to have a fountain-pen and pencil (of the best make) protruding from the breast pocket, and a notebook of prescribed size in the side pocket. As Mr Wright Mills points out in *The Power Élite*:

> The fit survive and fitness means, not formal competence—there probably is no such thing for top executive positions—but conformity with the criteria of those who have already succeeded. To be compatible with the top men is to act like them, to look like them, to think like them: to be of and for them—or at least to display oneself to them in such a way as to create that impression. This in fact is what is meant by 'creating'—a well-chosen word—a 'good impression'. This is what is meant—and nothing else—by being a 'sound man', 'as sound as a dollar'.[12]

'Soundess' in most British firms today is as highly-prized an attribute as it is in America although generally it will be termed 'reliability'. In many British, as in many American firms, moreover, there is a distrust of the man, however able, who has means of his own. There is a preference for knowing that a man has only the salary appropriate to his grade; his whole 'capital' is his standing with the firm itself. Independence, even in small measure, is not liked, even if the man has the good manners in no way to obtrude his advantages. This is truer of the new, light industries, or in retailing and selling, than in the older firms, or the older industries, and particularly in the City. Directors of the latter may agree with Lytton that 'the very possession of money in certain stages of life gives assurance to the manner and gives attraction to the address'.[13] Such a young man in the City is more likely to be invited to a week-end with one of the directors, or casually asked to make up a directorial lunch or dinner-party.

In some companies a man's private life is really his own, but even in those a reputation as a sound citizen who takes part in community activities is often a help provided there is no suspicion that work is neglected; in firms with social idealists at the head, it may be rather important. Most useful is prowess in sport; a good golf handicap is one of the best business recommendations. The secretaryship of the trade's golf association is said to be worth several years' business experience. Golf, too, offers one of the few opportunities to meet the top brass on an informal basis without too obviously trying to do so.

A man is known by his friends and contacts, and in business it is important to have the right friends. As Lorenzo Alberti, a business man of fourteenth-century Florence noted in his book on *Government and Family*: 'Children dear, be charitable as our Holy Church ordains. Nevertheless cultivate your fortunate rather than your unfortunate friends, and the rich rather than the poor'.[14] Friends who can arrange an apparently chance meeting with a director at dinner which may lead to his saying next day, 'Met a bright laddie last night, served in m'regiment, sound on India. Kind of chap our company needs, we might try him out . . .' This example may sound far-fetched but it happens to be true. Colleagues whose character and loyalty are beyond reproach and whose ability is well above their peers should be cultivated—though a man never must forget that his colleagues are his competitors. Outside contacts are even more important in many (not all) businesses, to be cultivated sedulously both as a source of other jobs and as a means of meeting senior managers—there again golf can be useful. This sort of thing is carried out rather more efficiently in American than British business.

> You never could tell when a little bread cast upon the waters might pay off. It never hurt to have too many friends doing the same sort of thing you were. Willis had told many of them a lot about himself over drinks in hotel suites, in corners of clubs and on golf courses, and a lot of them had told Willis a lot about themselves in return— of what they thought about so-and-so, about their yachts, about their hobbies, and their taste in women and liquor and automobiles. This sort of thing was the currency of business friendship. . . .[15]

The ambitious young graduate should remember that the ways of making a good impression in industry are different from those in university. He will not impress by having read the books on scientific management. Indeed, he can get to the top without having read a single book on management: courses and conferences will teach him enough of the lingo. Nor need he take a certificate in management studies to show his managerial competence, that is only for the plodder doomed to remain in middle management. The high flyer must be able to find more profitable ways of spending his evenings by working, developing his intellect or cultivating useful social contacts rather than sitting several evenings a week for a number of years in classes at the technical college.

A man climbing to the top will make himself familiar with all the ways by which a man's success in business is judged. Each large company has its own status symbols: desks, curtains, dining-room, make of car and location of offices are important, to mention only a few. A man must (this hint is superfluous to the public school boy) do his best to obtain them. A secretary, in herself a high status symbol, whether she is first-class or only an inefficient young girl, can usually be relied on to fight for these marks of prestige for her boss, as her prestige depends on his.

A man's ability will be judged not merely by what he has done, but also by what he appears to have done. It is therefore vital to fight to take all credit for one's own achievements; if one has subordinates, it is usually (not always) advisable to take responsibility for theirs also. A man should try not to let his superior sign his letters, but may be wise to introduce a rule when he becomes head of the department, that he must sign all letters (the writer being identified by a marginal initial only). In research departments this is, of course, a delicate matter. If the head of the department takes too much of the kudos he may lose, in these difficult days, his best and most inventive workers. Large companies are also finding this a nuisance; scientists are demanding credit and publicity for inventions which they are generously paid to make, and permission to write articles in learned journals on subjects which, in the directors' view, should remain—just in case they help a competitor—in the company's archives. Ultimately, of course, one must make a virtue of necessity, and encourage one's scientists to make a name for themselves. Such concessions are, however, less necessary in the executive team.

Men climbing to the top well know that they have the ability to do big things, but they may not have the time or the imagination to produce new ideas. This need be no handicap for a business man knows that *ideas* are two a penny, and so are *idea-mongers*; what is scarce is the ability to use them to advantage. One should have plenty of ideas in climbing up, and drawing attention to oneself; but they do not have to be one's own. The art of living on other people's ideas is a very old one in business; it began at least with the early inventors, who had holes bored in their houses by manufacturers so that their ideas could be taken up by those who knew how to use them.[16] On a different scale it is part of any emergent top executive's important equipment. At all levels in business, men take time off to listen to others—for their ideas—and then pay yet other men to market the ideas. Although some ideas may have to be paid for—those that are patented, subject to copyright or in the reports of consultants—business men in a candid mood admit that some of the most paying are to be had for nothing but a nose for the circles in which they are produced. To say that all an artist's ideas are those of other men is dispraise; to say that a business man's are those of other men, is merely to describe his function.

The use and handling of superiors is, of course, as important as that of using and handling colleagues and subordinates. The art of toadying is as old as human society, and is practised in business by many young men who want to get on.

> Frosty was a climber. As he said to himself, 'Figure out how the men above you are thinking and what they are like. If they like argument stand up and give it to them. But if they want to win it, let them. It depends just as much on how you say a thing as what you say. . . . As for the fellows below one . . . treat them politely but with reserve. The trick is to let them do the talking and you do the listening and thinking. . . .'[17]

Toadying is an art which requires delicate discrimination since flattery can take many forms. A few men, very few, are immune to all types of flattery—and it would be dangerous to attempt it—others may be suspicious of flattery about their work but love references to their prowess with women or their skill on the golf course. All but the most clear-sighted or modest of men are more susceptible to flattery on their weak points. Toadying does not necessarily require agreement; while some bosses only value 'yes-men', others appreciate those who stand up to them.

Three-quarters of the way up the ladder of a big bureaucracy a man's personality must expand and his aura must become one of confidence and comfort. At this stage, very often, he becomes what Mr Wright Mills calls the 'Maybe-man'—

> So speak in the rich, round voice and do not confuse your superiors with details. . . . Execute the ceremony of forming a judgment. Delay recognizing the choice you have already made, so as to make the truism sound like the deeply pondered notion. Speak like the quiet

competent man of affairs and never personally say No. Hire the
No-man as well as the Yes-man. Be the tolerant Maybe-man. . . .
Practise softening the facts into the optimistic, practical, forward-
looking, cordial, brisk view . . . Have weight; be stable; caricature
what you are supposed to be but never become aware of it much
less amused by it. And never let your brains show.[18]

4. RECKONING THE ODDS

Whether a man is building up his own business, or working his way up
in someone else's, chance plays its role, especially near the top. 'It
would surely be manifestly absurd to suggest that mere luck is not a
very great factor in the making of enormous fortunes,' said John Spedan
Lewis.[19] In big companies, few of which have any policy to limit the
effects of chance on promotion, advancement is often simply a tactical
question of being in the right place at the right time and, most important
of all, at the right age. The vital years in business are late twenties to late
thirties; if a man is to reach the top he must in those years as one young
man put it, 'go like a rocket'.

One important hazard is one's immediate boss. An able superior who
takes an interest in his subordinates' career can help them immensely
—not least by being promoted himself. Attaching oneself to a rising
man is an important way of getting a move on during the early stages.
A boss who is moving from one big job to the next often likes to take
his proven young men with him, and they can pick up plums and get a
chance to distinguish themselves. A jealous or indifferent superior, and
particularly one who has reached his own limit, may fatally obstruct an
able junior. Valuable time may be lost by an able man blocked behind
a boss who does not like him, or who does not want to lose him.

A good business man must take risks with his career just as an
entrepreneur must take risks in producing for the market. It is essential
not to be overlooked, and it may be wise to refuse a good job which
seems out of the main stream of promotion, and prefer something
smaller which brings him in close touch with top management. Though
he must be ready to prove himself in a minor command, the headship
of even an important department which itself is a dead end must be
avoided. (The men who transferred fairly early from running a district
to the central secretariat of their colony have done best in the colonial
service; this is the first move to a governorship.) A careful survey of a
business organization is necessary to make sure which are the most

likely routes to the top. In one company it will be via sales—if market-ing people travel first class and production men second the deduction is clear—in others, production will be more important, or design; in others again, the office or accounts. An ambitious engineer will avoid firms which favour accountants for top posts. But companies change—a new chairman may upset many career expectations by favour-ing technologists rather than accountants or lawyers for his top manage-ment. The political situation at the top must be watched with care at all times, and advance information is always valuable to the climber.

Some firms try to plan promotion and talk about promotion ladders; but most of these ladders only lead a limited distance. No man who wants to get to the top can afford to go up rung by rung. This is usually recognized by companies with management development schemes for they will often have a separate group of high flyers: men who they think have potential for top management. The 'crown prince' is picked young in such companies—either when he first enters as a management trainee or after the first few years proving himself in some professional job. It is essential for a young man to find out whether he is considered to be a high flyer. Good indices are: top management attention, frequent job moves, posting to jobs which have a good record for promotion and which are obviously used for training for top management, foreign visits and attendance at the more advanced management courses—if he is sent to the Administrative Staff College at Henley, senior promotion is almost assured. (The firm which does not provide rapid promotion after Henley merely provides itself with a discontented executive.)

More and more firms are taking training seriously in recent years, and are worrying about how to 'broaden' their potential top managers. They differ in their choice of methods and in the length of time they allow (some boards think that a three-weeks' course can do all the polishing and widening of a business mind that is really necessary). Though the heads of businesses may have doubts about the usefulness of the case-histories which are studied at such courses by seminars of rising executives, they often feel that the contacts which their men make are useful. Particularly do they feel they are valuable for the man who has been promoted from a long way down the ladder; for him the business course takes the place of finishing school. Some companies also use such courses as rewards for tired executives who have no real chance of further promotion and are in need of reassurance that their services are still valued.

The ambitious man should consider carefully why he has been asked to go on some conference—whether on labour relations, automation or higher accountancy—such as are becoming more and more a feature of British business life. It may be an honour—a sign that he has been noticed and is being given a chance to spread his wings. It may be because he is written off as an incorrigible gas-bag and is being sent because it is felt that, while the firm must be represented (because Sir Somebody talked the chairman into it at a Guildhall dinner), his absence from the office will have the least deleterious effect on the really important things in life. Broadly, the more specific the conference—on how to use new marketing techniques, for instance—the younger and more serious-minded the executive types one finds there. The less specific and the more worthy the objects of the conference, the more one finds in attendance the elderly has-beens of the firms composing it (ambitious young men will avoid these). If the conference though vague in object happens to be in the public eye, so that its proceedings may produce publicity for certain types of tycoon, then a sprinkling of really influential directors and top executives may be present, and the ambitious man may very well draw favourable notice to himself there. No ambitious man, of course, will miss any opportunity to attend a general get-together of the firms in an industry where a few general topics may be discussed, but the real objective of which is to meet over drinks to talk about pricing policies or joint representations to the government: practically all the big shots will be there.

5. CHANGING ONE'S COMPANY

The aspiring business man in a big business bureaucracy cannot afford to get stuck too long in one job. Three to five years is the longest that can safely be spent in any one post, and the lower the rung the shorter should be the time one is poised on it. A young man who has been in the same job for more than three years probably should begin to look elsewhere; if he has been there more than five years, he certainly should. The decision whether to move or stay is bound to be an agonizing reappraisal of one's business prospects.* A man's background will affect the decision. It seems to be a general rule (as the Acton Society's study on Management Succession showed) that the more lowly a man's social origins, the more advantageous it may be for him to move. A

---

* The proportion of successful business men who have changed companies is analysed in the next chapter.

boy who starts in a firm as young Bill may be in danger of remaining
'Our Bill' all his life; but if he moves he can start anew as Mr Jones.

However, wanting to find a new chance to make a break-through
and finding one, are different matters. The workman on £12 or £15 a
week can ask for his cards today and be happily suited tomorrow; not
so the manager on £40 to £60 a week. Yet if, as some people maintain,
management is becoming a profession a competent manager should
surely find a ready market for his skill. Even at a time when so many
company chairmen bemoan the shortage of good managers, this is
far from being so.

> Whatever their reasons, nearly all executives anxious to change jobs
> can expect to find the process a lonely, miserable experience. Indeed
> finding a new job is about the most difficult, embarrassing, and
> patience-exhausting venture an executive can undertake[20]

said the editors of *Fortune* recently, and this is even more true in
Britain where management brokerage is in its infancy. In neither country, however, is there an effective management appointments register on
which a manager, dissatisfied with his place, can put his name with a
fair hope of finding a better job (of course it is easier to step down than
up).

It is when a change is desired that the managerial job with a wide
range of contacts proves preferable to the one in which a man is encap-
sulated in a narrow circle of technicians and technology. Just as top
management demands 'loyalty' as the most important virtue, so self-
preservation requires that the man who knows he can make the grade
should get to know his firm's competitors in a friendly, non-committal
but prudent way. One good way of learning the political set-up, as well
as the technical layout, of an industry, and to acquire valuable contacts,
is to work with a firm of management consultants for a few years. Management consultantcy firms for this reason rarely keep their staff for
more than five or six years—they get too rewarding offers from
clients.

In the United States, high-level employment agencies have specialized
for some years in finding managers—and even directors—for clients.
The first British agency of this sort, Management Selection Ltd, was
only started a couple of years ago. Such consultants can advertise the
vacancy for a client, deal with the applications, interview the possibles,
and finally prepare the short list. This service can be very useful for
companies but it hardly helps the man 'looking round' unless he has the

qualifications for an advertised vacancy. Because executive employment is unorganized there is no information about how long it will take even a well-qualified man to find a job either in Britain or the United States. In Holland the average length of unemployment for a manager is one year.[21]

Managers do change their jobs—but not often; when a manager 'asks for his cards' (or rather, repayment of his pension fund contributions) it is likely to be at one of the two or three climacterics of his career upwards. Those who study the lives of successful men, with a view to learning the secret of their success, will examine with most profit the turning points in their careers—the moments when they lost office, or elections, or fortunes, changed jobs, took risks, seemed to have come to a dead end. Proven ability, sound technological or professional qualifications, and a firm grip on the old-boy network, are the most important requisites when the time comes to show one's board of directors that they are not indispensable. Those who have rare skills—thermonuclear or otherwise—which expanding industries covet, are in the strongest positions provided they know how to contact their company's competitors, and provided that they know negotiations will be treated confidentially. In a few industries there are gentlemen's agreements among the bosses not to poach, but these are not widespread enough to be a serious handicap. Generally speaking, a man can exploit really valuable specialized talents, and exceptional organizational ability; but there is often a good deal of narrow specialization in large companies which severely handicaps a 'captive' trying to go outside, especially if he has no professional qualifications. Such a man may find that he has no assets which are marketable for a figure near, and certainly not above, his present salary.

The most critical moments in the way to the top are, of course, the transition from being an employee, however senior and valued, to being a general manager, director or boss (however much one may still be, technically, an employee). At this stage, no holds are barred. Merit and luck may take a man across this divide, and some men even get carried across it by merit and luck without particularly desiring the transition. But for most it is an all-in fight as fierce, in its own way, as the fight of a rising M.P. to get into the Cabinet. This is the moment when a man may have to repeat to himself Cromwell's words 'regrettable necessity', as he sacrifices friends, betrays confidences, turns the screws with threats, unmasks unexpected batteries of blackmail, enters into pacts with enemies, even men he despises and regards as wholly disastrous to the company. An orderly system of management succession which reaches this point is most exceptional. The observation that 'There's plenty of room at the top' was first made by the Delphic Oracle. So there is for outstanding talent and climbing skill. But that leaves unchanged the fact that the profession of being the managing director or chairman of large and prosperous concerns is the most competitive of all, and one that has the highest proportion of failures and near misses than any other.

NOTES

1. Crittall, F. H., *Fifty Years of Work & Play*, London, Constable, 1954, p. 83.

2. Fry, R. H., *The British Businessman* 1900–49, Explorations in Entrepreneurial History, Vol. II, No. 1., 1948.

3. Westropp, E., *The Way to Fortune*, London, Oldbourne Press, 1957.

4. Committee of Public Accounts, 1st, 2nd and 3rd Reports, Session 1955–6, p. XXV.

5. Cf. *The Director*, July 1954.

6. Fry, R. H., op. cit.

7. 'Man of the Month: Montague Gluckstein', *Scope*, July 1954.

8. Brech, E. F. L., *Organization The Framework of Management*, London, Longmans, Green, 1957, p. 352.

9. Ibid., p. 179.

10. Cf. Edwards, J. D., *Executives: Making them Click*, New York, University Books, 1956, p. 70.

11. Courtauld, Samuel, *Ideals and Industry*, Cambridge University Press, 1949, p. 82.

12. Mills, C. Wright, *The Power Élite*, New York, Oxford University Press, 1956, p. 141.

13. Lord Lytton, *Lucretia*, quoted in *Business*, by 'A Merchant', Edinburgh, Edmonton and Douglas, 1873.

14. Alberti, Lorenzo, 'Government and Family', quoted in Sombart, *The Quintessence of Capitalism*, op. cit.

15. Marquand, J. P., *Sincerely Willis Wayde*, London, Robert Hale, 1955, American Edition, 1955.

16. A mannered account of it is given in *Business* by a Merchant, op. cit.

17. Twayne, Lester B., *The Weatherby Crisis*, New York, Twayne, 1956.

18. Mills, C. Wright, *The Power Élite*, op. cit., pp. 142–3.

19. Lewis, John Speden, *Fairer Shares*, London, Staples Press, 1954.

20. Editors of *Fortune*, *The Executive Life*, New York, Doubleday, 1956, p. 46

21. 'De Werkloze Baas' (The unemployed boss), *Management Abstracts*, November 1956.

CHAPTER V

Who Gets to the Top

'Unto every one that hath shall be given, and he shall have abundance.'

MATTHEW, xxv, 29

'... it is the first £1,000 which counts ... a man must feel those early deals right down to the pit of his stomach if he is going to be a great man of business. They must shake the very fibre of his being as the conception of a great picture shakes an artist.'
LORD BEAVERBROOK, *Don't Trust to Luck*

IT IS ONE THING to plot the route by which a successful man climbs the promotion ladder in big business, but it is another and harder task to discover the real qualities which have actually taken men to the managing director's chair. Business mythology has a simple answer— successful men started at the bottom and worked all the daylight hours which God gave and many of the night-time ones too. In the previous chapter we saw that hard work though necessary, especially for all men who make a fortune on their own, is by no means the only or the most important quality.

1. PRIVILEGE OR OPEN COMPETITION?

What of the other part of the business myth that all successful men came up the hard way? In a subject where so much is veiled, here we fortunately have some useful figures. Three studies in this country give an indication of how far this is true. They are the study of the careers of more than a thousand company directors by Dr G. H. Copeman,[1] of more than 400 top managers by the Acton Society Trust,[2] and of more than 670 managers at all levels by R. V. Clements.[3] They show that about a third could be said to have started their working life with no special advantages, but that those with a public school education and business connections had a much better chance of getting to the top.

All three studies show that a public school education was a decided advantage in getting to the top of British business. At least half of the directors studied by Copeman went to a public school and so did one-third of the top managers in the Acton Society study. The advantages associated with going to a major public school were even more marked, as twenty-eight of these schools provided one in ten of the top managers. Indeed, if there should ever cease to be a long waiting list for Eton, the governors might stimulate recruitment by advertisements on *The Times* pattern—'Top people went to Eton'; one in twenty of the directors in Copeman's study made his first useful contacts there, and in a random sample of 100 business men in *Who's Who* studied by us, 19 had been to Eton, which suggests that the advantages of being an old Etonian become more marked the higher up you go.*

Family influence is still a predominant factor in promotion in many small and medium-size companies, although in large companies top posts are more genuinely open to competition. The study of directors showed that about 60 per cent started their careers with the advantage of having business connections in the family, and nearly half this number went into the family business. No figures are obtainable for the top managers included in the Acton Society study.

Clements distinguished six basic career patterns. The first started as 'crown princes'; that is, they went into the family business which, as we have seen, accounts for 4 per cent of the managers in his study and for nearly 30 per cent of the directors. The second were managerial trainees who entered other companies and were trained to be managers although usually there was no guarantee that they would be given a management post. Ten per cent of the managers in Clements' study and a fifth of the top managers and directors started their careers as management trainees but the last two would include some who joined the family firm. The third group, accounting for 20 per cent of Clements' managers, consisted of those who entered industry after they had acquired professional qualifications and who tended to be promoted up their specialist ladder and sometimes from there to general management. About half the directors started their careers in this way, although again this might include some who were 'crown princes'. The fourth category, comprising 12 per cent of the managers studied by Clements, is for

* In financial circles the proportion going to Eton is even higher. A recent study showed that about a third of top financiers had been there, cf. Lupton T. and Wilson, Shirley, *The Social Background and Connections of Top Decision Makers*, The Manchester School of Economic and Social Studies, January, 1959.

other types of entrants who did not start at the bottom, such as premium apprentices* and sales trainees.

The fifth and sixth categories are for those who came up from the bottom, the first for later school leavers, which would usually mean those who started as clerks, and the second for early school leavers, who would usually be those who started as manual workers. Just over half Clements' managers started life as a clerk or manual worker, about one in five of the directors and more than a third of the top managers.

Thus the proportion of those who came up from the bottom—that is, who started their working life as a clerk or a manual worker, may seem quite high, and so may the numbers who did not go to a public school; but the advantages of privilege become more marked when it is remembered that most of the population starts work on the shop floor or as a clerk or office boy, and that therefore their chances of promotion were much less. According to the Acton Society Trust, opportunities for a public school boy to get into management were about ten times that of the general population and his chances of getting to top management were even better.

It is difficult to tell from these studies how many men had made their main career outside industry and joined their firms in a top position late in life; although we know that 26 per cent of the directors started work outside industry, we do not know the age at which they went into it. An analysis of 100 business men in *Who's Who* suggests that the civil service and the Bar may provide the largest group of those joining business late in life. Certain types of business deliberately recruit a high proportion of their boards from men who have had distinguished careers outside business—such as outstanding generals or admirals, colonial governors, ambassadors, top-ranking civil servants or, occasionally, academics. Banks are a notable example. The method of choice is, however, obscure.

There is widespread concern today about ensuring a much greater supply of technically trained people. Yet in the past at least the practically trained man was at a disadvantage in promotion. The man in the office fared much better, as is shown by the fact that between 60 and 70 per cent of the directors studied had spent their working life in the office. In the study of top managers, non-technical qualifications such as accountancy, law and secretarial, were also found to be more advantageous than technical qualifications such as engineering. It may

* i.e. boys whose parents pay for their apprenticeship—a declining category.

be that technologists failed to rise higher because they were too useful to be taken from their own work for administrative duties; this left them at a disadvantage in term of careers and rewards which inevitably affected the supply. The existing shortage continues to work against them when the question of promotion comes up.

Clements suggests that the recruitment of managers from those who started as management trainees is likely to increase, as is the proportion of later school leavers who come up from the bottom. A decrease is likely in the proportion of those who started as special entrants. As management recruitment becomes more systematic 'crown princes' will probably remain a small but important group. With better educational opportunities and greater specialization the proportion who left school early and worked up from the bottom is also likely to decrease.

The average age of top managers studied was fifty and of the directors fifty-five. The most striking contrast comes in the sixty and over age-group, which contained only 10 per cent of the managers compared with 31 per cent of the directors. This shows that while nearly all top managers have to retire at sixty or sixty-five to make way for those who are younger, directors often stay on much later. Twelve per cent of the top managers were under forty and 9 per cent of the directors. In the sample of 100 business men in *Who's Who* only 5 were under fifty while 27 were over seventy and still retained their official positions, if not always perhaps their power. A few young men get to the top, if not into *Who's Who*, but industry generally cannot have a young top management unless it kills off all the successful ones through overstrain or retires them early. Otherwise, a man who is promoted to the top in his early thirties is likely to be there blocking promotion for the next thirty years. Perhaps industry should follow Parkinson's[4] suggestion that men at the top should retire at sixty even though they are still able to do the work better than anyone else, since if they do not, their subordinates will go through Parkinson's four stages of frustration, jealousy, resignation and oblivion, to become prematurely unfit for senior responsibility.

One of the most thought-provoking facts which emerges from all three inquiries is that those who have been successful in business have rarely changed companies. Forty-one per cent of the directors had remained in the same company and a further 31 per cent had made only one change. This compares with 44 per cent of the top managers studied by the Acton Society who had spent all their life in the same company, and another 33 per cent who had joined their present company before they were thirty, 19 per cent of them before they were twenty-five. As Clements points out:

> All in all, top managers have not had marked experience outside industry, outside their own firm, or outside their own line of work. Specialisation whether trained early to a high pitch or gained by long experience is the hall–mark of most careers, and those of top managers are rarely exceptions to this rule. From the outside the careers of the top managers who were interviewed often appear in no way exceptional, except in the heights to which they attain, and usually in the speed of promotion. On the whole, the most successful do not appear to be the most devious careers, though again there are exceptions.[5]

These three studies agree that, while some men have managed to get to the top without special advantages, the odds were heavily against them. The men who were most likely to succeed were those with family connections in business, although this was less important in the larger firms, and those who have been to public school. Most likely of all were the old Etonians.

2. FACTORS IN SUCCESS

The figures in the previous section give a rough indication of the importance of birth and education in getting to the top. But this leaves unanswered two questions: 'What characteristics make for success?' and 'How far are changes in business organization favouring new types of men with different personality traits?' The economists, who have built their science of choice on the simplest hedonism, are content to instance 'the broad faculties of judgment, promptness, resource, carefulness and steadfastness of purpose'[6]—'the greatest degree of commonplace capacity', as Hazlitt put it.

Psychologists may be expected to use more scientific terms than this discredited mid-nineteenth-century psychology of 'faculties', though whether they succeed in being more exact may be doubted. As one British psychologist sees it:

> ... it usually takes a long time to reach the head of any concern and so the personality factors that drive a man to the top must be consistent and sustained; he has persistence. In the particular field of his work he has a dominant disposition, for he courts great responsibility and must be able, despite setbacks, to pursue the thing that he knows

consciously or instinctively is wanted. This dominance may be exerted by virtue of intellectual power and inherited position, or through force of character, with associated physical and material factors, such as appearance, clothing and eccentricities that make him a 'character'.

Initiative and originality are likely to have set the top executive apart from others, and though it is not inconsistent for him to be a domestic mouse and socially gauche, he must be able to co-operate and participate so as to maintain contact with specific groups of people or institutions, both, within and outside his firm. Self-confidence in his sphere, however, is essential . . . insight and judgment are also needed, to economize his energy. . . .[7]

American social scientists have tried to pin the successful executive down more firmly; and have even devised techniques for getting at his deeper motivation during the apparently innocent interview to which American bosses seem so much more readily to submit. According to W. E. Henry[8] for example, they are men with 'high drive and achievement desire' who must visibly 'accomplish to be happy'; doers not dreamers who feel the necessity of 'moving continually upward'. They are men who like the authority of superiors, with whom they easily identify themselves and can accordingly themselves step readily into authority; they have 'a high degree of ability to organize unstructured situations' and do so with decisiveness—and if they once lose this conviction and sense of certainty they quickly disintegrate (like Dos Passos's Charlie Anderson). As active and aggressive personalities they easily become paranoid if the way ahead is blocked, and in any event get restless if they feel they are not getting ahead, in their position and with their work, fast enough; and because they are only interested in practical and immediate results they have shallow relations with most human beings other than their superiors or heroes, in particular seeing their subordinates as doers of work rather than as people. Superimposed on an Eton education this may also be the recipe for British industrial success. Professor Marshall would not have put things quite like that, but probably he would have recognized, and admired, the type.

Those who find their attention straying when confronted with the jargon of the social scientists may prefer to turn to management literature or success books for their study of the boss mentality. But there they are likely to find an array of qualities which would belong to a paragon of all the virtues.* The list may be formidable. One manage-

* Listing the qualities of a good manager makes an excellent parlour game in business circles. Soon all the main virtues will be mentioned and who is to say that any of them, except chastity, is not desirable?

ment consultant[9] recommends evaluation under fourteen heads, beginning with policies ('knowledge of company's policies and success in "selling" them') and going on through organizing ability, speed of work accuracy and housekeeping to initiative, judgment, leadership ('possesses that indefinable quality') imagination, language, technical knowledge and outside interests ('that enable him to view his job in relation to wider trade and social events that give him a broader concept of his work'). A recent questionnaire sent by Fortune, the American business journal, to 75 top executives listed 14 qualities: judgment, initiative, integrity, foresight, energy, drive, human relations skill, decisiveness, dependability, emotional stability, fairness, ambition, dedication, objectivity and co-operation. Nearly a third of the executives said that they thought all these qualities were indispensable. But this survey showed the subjectivity of all such lists as the word 'dependability' alone was described in 147 different ways by those who returned the questionnaire.

Another way of trying to discover the characteristics which make for success in business is to read the biographies of outstanding business men, although unfortunately this is rarely as helpful as it should be. Too often we are only shown pasteboard figures, painted by their opponents as ruthless, ambitious and grasping; by themselves as terrifically hard-working, devoted to the service of the community and guided by common sense. Neither adequately suggest the complexities of human nature. Two qualities, however, stand out from the literature as being the most important for success: optimism and self-confidence —qualities which rarely find their way into books on management. The artist may produce his best work when he is tormented by doubts and fears but the business man must have faith in his own judgment since he has so little else to go on: imaginative self-doubt is a luxury which no business man can afford. As Munby points out:

> The world, in which the businessmen has to operate, is a world in which accurate forecasts are impossible, and the future is unpredictable. A businessman is a man who has to take decisions in the dark and bet upon his nerve and his fortune. Chance and luck play a part more important than plan and foresight; a cool nerve is a more valuable asset than a wide-ranging capacity to see all sides of a problem; the power to take rapid and firm action is more likely to be successful than the ability to judge wisely. Success in business, in contrast to academic study, depends on the power to shut a blind eye to the immediately irrelevant.[11]

The optimism and self-confidence of the business man can be illustrated by two very different personalities. It was said of Lord Nuffield:

> With complete faith in what he wanted to do, he has always had an
> unwavering confidence in his own abilities and judgment. Seldom
> seeking positive advice from others he listens to argument, but
> makes up his own mind.[12]

And of Selfridge that he:

> struck me as a natural force—like the wind. He blew and the whole
> store registered the force. It drew its power from his tremendous
> optimism. 'Optimism is the foundation of this business, Williams'
> he said on one occasion.[13]

Some business men have succeeded because of their imaginative
ideas, their ability to see a marketable need before anybody else. Here
self-confidence and optimism were also vital in backing their own
judgment. It was said of Ford, for instance, that:

> He evolved from his intuitive processes of thought certain large
> conceptions which, more than anything else, account for his spectacu-
> lar early success. One, of course, was his idea of a car for the masses,
> built in quantity and sold at ever-lower prices as consumption
> grew. Another was his determination to expand his plant, his pro-
> duction and his sales at a steady pace, in defiance of those who wished
> to call a halt. He meant to make as many cars as possible at the
> lowest prices; the ordinary manufacturer worked to restrict produc-
> tion and raise prices.[14]

In other words, he foresaw the shape of the demand curve of a product
before any economist had worked it out for him.

Unfortunately many men have all these qualities but do not succeed
in business; one reason why it is so hard to define the qualities of
successful entrepreneurship is that no tally is kept of the men who
seemed all set for success, but failed. There are no case-histories of
failure—of honourable failure, that is; the unsuccessful business man
sometimes dimly appears as a minor character in novels, or is the
briefly-described father of somebody far more eminent in another walk
of life in biographies. What is perhaps more interesting is the remarkable
similarity of the characters of successful business men and those that
are successful until they are found out to be frauds. Ivar Kreuger is the
obvious example. Such men—Bottomley, Hatry, Insull, Bishurgian—
show all the right qualities—marked ability, optimism, ambition, mas-

tery of a winning idea, swift capitalization of an opportunity, self-confidence, application, determination—everything but integrity. One study of business frauds reached the conclusion that

> fall came from pride . . . the mystery remains why so few of them did not stop in time. In most cases it would have been possible, long before crash and disclosure, to retire from the ardours and anxieties of high finance, and cultivate a leisured garden . . . all suffered . . . from *folie de vitesse*. Products of an acquisitive society, they typified—in extreme degree—its madness.[15]

Perhaps. But perhaps their fate also shows that under private enterprise there are too many Napoleons for any one to inflict too much madness disastrously on the rest of society. What brings down the fraudulent business man is—the operations of other business men. This quality of knowing just what one is up against in the business community is one undoubted ingredient of achieving success with respectability.

3. SUCCESS HAS NO FORMULA

It is regrettably difficult to show in much greater detail what character-istics make for success in business. One reason for this was given by Marshall when he discovered that

> The abilities required to make an ideal employer are so great and so numerous that very few persons can exhibit them all . . . scarcely any two owe their success to the same combination of advantages.[16]

Samuel Smiles did not think the matter anything like so esoteric in reality. 'Anyone,' he said, 'who devotes himself to making money, body and soul, can scarcely fail to become rich. Very little brains will do.' But that was in 1860 or so.[17]

Another reason is that business men are inarticulate about their motives and feelings. Sometimes it seems that they are deliberately throwing up a smoke-screen, or are they really as simple as they portray themselves? Like the top executive who said:

> I was happy being an office boy, just as I am happy being the managing director . . . as a boy I liked pressing those letters in the big copy books. It just came naturally to want to press them well, and to press more than had ever been pressed before.[18]

Three reasons may be suggested for the business man's inarticulateness. First that he is a man of action, and has no time to analyse his feelings, that indeed success in business may be incompatible with self-analysis. 'Business men do and don't talk; statesmen talk and don't do', is the relevant and flattering aphorism. Second, though he is a man of action his action is generally unheroic; this may explain why we know more about a Tuscan merchant than we do about any modern business man since his life was made more interesting by the dangerous times he lived in. The third reason for this reticence may be that money-making, especially outstandingly successful money-making can be a dirty business, both in terms of the methods used and of the colleagues trampled upon, and therefore is never described with candour.

Yet another reason for the difficulty of defining what factors make for success is that though there is a basic business situation—keeping out of the red on the Profit and Loss account—the circumstances of every firm varies widely. There are so many routes to the top, so many ways of conducting oneself successfully when one gets there. As Clements has pointed out:

> It looks as if managers constitute many non-competing groups. Industrial management appears to be a host of diverse jobs, entailing diverse techniques and experience, different standards and types of education, and different attitudes and sets of principles. It seems that these differences even lead to recognizably different patterns of career, and that different social origins frequently coincide with these other differences. Has the extent to which these people form an homogeneous élite in the social body been exaggerated?[19]

Not merely will the career patterns and social background differ but the qualities required for one route may be very different from those required by another. The managing director of a heavy engineering works who makes for and sells to other companies will acquire a different outlook even if he does not start with one, from the head of a company catering for a mass and highly variable market where the primary emphasis is on selling stylistic changes, and both will be different again from the man who has climbed up the promotion ladder of a well-established store. Further, the personality traits required for succeeding in a mature company which has already solidified into a bureaucracy will be unlike those needed in a rapidly expanding company in a highly competitive industry, and both will be different again from those required by the man who builds up his own business.

The greatest contrast to be found is, of course, between the top manager and the self-employed business man. The former, to succeed, must subordinate his personality at least, to some extent, to the organization until he may become as much a product of it as the goods that carry its trade name. The independent business man is precisely the opposite. The top manager will need tact—he should be a good committee man and have at least an artificial air of bonhomie—his ego must not be too obviously in evidence. The self-employed business man, on the other hand, who is boss of his own show, can fire those who do not fit in with his own personality and may carry the others with him through deference to his energy and originality. The top manager must be highly literate although in many industries he need have no technical ability. He must be able to absorb information by reading and listening, for it is more important for him to be able to sift other people's ideas than to put forward his own. By contrast the owner manager can be almost illiterate*—but he will usually owe his success at least in part to his mechanical genius or his financial flair, and some of the most successful have had the imagination to see a marketable need before anybody else.

4. THE CHANGING FACE OF SUCCESS

It is often alleged that the characteristics of the successful business man have changed, that the days of the autocrats and robber barons have passed and that emotional maturity is now one of the requirements for a good manager. Emotional maturity is indeed one of the selection criterion for the Harvard Business School,† but it is one which

* Like the man in Mr Somerset Maugham's story who, sacked from his job for illiteracy, built up a chain of tobacconist's stores, and was asked by his banker where he would have been had he known how to read and write, and replied, 'A verger.'
A consultant known to us, when asked by a managing director of a business bureaucracy what qualities he ought to have, proceeded to eliminate those he did not need. 'To begin with,' he said to his client, 'you do not need to write or read; for you have no time to read and you dictate everything you write.' After thought the managing director agreed. A growing number of senior business men have personal assistants (with arts and science degrees) to read for them, and then tell them succinctly what is important in the press.

† Although a professor at the Harvard Business School told one of the authors that they had sent down a student for his emotionally immature escapades. He had later become an outstandingly successful business man. The qualities which made for his success were, the professor admitted, the same that had caused him to be sent down.

would have excluded some of the most successful business men. For example, Lipton with his quick temper, his resentment of opposition and his sofas containing microphones so that he could overhear what his visiting staff said, could hardly be passed as emotionally mature. Nor could Selfridge—gambling vast sums with one of his lady loves on the understanding that she took all the winnings and he made good all the losses. Nor yet Ford who created a police state in his Company. Yet these men built great businesses and were responsible for imaginative ideas—Ford for his conception of cars for the masses—Lipton for his understanding of the power of advertising and Selfridge for his grasp of the value of showmanship in retail trade.

This paradox suggests that the qualities required for a good manager in a well-established business serving a stable market may—indeed, must—be quite different from that of the business man who creates a business or who caters for a new or unpredictable market. The smooth, 'mature' manager may be one type of modern business man and undoubtedly with an increase in the number of long-established industrial empires we shall need many more of him; but the founders of new business may still in miniature resemble Ford rather than Heyworth. The modern Fords, however, are likely to be less autocratic, and it might be difficult today for the business man successfully to follow Lord Cowdray's advice to his son written shortly before his death in 1927:

> Do not allow any responsibility to be taken by any colleagues beyond that which you give them. Care will be necessary to keep them within the limits you allow. The limits you grant will be controlled by the personal demands on your own time. Probably a committee meeting, for a few minutes only, would be desirable at frequent intervals, if not daily, at which each would properly report verbally what he was doing. All decisions taken must be those which you fully approve. Do not hesitate for one second to be in opposition to your colleagues; or in overriding their decisions. No business can be a permanent success unless its head be an autocrat—of course, the more disguised by the silken glove the better.[20]

The opportunities for such unfettered control may not exist in the future; Andrews and Brunner have suggested in *The Life of Lord Nuffield* that:

> It is doubtful whether such a life will ever be open to others in this country again. By this we do not mean only the opportunity to amass such a personal fortune; Nuffield did not seek money as such and it

was rather the consequence than the cause of his endeavours. The monetary reward was a consequence of his business succeeding so vigorously, but he could not have built up such an enterprise and kept it under his control had he not been able to retain profits on the scale shown in the table. A new private business started nowadays, however successful, is bound to have a much slower rate of growth on the basis of retained profits because of the incidence of taxation. If capital is raised outside, ownership is divided and the question remains whether the Nuffield kind of temperament can make its mark without control over the whole of the developing stage of a business. He himself most definitely felt he needed his completely independent command.[21]

Although business men must perforce be less autocratic and less buccaneering, this does not mean that they are becoming a homogeneous species. Possibly they even represent themselves to be more homogeneous than they are. To give some indication of their diversity we shall round off this survey of what is known about entrepreneurial psychology with a few pen portraits in the next section.

5. PORTRAITS FROM LIFE

Successful business men sometimes sit for their portraits—by painters or journalists. Both find it advisable to idealize the subject. Lines of firmness and humour are touched in round the mouth; resolution is rescued from the jowl; the eyes set deeper, perhaps, to strengthen their visionary quality; the proportions of head and forehead fashioned to intellectuality; the career similarly adjusted, in accordance with the rules of the drama, to bring out prescience, mission, message, serenity in hard times and modesty in achievement. They create what is expected —and what is indeed seen in the shaving-mirror—

> 'a man of rapid decision, quick insight into character and iron will; he must have a firm jaw, tightly closed lips and a habit of brief and incisive speech. He must combine the qualities of a great general and a great diplomatist: ruthlessness in battle but a capacity of skilful concession in negotiation.'[22]

The result perhaps is no happier in terms of art than in terms of biography.*

* Cf. the following description of Sir Eric Geddes, 'ruthless' boss of Dunlops between the wars: 'His huge physique, clear grey eyes and bulldog jaw gave his

continued overleaf

Though captains of industry may have a good deal to say about national affairs at shareholders' and other meetings they are not, they insist, politicians or even generals to whom rules of 'fair comment on matters of public interest' apply with any rigour. They want publicity 'of the right kind'. It is therefore one thing to list or chart the qualities that bring men to the top in industry or commerce or finance; it is quite another to demonstrate them from the vivisection of a breathing industrialist. Everything that emerges in private conversation or press interview, other than the possession of stereotyped qualities, a steady accumulation of achievement and capital, and a set of opinions is generally off the record. Yet something ought, in conclusion, to be done to give a more lifelike picture of Who Gets to the Top than we have been able to do so far. Since so much is 'off the record' and the libel laws can be so punitive, recourse must be had to the revived Theophrastian method of the imaginary case-history[23] in which every detail is true of someone but the ensemble coincides with nobody. The gentlemen who follow are made up, as hospitals make up skeletons for burial from the anatomy-room, by taking a leg here and an arm there, but keeping everything in proportion as far as possible and not leaving out —as the bare bones of mere qualities would do—the odd quirks of motive or circumstance which affect every *curriculum vitae*. These case-histories will show you why you cannot quote from life.*

(a) HEAD OF THE FAMILY

Mr Henry Franklin Clammer is the grandson of the founder of Clammer & Co, the well-known makers of modern kitchen equipment. He was born in 1905; passed a carefree childhood in his parents' comfortable home in West Kensington, went to a private prep. and minor public

* The dangers of doing so were the *raison d'être* of *The Observer's* 1957 Christmas competition when readers were invited to draw imaginary profiles of successful persons with major faults of character which cannot be openly stated.

---

personality tremendous force. He was a mighty trencherman and a chain-smoker of strong cigars. . . . He rode large horses and drove large cars. . . . A rapid and tireless worker, relentless in his demands on his staff, he was not a comfortable man to work for . . . but he had inherited the high principles of his Scottish ancestry and insisted on complete personal integrity in personal relations and commercial dealings and on the best achievable conditions of employment for workers of all grades.' Sir Charles Tennyson, *Stars and Markets*, Chatto, 1957, p. 175.

school where, the emphasis being on games, he did not much distinguish himself. He would have liked to go to the university but his father thought he had had quite enough book-learning by then and he went into the business, starting as a warehouse-boy, delivery boy and vanman's help; in 1925 he became a salesman, and sold every kind of domestic ironmongery until 1930, when he did a spell in the buying department. During this period he quarrelled violently with his father, who saw no sense in his doing night-school courses in furniture design, and even less in his taking cookery lessons; who could not understand why he would not marry his charming and well-off cousin; and who disliked his taste in furniture and personal adornment, which ran him into debt despite his salary of £650 a year. Clammer senior repeatedly stepped in to stop Henry making a fool of himself and wasting the firm's money. His fad for 'bespoke kitchens' angered his father even more; and when Mr Henry called the firm 'a hardware shop', banished him to the small and unprofitable Bournemouth branch. Mr Clammer senior, however, had a serious operation soon after, and following two death-bed scenes there was a reconciliation and the heir was brought back to his beloved West End in charge of sinks and water equipment with his debts paid and a very small budget to develop his idea of 'Whole kitchen design'. As he exceeded this, family rows continued, growing worse after Mrs Clammer's death in 1937. Officially, and at shareholders' meetings, the business was showing 'steady and continuous expansion' and 'future prospects' were good.

In 1940 Mr Henry joined the R.A.S.C. and specialized in field kitchens with such astonishing success that he ended the war as a full colonel. He left the army, with some reluctance, in 1946 and rejoined his father, who was ill and depressed. His birthright could no longer be denied and he took over as managing director. The firm was shaky; there was plenty of trade, of course, but nothing much to sell; worst of all, the crowd of family hangers-on, at boardroom level, was fatal to efficiency. Mr Henry called in consultants, who tactfully but definitely advised that not only his father but his three cousins should retire from active participation. There was a new flare-up; the colonel was firm; the cousins went—and took their capital with them. Clammer & Co was now near disaster. Henry, helped by Dr Dalton, raised money feverishly from the bank; bought army surplus kitchenware and spray-painted it (often with his own hands) with surplus army paint, and began to do a roaring business. Now his plans bore fruit; he built his design department and staffed it with two close friends of his army days; he became

112

Britain's first 'Kitchen Consultant' and appeared regularly on tele-vision—showing how one could run a labour-saving kitchen—where his performance, wearing a frilly apron, became a byword for sheer enter-tainment as well as thorough kitchen-wisdom. He engaged a smart young man to write his kitchen articles for the women's magazines. He did an immense business in the new towns with his modular kitchen ('Britekits' and 'Merriwork'). In 1950 he easily raised £1,000,000 in the market and in 1954, he raised another million. The credit squeeze has not hit Clammers too hard, thanks to Sir Titus Bawlforth's brilliant advertising series, 'Give her a healthy kitchen first. . . .'

Mr Henry Clammer at fifty-two looks forty-five, is unmarried and certain to remain so. His outstanding social quality is his wit, exercised only in male company, which infuses an air of delicacy into even the most unadorned of after-dinner jokes. He gives wonderful parties, has a valuable collection of pictures, knows everybody, is right-of-centre socialist in politics and leaves his finance to a first-rate firm of merchant bankers. (The handsome cousin married a missionary and was killed by the Chinese communists.)

(b) CAPTAIN OF INDUSTRY

James Hampton Rich comes of a well-to-do middle-class family in Buckingham. Father was a solicitor, one of his uncles a well-known Harley Street specialist, another a large farmer. Born in 1897 he was educated at Eton and St John's, Cambridge. In 1914 he enlisted in the Ox. and Bucks, transferred in 1915 to the Royal Flying Corps, where he won the D.F.C., and was captured after being shot down. He made three attempts to escape. Back at Cambridge, in 1919, he took his science degree and, to his family's surprise, took the advice of an Eton friend on the board of the British Hot Air Company, then a £3,000,000 public company, and 'went into business'. He was run round the departments as a trainee (an early scheme, this), spending a year in the works management of the firm's three factories. From there he went to sales; and to service accounts.

In 1922 he was sent to India, where he arranged agents, shot two tigers, and sold two primitive tropical air conditioning plants, one to H.E. the Governor of Oudh and Tirhut, the other to H.H. the Maha-rajah of Rajastan. He obtained substantial government contracts for more standard equipment. In 1923 he returned and became head of

H   113

home sales, S.W. region. In 1925, he was made assistant works manager and (as a sideline) took up the problem of oxygen apparatus for pilots, balloonists and mountaineers at high altitudes. In 1929 he was promoted assistant to the managing director, where he again turned to overseas sales, visiting Australia by plane (his own) in 1932. During the slump he was at head office reorganizing and staving off bankruptcy; the tide did not turn for British Hot Air until 1936. Then J. H. Rich became general works manager, and the next year works director; B.H.A. was busy with war work. In 1946, Rich became managing director; once again recession and reconversion hit the firm. In 1953, he became chairman and received a rather belated knighthood. He has been liked by no Minister of Defence since Sir Thomas Inskip, except Churchill.

Most of this story can be found in *Who's Who*, as well as the fact that he married Lady Deirdre Tulkinghorn, daughter of the Earl of Aycliffe in 1924; has three children and has served on the Royal Commission on Industrial Pollution. In management circles he is known as an early enthusiast for scientific management, and has written three unusual papers on work study. He often takes the chair at meetings of the Market Research Society, and is a director of Export Intelligence Inc, jointly owned by B.H.A., and an American combine. In the firm itself he is known for certain things not widely known of him outside it. One of these is his standard procedure for committees. 'This is the committee age,' he says. 'Let's face it—and make it work as best we can.' He also is convinced of the need for management training and succession—but he has made no arrangement for his own. ('Neither did Alexander.')

But none of this explains Rich's later career: they have not even made B.H.A. particularly efficient. The *real* reason for his success was his relationship first with the chairman, Sir Dan Picton, and second with two big banks and one big insurance company who were the firm's major creditors from 1930 to 1942. Again and again, due to Sir Dan's earlier financial indiscretions, and those of his board, B.H.A. could have been bankrupt, and there might even have been scandals. Sir Dan, in and out of nursing homes, had to be kept at the head of affairs, and the board had to be kept from panicking more than once. Rich's objectivity and self-possession in tight corners gave him his ascendency over the chairman and the board, and engendered confidence in the creditors. Few even of his intimates know that while in India he met Colonel Yeats-Brown and took up the practice of yoga. Apart from

Lady Rich, only Miss Lymphe, his secretary since 1926, has seen him in *samadhi* and she would never speak of it to a soul.

(c) PRACTICAL BUSINESS MAN

William Ramsbottom started his business career as a craft apprentice at the age of fifteen in the Hercules Lathe Company in Manchester in 1923. His parents were working-class people; his mother having been a mill girl and his father, until he became paralysed after a stroke, a municipal tram-driver. After finishing his indentures, and taking night-school courses, he went in to the drawing office in 1928 and stayed there until 1930. He then went to another firm as a draughtsman but within nine months he was out, as its orders for drop hammers had dwindled to nothing. He then joined the British Automatic Machine Tool Company which made small tools—including some for amateur use—in 1934, as a draughtsman, almost its only one, at a meagre salary of £250 a year. He showed marked aptitude in developing these machines, and in his spare time took his A.M.I.Mech.E.

He married in 1937 when his salary had risen to £375 a year, and moved to a new surburban estate, putting down an initial building society payment on a house costing £565. In 1939, he moved to his present firm, Shafting & Transmission Ltd, as an engineer; almost immediately he became works manager of one of the smaller government shadow factories working on tank components. By 1946 his salary was £2,500 a year, and he went on the board of his company, which retained this factory as its main plant.

Between 1946 and 1953 he strongly opposed suggestions that Shafting & Transmission Ltd, should buy up an electronic outfit or merge with several other electrical firms, on the grounds that automation was nothing new, and that a firm making standard machine tools should stick to its own business. He was able to point to a steady increase in sales to the East, and to argue that they had everything on their plate that they could manage. In the end the directors who wanted to go into electronics resigned; at the same time the managing director who had used Ramsbottom to stave off their pressure, went on a world sales tour and Ramsbottom took charge as deputy managing director. On his return the managing director decided that he could attend to his other interests better as chairman of the company, and as the chairman resigned conveniently, both he and Mr Ramsbottom moved up one.

Mr R. then found his customers were demanding electronic controls on several standard machines and brought in a Dutch associate to work on this—which they did with great success. Mr R. is now cautiously developing an electronic division but sets his face firmly against anything spectacular. He is suspicious of any increase in numbers of men on the shop floor and is downright hostile to any increase in the offices which he is sure will be due to empire building, but he will occasionally 'buy an expert'.

He considers that there should be heavy tariffs on 'foreign' machine tools, and is a strong supporter of the British Machine Tools Association. He thinks his customers are often very unreasonable, but he takes a lot of trouble to give them—outside too much 'tapery and transistery'—what they want. He is a strong believer in starting young and thinks 'university types' are useless in engineering, and in most kinds of business. He has a contempt for the workers—who like him because he understands them—an equal contempt for the upper classes.

He now has a large surburban house and two cars—a Lagonda for himself and a Fiat 600 for his wife. His son has a motor bicycle but, though a satisfactory boy in most respects, is taking a degree in architecture. Mrs Ramsbottom is mainly concerned with getting the two girls married. Mr Ramsbottom's leisure is divided between his hobby—building model boats—motoring and the local, where both he and his views on the laziness of young men today—his favourite theme—are received with great respect. He leaves all public activities, which he considers a waste of time, to the chairman.

(d) CITY TYCOON

Graham Cornhill is the brother of Vernon Cornhill, the well-known actor. Like his brother he was educated at Winchester and New College; but, while his brother did brilliantly in O.U.D.S., Graham only did brilliantly in Oxford social life. He obtained a fourth in Greats with ease, because he improvised several undeniably brilliant answers in otherwise barren papers. His real interest was Italian, in which he was more than proficient; he professed his intention of becoming *Inglese Italianati* when he went down—but his father, who was a literary agent, died suddenly and unexpectedly, was found to have left only just enough for his widow (whom both boys adored) to live on. Both had to rise by their own efforts: Vernon in the Birmingham Rep., Graham in the

City. Graham's aunt, Leslie Colquhoun, the Society beauty, arranged for him to start as a junior in 1923 in Sir Pardoe Josephus & Co, the merchant bankers. Graham worked in the securities department, and went to many of the famous parties of the twenties. He held his job in 1929–31, as did his aunt, even though the bank, as paying agent for several foreign governments, saw all the foreign bonds which Graham was used to recommending fall to a fraction of their value. He suggested that the firm should now compete for some home industrial issues and was told he did not understand. But, as a matter of fact, he *did* understand. *Post hoc, ergo propter hoc* the adoption of tariffs in 1932, Sir Pardoe suddenly felt a new buoyancy in home business, and he brought young Graham in on the first of a new series of home industrial issues. One day, over a Napoleon, Sir Pardoe told Graham he was thinking of starting a subsidiary as a company nursery through which the bank could finance businesses not yet ripe for flotation. 'How long would that take, sir,' asked Graham. 'I think we could get going in two years, Graham,' said the banker. 'That will be too late, I'm afraid, sir,' the Junior replied. 'We shall be at war by then.'

Graham joined up as an aircraftman in the balloons, and finding them phoney, transferred to the Ministry of Economic Warfare; a girl friend effecting some necessary introductions. In 1941, he was proving invaluable to the Minister of Supply. He arranged government finance for firms that no merchant bank would have touched and quietly decided that, when war was over, he would specialize in financing just such people.

The problem was money. Even though he had been doing fairly well owing to capital appreciation, he had always been in debt, because of his tastes, which ran to country-house life, party girls and, even more expensive, jade. He married exquisite Marie Le Charpentier from Montreal in 1946, and was received into the Church soon after. Marie, as one of eight daughters, was not enormously wealthy, even with Le Charpentier copper at 1946 prices; but she was glad to buy Graham the Lynx Investment Trust, which had not grasped the principles of war finance and was going cheap. He immediately formed a finance company, New Era Holdings Ltd, as its subsidiary which enabled him to play the inland revenue both ways. His many contacts of the war years enabled him to seek out businesses that had to be financed internally because they were not ripe for public issue, and now he is quite a name in public issues too. As chairman of New Era Holdings, he does not invariably claim a seat on the board of those whom he finances, but he is flattered when he is asked, and when the old-established family business of Camberwell & Rutland, the world-famous pottery firm, had to become a public company to meet Mr Adolphus Rutland's death duties, he was honoured to be asked to become its chairman. Seventy per cent of this business is still in the family, but they find it useful to have an independent financier at the head of the board. He may not know much about ceramics—outside the antiques end of the trade—but he does understand financial control. Profit estimates every month—the general manager said it was impossible; but now they are the solid ground under his feet. Budgets of capital expenditure have shown him how to plan a rate of growth and to finance it without the recurrent crisis into which Mr Adolphus periodically ran. And the chairman always knows where to go for sound advice. The mere appointment of the right tax advisers is worth his chairman's fee. He knows everybody and he goes everywhere; he is certainly a man to watch. But it is better still to be asked to his estate in Caithness for the shooting; you may meet the highest in the land there, and really learn something.

NOTES

1. Copeman, Dr G. H., *Leaders of British Industry: a study of the careers of more than a thousand public company directors*, London, Gee & Co (Publishers), 1955.

2. Acton Society Trust, *Management Succession*, London, Acton Society Trust, 1956.

3. Clements, R V., *Managers: a Study of Their Careers in Industry*, London, Allen & Unwin, 1958.

4. 'Parkinson Looks at Retirement', *The Economist*, 16 February 1957.

5. Clements, R. V., op. cit., p. 151.

6. Marshall, Alfred, op. cit., Chap. XII.

7. Tronchin-James, Dr Nevil, 'The Changing Manager', *The Manager*, March, 1957.

8. Henry, W. E., 'The Business Executive: the psychodynamics of a social role', *American Journal of Sociology*, January, 1949.

9. Whitehead, Harold, *How to Become a Successful Manager*, London, Allen & Unwin, 1957, p. 51.

10. Stryker, Perrin, *On the Meaning of Executive Qualities*, Fortune, June 1958.

11. Munby, D. L., *Christianity and Economic Problems*, London, Macmillan, 1957, p. 51; 1956, p. 164.

12. Andrews, P. S. and Brunner, Elizabeth, *The Life of Lord Nuffield: a study in enterprise and benevolence*, Oxford, Basil Blackwell, 1955, p. 4.

13. Williams, A. H., C.B.E., *No Name on the Door: A Memoir of Gordon Selfridge*, London, W. H. Allen, 1956, p. 22.

14. Nevins, Allan, *Ford: The Times, The Man, The Company*, New York, Charles Scribner's Sons, 1954, p. 577.

15. Vallance, A., *Very Private Enterprise*, London, Thames & Hudson, 1955, p. 11.

16. Marshall, Alfred, op. cit., loc. cit.

17. Smiles, Aileen, *Samuel Smiles and His Surroundings*, London, Robert Hale, 1956, p. 107.

18. 'Man of the Month: Leonard Sinclair', *Scope*, April 1954.

19. Clements, R. V., op. cit., p. 159.

20. Spender, J. A., *Weetman Pearson, First Viscount Cowdray*, 1856–1927, London, Cassell, 1930, p. 278.

21. Andrews, P. S. and Brunner, Elizabeth, op. cit.

22. Russell, Bertrand, *Power: a New Social Analysis*, London, Allen & Unwin, 1938, p. 46.

23. *The Economist*, 21 July 1957.

CHAPTER VI
Life at the Top

'Where your treasure is, there will your heart be also.'

MATTHEW, vi, 21

'The typical picture of what goes on in the "front office" or on the "fourteenth floor" in the minds of otherwise sane men ... bears striking resemblance to the mediaeval geographer's picture of Africa as the stamping-ground of the one-eyed ogre, the immortal phoenix and the elusive unicorn.'

PETER DRUCKER, *Practice of Management*

LIBRARIES FULL OF MANUALS on economics, business administration and boardroom procedure have been published; but the top business man remains—let it be repeated—the man nobody knows. Bafflingly little light is available on the sort of life he lives—at all events in Britain. Of the kind of decisions he and his kind have to make and what comes of them plenty is known—to economists, to stockbrokers, to management consultants—but of the atmosphere in which they work, of the impact of their duties, powers and privileges upon them as human beings, of their secret thoughts and doings as distinct from the front which their poker-faced impassivity or romanticized publicity puts up to the public, almost nothing. Apart from the shiny business journal *Fortune*, and a few novelists, who also write only of the American business man, hardly anybody has sought to describe what life at the summit is like in business. Private enterprise remains extraordinarily private; and it is a privacy which not even the social anthropologists have sought to lay bare. We know far more about the motives, habits and most intimate arcana of primitive peoples in New Guinea and elsewhere, than we do of the denizens of the executive suites in Unilever House, or of the directors' offices of the Allsorts Engineering Company's works at the bottom of the road.

1. SWEETS OF OFFICE

We know firstly, however, that it is a very enjoyable life, whatever may be the motives that consciously or unconsciously activate the individual chairman or director. Though many business men complain that people nowadays 'are unwilling to shoulder the burdens of responsibility', and many affect the air of the weary titan themselves, all the evidence points to the fact that they find the burden of responsibility enjoyable, or at least infinitely desirable.

What is the satisfaction, what the fascination, of lives which are nowadays said to be loaded with overwork, worry and responsibility? We shall see in a later chapter that in British business the opportunities to get really rich have been narrowed, although the average top executive is the best-paid man in the country, outside the top rank of entertainers; though a few can still become millionaires, it is now easier for a camel to go through the eye of a needle than for a British—as opposed to a Greek or South American or Syrian—business man to become a multimillionaire. It is not to be denied however that people still go into business to make money; that the making of money is an immense pleasure; that almost all business men want to handle as much of it, and keep as much of it, as they can. Making one's pile (like the dung beetles in Capek's *Insect Play*) is a larger or smaller part of almost every business man's drive. He may rarely admit this, but rarely will the repudiation of any interest in money be quite sincere, though there are no doubt a minority who can say with Cobden

> What is all this yearning after? I can scarcely give myself a satisfying answer. Surely not for money; I feel a disregard for it, and even a slovenly inattention to its possession, that is quite dangerous . . . I do not think that the possession of millions would greatly alter my habits of expense.[1]

Those that can, may covet a political cause, not commercial success.

If making money is no longer as great an incentive, what others are there? Fame is hardly the spur. A few business men achieve notoriety, but not if they are successful. The fame attaching to a successful business career is very modest. Hence those who wish for public recognition have to seek it outside business, in politics, public works or philanthropy. This search may have unfortunate effects for their subordinates, for the business whose chairman or managing director is kept waiting for a public honour, which he feels has been too long delayed, is likely to suffer from a rapid turnover of top executives. Sir John, unless he now wishes to become Lord, is often a much more relaxed and easy man to work for. 'Gongs' have in the past not been awarded for business success as such; but for the good which a man has done with the money he has made, or the influence he has secured. This is tending to change, and many business men wish the change could be speeded up, arguing that to do the necessary outside committee work, like the vigil before knighthood in medieval times, is rather meaningless and distracts a man from his proper job. As, they say, now there is so little to be made out of business, it should, in the matter of honours, be put on more of an equality with the civil service. They argue that their productive record may be as good as, or better than, that of many civil servants, and probably worth far more to the nation than the running of a few philanthropic works. 'Just because Bill runs the Homes for Khaki British Babies,' they growl, 'he gets his K. What about those two power stations I got for British industry in Byelo-Russia this year? A cool twelve million. Don't they think that's worth anything?'

What then can be said of power? The head of a £10,000,000 soap firm no doubt has power; but a successful career in politics or the trade union movement is today likely to yield a man far more power than a career in business. Though some industries, and even certain large firms, are of national importance, their heads can no longer expect to be able to exert pressure on governments; the days of great business autocracies are over. A small group of newspaper proprietors can perhaps claim considerable influence with the public, but this influence is probably in most matters in inverse proportion to the commercial success of their product. It is almost unthinkable today that a business man could make a private treaty with a foreign government, duly ratified by its parliament, as Sir William Lever did with Belgium over concessions to his firm in the Congo in 1911, and derive a very special thrill from it:

> My happiness (wrote Lever) is my business. I can see finality for myself, and end, an absolute end; but none for my business. There one has room to breathe, to grow, to expand, and the possibilities are boundless. One can go to places like the Congo, and organise, organise, organise, well, very big things indeed. But I don't work at business only for the sake of money. I am not a lover of money as such and never have been. I work at business because business is life. It enables me to do things.[2]

It certainly enabled Rhodes to do even bigger things than it did Lever; but business men are unlikely again to find themselves part of the scramble for Africa, or the conquest of the American frontier. Indeed, no business can now dominate a colonial or semi-colonial country; and the *burra sahib* of yesterday is today the bowing and sirring commercial delegate of London Office in the presence of the new Asian or African Prime Minister. At Abadan the mighty oil companies were shown that they existed only on terms that suited the foreign government; today they are leaning backward to be purely commercial. British oil companies with British government directors indeed, take orders to close down their Israeli departments at the brusque behest of the Sheikh or Sultan. 'Importance' the bustling British top oil executive can feel, as he hurries to and fro in the service of the oil business; but power to organize, organize, organize, well, very big things indeed? No: this is a matter for the Foreign Office.

The belief still lingers in some circles that big business men do, both individually and as a group, exert great and sinister power behind the scenes of public life. In the inter-war years socialist writers discussed how to prevent a business men's *coup* against attempted nationalization. The post-war years have shown how vastly they overestimated their opponents. Nationalization, high company and estate taxes, restrictions on selling in the home market and anti-monopoly legislation have all, as we have seen, demonstrated the limitations of business men's influence on the government. This is true of legislation under Conservative as well as under Socialist governments. Shaw's Undershaft never existed in the flesh even in the days when governments were pinning decorations on Hiram Maxim for every advance he made in gunsmithery. Today the business man who wants scope for policy-making on a national scale must go (like Lord Mills) into politics (and some day, perhaps, into the nationalized industries). Mr Oliver Lyttelton, as Colonial Secretary, had far more power—for good and ill—than as Lord Chandos, Chairman of Associated Electrical Industries, he will ever have again. Even the Federation of British Industries now mainly deals with masses of administrative minutiae, and its efforts behind the scenes often concern no more than minor amendments to bills every clause of which may stink in its members' nostrils. There is a sense of self importance to be had, no doubt, from serving on the committees of such bodies, but little of personal power; and their officers mainly live and think much as their opposite numbers, the civil servants of Whitehall, do. Business political influence is in fact exerted through pressure groups, which are composed of the trade associations concerned, such as the National Union of Manufacturers, and which appeared in recent years to have only a very limited success in achieving their objectives.[3]

Power in business is, in fact, limited and confined; but in the small world of the individual firm or industry it gives enough scope and pleasure to many men whose ambitions are moderate and practical. Men with the abilities to make a success of politics often say they prefer business because, though the stage is smaller, one has greater power in that smaller area and therefore more chance of getting things done in one's own way. Many men would rather double the size of a firm than spend half a lifetime over the compromises necessary to get a few bills through Parliament—bills which will become law in a form very different, perhaps, from that first planned in hope. Business, with all its hazards, is more predictable, more under control: success is more probable for the man with flair than in most other avocations.

The pleasure of top business is very much the pleasure of a game, as many have noticed;* a game of poker to be played for its thrills even more than its rewards, though to impart the thrills the stakes must be fairly high. The essence of adventure is risk. Some find it in physical danger. Some in politics. Others find it in deals and financial speculations, great or small, in which their wealth, sometimes their livelihood, and occasionally their reputations are staked. Even if the money is not your own, big deals are still immensely exciting; the audience is a select circle of other business men who well know who has come out on top. In this sense fame is the spur, not public fame, but the knowledgeable appreciation, admiration and perhaps sweetest of all, fear, of rivals and colleagues. Failure means adverse comment in financial circles in the know—and bad failure may even mean a row with the shareholders and unpleasant publicity. Competitive games are, in a real sense, tamed war; so are business and competition, and business men often get the same sort of satisfaction from it, as do generals—if more safely.[4]

But while many business men frankly admit that business is a game, they do not of course admit that it is just a game; they readily combine

* So much so that the newest school of mathematical economics takes· this concept, not the orthodox dynamics of the market, as its starting point, cf. John Von Neumann and Oskar Morgenstern, *The Theory of Games and Economic Behaviour*, Princetown University Press, 1942. A simplified statement of the idea will be found in J. Macdonald, *Strategy in Poker, Business and War*, Norton, New York, 1953.

gamesmanship with lofty views of the value to the community of their play. Lord Rhondda, for example, said:

> I am out for the game and not for the stakes, and while I admit I find business a very fascinating game, I contend that by increasing the means of subsistence of the people, I have in the aggregate contributed more to the material happiness and well-being of Welsh colliery workers and their familes than have all the miners' leaders combined, though moved by the best intentions.[5]

The fact that work is a sort of game for those at the top rather than a form of compulsory activity is, as Lord Halsbury has suggested with shrewdness, that which divides them from those lower down. As one managing director confessed to *Scope*: 'I never have a dull moment in my business. But if I was one of many I don't think it'd be such fun.'[6] Because work is such fun to the boss, he can work long hours absorbed, happy and tireless. Few bosses realize, however, that they enjoy this pleasure at the expense of everyone else; that, lower down, to do half the boss's stint is thrice as tiring. On the contrary, it is a wonder to most business men who have wealth and sit permanently in the driver's seat that everyone else—at least among their executives—is not just as 'keen'. Bosses commonly talk of 'shared adventure' of their enterprise. Yet it cannot really be shared—though nobody will dare to tell the boss that horrid truth. For someone else to have the authentic thrill the boss must give up the steering-wheel for a bit.

For this reason one of the greatest incentives to get to the top in a large organization (though it is never mentioned in books on business) is the desire to reduce the number of people above one; to escape to an increasing degree from the frustrations of being bossed, from the harassment of having to placate and impress one's superior. The higher you get, the brighter life becomes, care and responsibility notwithstanding.

Put positively, the urge to get to the top may be strongly influenced by the desire to get one's ideas carried through instead of having them squashed or spoiled, ignored or mislaid in the management hierarchy above one. Even the brightest brains must wait in a large company before they can push through the top crust. A senior manager in the United States was asked what opportunity his company provided for a Winston Churchill to have a top post by thirty. The answer was, none; yet Churchill at thirty was a cabinet minister.[7] The great attraction of the small company is that this barrier is so much thinner, and can indeed be narrowed down to a personality or two who can be persuaded or fought, hated and put down. According to medical authority[8] the man who is trying to get a new idea across has to use many times as much energy as the man who wishes merely to obstruct him passively —a fact of which the insecure senior, past his prime, makes abundant use.

As in other occupations, to be in the top rank in business is its own reward apart from any other advantages it confers. The bigger the business, the greater the pleasure of arriving and in the recognition of others that you have arrived.[9] This is of outstanding importance to some men, and it is a rare man who does not enjoy it. As the head of one of America's largest corporations is reported to have said:

> 'When I walk out of the building a lot of people turn and stare at me, and whisper that there goes Mr Big. My friends think this probably annoys and embarrasses me. Frankly, I thoroughly enjoy it. Why shouldn't I?'[10]

or as Daphne du Maurier has put it in *The Progress of Julius*:

> It was good to be envied by men, it was good to be feared, it was good to experience deeply the sensation of power by wealth, the power of money tossed to and fro lightly in his hands like a little god obedient as a slave. The voices around him were warm and thrilling to his heart because of their envy. He knew the meaning of the whisper and the glances, 'Julius Levy . . . there's Julius Levy.'[11]

In Britain adulation for the successful business man is more muted, but in narrower circles it is there to be enjoyed. The sense of pride in achievement is, however, as common here as in America. The thing which kept Mr Bullard, the key figure in Cameron Hawley's story *Executive Suite*, going, for instance,

> was his terrific pride in himself—the driving urge to do things that no other man on earth could do. He saved the company when everyone else had given up. He built a big corporation in an industry where everyone said only small companies could succeed. He was only happy when he was doing the impossible—and he did that only to satisfy his own pride. He never asked for applause, appreciation or even for understanding. He was a lonely man but I don't think his loneliness ever bothered him very much. He was the man at the top of the tower—figuratively as well as literally. That's what he wanted. That's what it took to satisfy his pride.[12]

And, in the novel, his successor's ambition was—simply to enlarge the firm's size of the furniture market at the expense of all the little firms. This ambition made him logically the heir to the lonely throne. The thought of the loneliness of leadership is, indeed, a very appealing one to business men. As Mr A. P. Young, a former managing director of British Thomson Houston Ltd, indeed considers,

> the successful Manager of the future will have to combine in his make-up those finer attributes of the human mind and spirit which have at all stages of history been the mainspring of human progress. Silently and alone in that valley of loneliness inseparable from true leadership, he will wield his power, not in any obvious or fussy fashion, but imperceptibly and intangibly in the spirit of the truth that 'Whosoever would become *great* among you shall be your *servant* and whosoever would be *first* among you shall be the *bond servant of all*.'[13]

It is surely a fine thing for the head of a large engineering works or ladies' underwear factory to be able to feel that he is visibly inspired by such sentiments; and business offers a fair number of positions, after all, where they can be satisfied.

Many managing directors, if not chairmen, are content with more purely professional incentives. These are apparently more in evidence in manufacturing than in trading or finance. They touch the specialist, particularly if he be a scientist or engineer. The works manager may take a professional pride in *his* week's output; he may experience a craftsman's sense of well-being when production of crank-shafts at last goes over 10,000. But the professional satisfaction is largely a *management* incentive, and even there it has, perhaps, been overrated by those who want to make out that management has become a profession like medicine or law. For men at the top the professional incentive, in so far as it exists, seems to be inextricably mixed with other motives. Samuel Courtauld wrote,

> Live industrialists are inspired by the desire which inspires active men in every career; the desire to try out their ideas, to prove themselves the best men in their profession, to be in command of the best run and most efficient enterprises which will contribute to the general well-being and progress of the community as well as to their own reputations.[14]

A very similar mixture of motives is ascribed by his biographer to another remarkable industrialist, Hans Renold, the founder of the Renold Coventry Chain Company, one of the first to apply the ideas of F. W. Taylor in England, and one of the few who, believing business was a profession, thought that the proper and wise thing was to show one's competitors everything.

> He enjoyed money when it came, but commercial success was of quite secondary interest. What drove him on was the joy of creation —of doing something just as well as he knew how. . . . He valued and respected people according to the quality of their work.[15]

Many business men will argue that their real motives are simply those of responsibility to the job to which fate has called them; a responsibility to the public, to the workpeople and to the shareholders. Business men with these feelings share the inner, compulsive drive of the senior civil servant to keep public affairs moving. They will recognize their own Kafkaesque mentality in this description of the motive-power that lies behind the devoted work and extra-trade union hours of the departmental administrator:

> one's official work . . . can be regarded as a tremendous and continuing task which is never finished. At any given moment there are parts of it just finished, parts half done, parts just begun. Subconsciously one is always trying to get this great task done; but it is never done. So one drives oneself along, day after day, to reach a point which is ever receding.[16]

The criteria of success in business provide one of the strongest arguments against regarding management, certainly top management, as a profession, however powerfully professional motives may move some of its practitioners. Success in business is primarily a matter of getting on, making money and, in a large company, being promoted rather than doing good work for its own sake and irrespective of who gets the credit. In a large firm a man's position on the promotion ladder is the mark of his success, not necessarily how well he does his job. Hence the emphasis is on promotion and a manager who does not get promoted tends to be regarded as a failure and, unless he is unusually philosophic, to regard himself as a failure *as a business man*. We know of one manager of academic antecedents who at a critical point in his own career and that of his firm, when he refused on professional and moral grounds to take the action demanded (and which would have put him on the board), drew the contemptuous comment from the man who *did* get on the board, 'Why are you in business? You are only fit to be a schoolmaster!'

Any observant visitor to large firms must be struck by the variety of the symbols of status which in some companies are used to distinguish each tier in the organization. The commonest is the eating-place. Separate eating-places will usually be provided for manual workers,* staff and senior management or directors. But there may be as many as six or seven grades of eating-place, and one company known to us was even thinking of introducing five different managers' dining-rooms to enhance the sense of rank and emphasize the value of promotion. Office furniture, particularly the type of desk and whether there is a carpet and hat-stand—distinctions which have proverbially obsessed the civil service—is now often a reliable index to rank in private industry.

There are many other status symbols which the innocent abroad in the world of big business may not suspect: where one parks one's car (and what make of car one has), which entrance one may come in by, whether one can press the directors' lift bell, and which lavatory one uses. There are usually several grades of lavatory in any sizeable business house, and directors and a few other privileged élite may have a special lavatory to which they have a key. Indeed the lavatory is quite an important status symbol.†

The badges of rank may be awarded to all members of a particular grade; but they may also develop without official encouragement and even in many subtle ways in opposition to a company policy which discourages them. They will then tend to be not so much an alternative to economic incentive as an external support for authority and especially as a protection against feelings of insecurity. There seems to be a general belief that in the anonymity of large business organizations the feeling of insecurity among executives is growing. Since it is harder for a company officer to obtain respect and recognition for his intrinsic qualities as an individual, and even as an able executive initiating policy, he turns to such outward symbols of arrival to protect his position. He does not necessarily lose his need of them at the very top. On the contrary, there are a large number of top business men who depend upon them for reassurance that they really are the big men they are supposed to be. . . .

---

* Quite apart from a distinction made sensibly enough at some works between canteens for those eating with only roughly washed, and those eating with clean hands.

† Exponents of the Freudian school will expect this to be specially so in banks.

2. WORK AND WORRIES

The board will none the less claim that, whether it be a pleasure or toil and sweat, they do their job and work hard at it. Hard work has been the gospel of the business man for three hundred years. Many business men are fond of talking of their 'fourteen-hour day'. How hard, however, does top management in Britain work? It is not possible to give a precise answer. A study of American executives, made by *Fortune*, revealed that the minimum average hours worked by men at the top was 57 to 60 per week, including official entertaining—a flexible item—but when there was a week-end conference or a crisis this could go up to 70 or more.[17] A time-study of a small sample of managing directors in Sweden, though it did not give the total hours, suggested that they were very overworked.[18] In Britain the number of hours worked, so far as one can judge, varies enormously from industry to industry and firm to firm. For line managers, a continuous industry like steel, where managers are always on call, means harder work than a factory on a one-shift five-day week. In some companies, both large and small, top executives may work nearly all their waking hours but in others, especially sometimes it seems in family businesses and in service trades and finance, a business man may comfortably conduct his organization and make his pile by working two or three days a week. Even so, such men often plan their deals on the golf course. Some business men, though perhaps a dwindling minority, take pride in being extremely efficient while achieving a maximum of leisure for themselves—leisure to think, to work for the public weal (a long line of business men have combined directorial duties with membership of Parliament or of the Borough or County Council) or merely to enjoy. Some people choose a business career for the leisure it gives. But these are in the minority.

Business men are in general devotees of the gospel of work for work's sake which stems from the puritanism of the sixteenth and seventeenth centuries, though this gospel may not be applied in some British businesses with the same zeal as by Americans and Germans. It was the apotheosis of the American business man Henry Ford, who said the definitive word on the subject:

> I do not believe a man can ever leave his business. He ought to think of it by day and dream of it by night.[19]

British business men echo him. The late Sir John Craig of Colvilles told *Scope* in an interview:

I say there is no joy in life to compare with work . . . as I grow older, the pleasure work gives me becomes keener and ever keener. I would rather be at my desk or the works than anywhere in the world.[20]

Nor do British business men admit to working less hard—and certainly not to working any less effectively—than Americans or Germans; and in a high proportion of them can be observed the same masochistic enjoyment in being overworked.* The actual proportion of the time put into solving purely business problems in the economists' or business consultant's sense is another matter. As Mr John Marsh, director of the Industrial Welfare Society, has pointed out, 'the late hours and seemingly important social engagements at which the chief executive is present, are often due to a desire to keep one's end up rather than to further an immediate project.[21]

The owner of a small business may tend to work longer hours because he carries all the responsibility and makes all the decisions, and also because he has to search harder for the information he needs. The top manager in a big business, who has so much laid on to his palatial office, may have to spend more time on community affairs and on industrial activities outside his own company; though in industry as elsewhere there is a distinction between the men who are on everything and those who keep their leisure for the garden or their family. Once a business man concedes that, for business or other reasons, he must take an active part in public affairs, a great variety of bodies will claim his time—even leaving on one side the charities in which a few business men take an interest. There are the trade associations to which his firm belongs, and at a national level the F.B.I., the B.I.M., and such bodies as the Ministry of Labour National Joint Advisory Council. Such committee work can choke his engagement book and swallow his leisure. Two examples must suffice of the range of public activities of many of the leading business men.†

* According to Mabel Newcomer in *The Big Business Executive* (New York Columbia Press, 1955):

'. . . although there is an occasional defection from the ranks, there is every indication that the majority of executives work overtime—not because it is necessary in order to keep the job but because they are absorbed in their work. Complaints about long hours and short vacations come from their wives and subordinates rather than from the men themselves.' (P. 122.)

She quotes an inquiry summarized by *Time* magazine which showed that those top executives who worked overtime were happier than those who didn't though their wives were not.

† Information kindly communicated by Sir Hugh Beaver and Sir Frederic Hooper.

List of Public Committees on which Sir Hugh Beaver served in 1957:

Federation of British Industries.	President (from April 1957).
British Institute of Management.	A Vice-President.
'Operation Britain.'	Founder Member.
Brewers' Society.	Chairman of Central Panel.
Brewers' Society.	Member of Council and various other committees.
Industrial Fund for the Advancement of Scientific Education in Schools.	Chairman.
Institute of Chemical Engineers.	President (from April 1957).
Clean Air Council.	Member and Chairman, Research Committee.
London School of Economics.	Member, Court of Governors.
London School of Economics.	Member, Building Committee.
Public Schools Appointments Bureau.	Chairman of Council.
Wellington College.	Governor and Vice-President.
British Institute of Archaeology at Ankara.	Chairman, Council.
Corporation of Church House.	Member of Council.
Nursing Sisters of St. John the Divine.	Hon. Treasurer.
Shoreditch, Hackney & Highbury Housing Association.	Chairman, Committee of Management.

List of Public Committees on which Sir Frederic Hooper served in 1957:

Advisory Board of the Regular Forces Settlement Service.	Chairman.
Consumer-Advisory Committee of the Advertising Association.	Chairman.
Public Affairs Advisory Committee of Advertising Association.	Member.
Council of Institute of Directors.	Member.
Policy Advisory Committee of 'Operation Britain'.	Member.
Executive Committee of Building Centre.	Member.
Executive Committee of National Institute of Industrial Psychology.	Member.
Finance Committee of Royal College of Nursing.	Chairman.
Finance and General Purposes Committee of Royal College of Art.	Chairman.
English Stage Society (Royal Court Theatre).	Treasurer.
Finance Committee of Royal Academy of Dancing.	Member.

Top managers usually work longer hours than their subordinates; some of them worry even more. If they do not take work home in their brief-cases, they almost certainly take it home in their heads. Running a business requires more of a chess-player's mentality than it used to do. Once it was enough to watch the market and worry about the ups and downs of the prices of materials and finished goods. Today there is the maze of restrictions which must be related to every move: restrictions on where a firm can build and what, how much money it can raise, where it may sell, how it may describe its goods, and what it may charge for them. Much of top management's job is still finding out what restrictions lie in the way of each shot down the fairway.

Still more important for the manufacturer are the trade union restrictions; the new theory of management requires that all new projects—such as changing a model, shifting work to another factory, putting in automation—must be discussed with workpeople.* To many business men, especially small men, who are out of sympathy with modern trends, these government and trade union restrictions together may exert an almost unbearable strain on their blood pressure. Nor are these the sum of the limitations on a business man's freedom of action in his own factory or office. In the more democratic atmosphere in some sections of industry today the man at the top often has to consult not only the trade unions, but even his junior officer. In America where group management is the vogue, this means as *Fortune* has pointed out in *The Executive Life* that:

> 'You have to *ask* a guy now' goes a characteristic complaint. 'You can't tell him. It would be a lot easier than all this damn sitting and talking, but if you did—well, nobody would co-operate and the thing wouldn't get done right.' All of which makes for more, and harder, work. Democracy, as executives can observe, is a lot more fun when you are going up than when you get there.[22]

However, such group management has not yet penetrated very deeply into British business.

The main worry of the top executive manager has ceased for some years to be either production or profits or even selling: it is people and their growing cussedness. We have heard business men say that the most saddening news about automation was the claim of Mr John Diebold and its other exponents that it would not make workpeople redundant. If only it would! The thought that on top of the job of putting it in, comes the job of re-training a lot of British workmen

* See below Chapter VIII.

to do something different fills some business men with gloom. In an article entitled 'What Corporation Presidents Think about at Night', John L. McCaffrey, then president of International Harvester, said:

> The biggest trouble with industry is that it is full of human beings. The longer you are a president, the more firmly that fact will be riveted in your mind. That is why you will lose sleep.
>
> You will learn to your sorrow that, while a drill press never sulks and a drop hammer never gets jealous of other drop hammers, the same cannot be said for people. You will learn that a turret lathe may run one part for ten years without affecting its ability or its willingness to be switched at any time to another part. But men are not that way. . . .
>
> You will learn that you have with people the same general problems of preventive maintenance, premature obsolescence or complete operational failure that you have with machines. Only they are very much harder to solve.[23]

Some chairmen and directors in Britain (as elsewhere) get along pretty well however without worrying too much about human beings. City magnates, of course, have few contacts with factory folk. But even industrialists sometimes hardly realize that there is a problem, since they model their high command on the simple Oriental pattern of an autocrat surrounded by yes-men. This may mean that they will have to spend a good deal of time buying out efficient firms and rigging prices with competitors to offset the managerial inefficiency of the parent stem, but both occupations give agreeable scope for an able and dominating personality. Those who work on the basis of being *primus inter pares* in a team may have an efficient firm, but may spend so much time keeping the human wheels running as to fail to keep out of the clutches of the no-nonsense autocrat with more time to be a business man.

3. THE PRICE OF SUCCESS

In all this it must be borne in mind that there are business men, and a very considerable proportion of the total, who take their high destiny lightly and find plenty of time for other pursuits. When the business man wants to 'get away from it all' he nowadays alone has the money for shooting, hunting, fishing, yachting or other traditional patrician pastimes; and the money too, for the traditional 'separate establishment' if his tastes incline that way. It is often said that to the British

business man, business is merely a means to an end, as compared
with the American business man, for whom business is a way of life.

> Sir Francis sighed. 'Now I, on the other hand, am not interested in
> business at all, from that point of view. I am interested in a number
> of other things—medical research, Renaissance painting, juvenile
> crime and so on. Business simply gives me the—the resources with
> which to pursue these interests. . . .'[24]

The contrast in these attitudes cannot be escaped in any comparison
between British and American management. Yet our impression is that
the proportion of British business men who become wholly absorbed
in business, and sacrifice leisure and other interests to its demands and
its fascination is growing. Even these may find time for golf, which is
the business man's game—partly because it is a game at which he can
meet customers, suppliers and colleagues. They have little social life, it
appears—a couple of dinner parties a year; lunch is for clients; spare
time for national work which will be good public relations for the
business, secure a 'gong', or assuage a sense of a wider mission than
profit making. They live from one appointment to the next.[25] Although
as has been said above, plenty of business heads take far more than the
traditional fortnight in the year away from their offices, a very large
number take no more, and are continually amazed that young executives fresh from university with their way all to make, want three weeks.*

Indeed, the young executive who gets close enough to the top to
look closely at the lives of some big business men, in some—mainly
very large—corporations may even flinch from the prospect in terms
which echo those of the Man in the Grey Flannel Suit:

> 'I don't think I'm the kind of guy who should try to be a big executive.
> I'll say it frankly: I don't think I have the willingness to make the
> sacrifices. I don't want to give up the time. I'm trying to be honest
> about this. I want the money. Nobody likes money better than I do.
> But I'm just not the kind of guy who can work evenings and week-
> ends and all the rest of it forever. I guess there's even more to it than
> that. I'm not the kind of person who can get all wrapped up in a job—I
> can't get myself convinced that my work is the most interesting thing
> in the world.'[26]

* This becomes particularly irritating to business men when a brilliant scientist
prefers a smaller salary at a University which so unfairly overbids business in the
matter of vacations. 'Why can't scientists behave like adult business men, instead
of wanting to mess about in labs. on "their own work" for two months a year—
and wanting another month to recover from that?'

But most men in the chairman's or managing director's position have so convinced themselves; some consciously surrender almost all other interests in life on the grounds that their positions call for complete self-dedication—a single-mindedness almost as complete as that of a religion. They consciously reject the hope of being 'whole men', certainly of any attempt, with the good things that are theirs, to work out for themselves some part in 'the good life'.* They say that business today demands such specialization, such self-immolation if the job, in everybody's and particularly in the national interest, is to be done. They echo the American corporation president who said 'what you ought to ask me is not how I live, but how I stay alive'. Their retort to the Man in the Grey Flannel Suit is that of his own boss:

> *Someone has to do the big jobs!'* he said passionately. 'This world was built by men like me! To really do a job, you have got to live it, body and soul! You people who just give half your mind to your work are riding on our backs!'[27]

To give one's whole mind to the problems of a growing or of a great and established industry may well mean giving none of it to the graces generally—to art, culture, sport, social affairs, to one's family, to personal friendship. Indeed such sacrifices may often be a prerequisite of success. As one American who had built up his own firm admitted:

> The pressure of business can destroy your family life . . . even when you are with them you are preoccupied and a damn bad husband because of the terrific excitement . . . I like golf but it killed me to think of the real good fun I could have been having at the office.[28]

One of the business men interviewed by the American writers Warner and Abegglen was asked whether he had any close friends, to which he answered:

> 'Who has any good friends? Maybe one or two but if I left the present company I'd find new ones and the old ones would be forgotten. So would I. Oh sure, I have plenty of friends. I could call any bank president in St Louis and you'd have dinner with him because of my friendship with him. But it doesn't mean anything. I learned a long time ago not to form close attachments. It is easier to fire the guy when you are moved ahead of him. I think that's very important.[29]

Few business men make such an arid business of life, perhaps: but the degree of self-dedication is frequently remarkable, even in England.

* In doing so they may take as their motto W. B. Yeats's lines 'The intellect of man is forced to choose Perfection of the life, or of the work'.

Here too may be seen, in some measure, 'the terrifying fanaticism that would make a man offer up his life as a human sacrifice—and all for something of no more consequence than a gadget to spray ink on wallpaper'.[30] But to establish and make a profit out of such a device in the business climate of post-war Britain may possibly require in one man, even in several, just such a fanaticism.

The strain of being a successful business man is a cliché. It is, of course, no new thing. Yet it is really a matter for surprise. Creative fury in other occupations may exhaust a man temporarily, but the creative artist or craftsman is noted for his vigour; his ability to survive and enjoy exhausting bouts of labour. Business and perhaps the civil service seem to be in a different category. A Dr Gregg, lecturing to the Royal Institution, noticed this as early as 1875 in Britain and concluded that 'success in professional, public and commercial life demands more strenuous and exhausting toil, sterner concentration and a more harsh and rigid sacrifice of the amenities which time offers the easy-going than was formerly the case'. Sombart noted that the business man had, however, imposed this type of ceaseless haste, this endless going to the limit of technical or administrative possibilities, upon the world in the nineteenth century. The concept of the 'tired business man', incapable of anything but the lightest amusement in his rare hours of leisure, goes back before the First World War; 'management fatigue' to the Second. The business man may claim to have brought leisure and freshness after work to everyone but himself. Once the workmen looked tired when they left the factory gates; now it is the boss who returns to his wife 'all in'.

> No other profession, apparently, equals business in its power to wear men out. Certainly there was no such generic term as the tired soldier. Politicians lived to a great age. Priests flourished on a meagre diet with flagellation. Farmers bore toil and misfortune, growing stronger. All through the eras of epic carnage and herculean labours, explorers and pioneers kept burly and jolly. Only the effort to organize and calculate brought forth that strange phenomenon, the Tired Man

concludes Dr Beard in her history of the business man. The impression is perhaps sketched with a rather broad pencil. But there is something in it.

Yet, for all the talk of ulcers, the business man today, weary as he may be, enjoys goodish health, actuarially speaking. Contrary to public belief the business man up to the age of fifty-five has a death-rate 2 to 3 per cent lower than that of the average of all male workers. But above fifty-five he has only the same expectation of life as an executive of thirty years ago, although in other male occupations the expectation of life has been increasing steadily.

Why has the business man in his later fifties not shared in the improvement won by the miracles of modern medicine for others? Is mental strain responsible? In part, the others are simply catching up on where the business man was when he could have the best doctors and a 200-guinea cruise when they imperatively ordered it. But there are two major strains on the business man's health, apart from the overwork with which he indulges himself. One is the unnatural life he leads—mostly sitting, going everywhere in a car driven by someone else, eating, drinking and smoking more than is good for him; few business men train up to the job on carrot-juice as the stint they set themselves really requires. The other strain is the suppression of irritation which is demanded by the modern business cult to surface pleasantness—a harder mask for the executive than even the ingratiating smile of the salesman.

Both of these strains help to account for the business man's diseases —high blood pressure, nervous lesion, diabetes, liver and gall-bladder diseases, hardening of the arteries and coronary thrombosis. In 1951, these diseases were responsible for 1 out of 4 deaths among business men below sixty-four compared to an incidence of 1 in 8 deaths of unskilled workers. The business man is correspondingly less prone to TB., pneumonia, bronchitis, stomach ulcer or prostate disorders.[31] Some firms worried about the health of their top executives have made it a rule that they should have a medical overhaul every six or twelve months. Senior members of the Bart Schwartz International Textiles in New York are given a mandatory week's holiday with full pay every seventh week to try and reduce the number of heart attacks and ulcers.

For many senior executives, there is also the strain of keeping up with the job, which diligence or top businessmanship has won, when mental powers begin to decline. 'Of the breakdowns which occur (among senior managers),' wrote a medical authority recently, 'a great number are directly related to a failure to adapt successfully to change, or the need for change.'[32] And he adds, 'among those in senior positions in an organization, the tendency to hold on to power as such is apt to increase as real capacity diminishes'. It is not merely the unsuccessful or failing who break down; 'some very successful business men with a very sure touch in their business affairs require in their private lives to be propped up by psychiatrists, astrologers, diets and wives'. Some men suffer especially from the fact that their energy comes in waves, but routine is an inexorable daily pressure; the business man cannot throw aside his canvas as an artist can and go for a walking tour when he is drained of virtue; besides the business man may take on more when he is 'high' than he can handle when he is 'low'.

The symptoms of strain in top executives are well known and recognizable to everyone in a more junior position:

1. Poor sleep; bad temper, continual grumbling; longer hours of work but less achieved. Symptoms usually attributed to overwork.

2. Repeated minor sickness. Consulting specialists and self-medication, often accompanied by an interest in life assurance and financial security.

3. Procrastination. Working from in-tray to out-tray and losing sight of long-term aims. Working by the clock rather than the interest in the job.

4. Feeling of frustration and persecution by colleagues. Complaints of lack of co-operation.

5. Increase of alcoholic intake and verbal output. Technical jargon and catch phrases replace original thought.

Such facts point to the advisability, in general, of earlier retirement or at least relinquishing of supreme control in the later fifties. Yet many top business men fear retirement more than anything else, more even than a bad American slump, a Labour government or competition, recognizing in retirement the worst danger to health of all. Fear of retirement 'for which no mental preparations have been made' is a cause of any or all the symptoms of breakdown listed above. This problem was not unknown to nineteenth-century writers on business men. They quoted, with melancholy, Cooper's lines:

> Tis easy to resign a toilsome place
> But not to manage leisure with a grace.

For a man whose life has been his work and nothing else, the strain of retiring is often greater than that of going on working; retiring to him is the end of life, death.

Indeed, one of the advantages of being the boss is that you can resist retiring, and thus resist becoming old; you merely enjoy what the Americans call 'the later maturity'. Business has no use for old age, either in the firm or in customers; old men cannot 'do' things or 'consume' in bulk. Twenty British directors selected at random were asked by us if they had any plans for retirement; not one had made any. What is golf for its own sake—golf without a business colleague for partner, and a sense of shared and well-earned recreation in preparation for a return to business? It was easier for the head of the family firm to retire—though many hung on, and are hanging on, unconscionably—because he could take pleasure in seeing his son continue the line, as a farmer can retire to the inglenook. For the modern top-business bureaucrat there is nothing but demotion to a high-sounding job with minor responsibility, or service on voluntary bodies and institutions. The man who owns his own firm and can work till he dies may well greatly extend his life expectancy if not that of his firm.

Towards the end of his life, indeed, the successful business man may be up against determined efforts to unseat him and get rid of him. This is not easy, he may comfort himself. Unless his firm is 'raided' and he is displaced by take-over bidders, he can usually defeat any internal cabal. Rarely need he fear his shareholders; his job, unlike the Prime Minister's, cannot be terminated by an election—he will not get five years in opposition to freshen himself up.

The determination of top business men not to retire is, however, not merely a consequence of the absorption of their lives in a business. It is also the clearest evidence that chairmen and directors find life at the top with all its penalties enjoyable, exciting and worthwhile. To their critics business men will retort that they have a supremely difficult job of national importance to do for which they may well have to stunt their lives and for which they are not well rewarded nowadays. But they do it. To these criticisms we must now turn.

NOTES

1. Morley, John, *The Life of Richard Cobden*, London, T. Fisher Unwin, 14th edition, 1910, p. 20.

2. Wilson, Charles, *The History of Unilever*, London, Cassell, 1954, Vol. I, p. 187.

3. Stewart, J. D., *British Pressure Groups, Their Role in Relation to the House of Commons*, Oxford University Press, 1958, p. 36; Finer, S. E., 'The Federation of British Industries', *Political Studies*, February 1956.

4. Cf. Churchill, W. S., *History of the English Speaking Peoples*, London, Cassell, 1958, Vol. IV, p. 136.

5. Quoted in Creedy, F., *Human Nature in Business*, London, Benn, 1927, p. 163.

6. 'Man of the Month: George Measham', *Scope*, June, 1954.

7. American Management Association, *Management Education in American Business. General Summary*, by Lyndall F. Urwick, New York, American Management Association, 1955, p. 44.

8. Kennedy, Dr Alexander, 'Individual Reactions to Change as Seen in Senior Management in Industry', *The Lancet*, 2 February 1957, p. 261.

9. Cf. Galbraith, J. K., *American Capitalism,* New York, Mifflin, 1952, pp. 28–29.

10. Quoted in The Editors of *Fortune, The Executive Life*, op. cit. pp. 67–8.

11. du Maurier, Daphne, *The Progress of Julius*, London, Heinemann, 1933.

12. Hawley, Cameron, *Executive Suite*, London, Hammond, Hammond 1954.

13. Young, A. P., *Forward from Chaos*, London, Nisbet, 1933, p. 110.

14. Courtauld, Samuel, *Ideals in Industry*, op. cit., p. 105.

15. Thripp, B., *Renold Chains*, London, Allen & Unwin, 1956, p. 33.

16. Munro, C. K., *The Fountains in Trafalgar Square*, London, Heinemann, 1952, p. 79.

17. Editors of *Fortune, The Executive Life*, op. cit., p. 65.

18. Carlson, Sune, *Executive Behaviour*, Stockholm, Strombergs, 1951, p. 75.

19. Nevins, Allan, *Ford; The Times, the Man, the Company*, op. cit., p. 579.

20. 'Man of the Month: Sir John Craig, C.B.E.', *Scope*, August, 1947.

21. Marsh, John, 'Realities in Human Relationships. (I) Power Politics', *Industrial Welfare*, September/October 1956, p. 129.

22. The Editors of *Fortune, The Executive Life*, op. cit. p. 76.

23. McCaffrey, John L., 'What Corporation Presidents Think About at Night', *Fortune*, September 1953, p. 128.

24. Balchin, Nigel, *Sundry Creditors*, op. cit.

25. Copeman, G., 'The Daily Life of Six Directors', *The Director*, December 1952.

26. Wilson, Sloan, *The Man in the Grey Flannel Suit*, New York, Pocket Books 1956.

27. Ibid.

28. 'Young Presidents Look at Themselves', *Fortune*, August 1956.

29. Warner, Lloyd W., Abegglen, James C., *Big Business Leaders in America*, New York, Harper, 1955, p. 92.

30. Hawley, Cameron, *Cash McCall*, London, Hammond, Hammond, 1956.

31. *Scope*, April 1953.

32. Kennedy, Dr Alexander, op. cit.

CHAPTER VII

Commercial Spirit

'By their fruits ye shall know them.'

MATTHEW, vii, 20

'The market is a place set apart where men may deceive each other.'

ANACHARSIS, *Diogenes Laertius, Anacharsis, Sec.* 5

WE HAVE CONSIDERED how business men make a start, rise, succeed and live with the privileges and responsibilities of their success; and how the conditions of success are changing. How men rise affects their character; the British business man no less than the Russian party boss. But business men are also intellectually the product of free enterprise. The background of their thoughts and actions is an important part of their psychology, particularly in their attitude to the public. It is a rare business man who can read the late Professor Schumpeter's prophecies of the ultimate replacement of private enterprise by socialism, and return to his desk quoting Alexander Borgia, 'Since God has given us the papacy, let us enjoy it.' The practice of business, like the practice of a profession, generally causes the practitioner to identify himself with the institution he serves; to uphold it and to believe in it. There was common sense in an observation of Mr C. O. Stanley of Pye Radio to the Institute of Directors that 'we must fight for the thing that makes directors possible, which is the free enterprise system'.[1]

What is the free enterprise system which makes the business man possible? It is one thing in the textbooks; but it is apt to look different to the public and to the business man. The latter may think that it is a system in which he is able to respond to the needs of the public through the working of the free market. He may see himself thereby as an honest servant of the public's needs; the market as a neutral instrument for measuring those needs. Yet this would be a very naive view of the dynamics of capitalism. Business men know, as Lord Leverhulme said, that they are creators; and indeed, the market, the rules of the business

142

game as we know it today and even the shopping public are very considerably their collective creation. They, in turn, are what business makes them, and it is thus that the public sees them. The relation between the business man and the public is determined both by what business does to the public and by what business does to the business man. Business public relations are not often based on a clear-eyed recognition of this fact, but in so far as any advertiser ought to know the product he tries to sell, they should be. The greatest influence upon business men is that they are in business.

In the past business men would have repudiated this idea. Like Chaucer's Merchant they would have said that they were on the same pilgrimage as men of other avocations; business was a matter of circumstance and aptitude to the calling. Yet even a superficial study of the history of the business man shows that his profession moulded him to a great extent; he chose from the ideas of the day those that most suited business interests; the man who, like Robert Owen, could break completely away from the current framework of ideas has always been rare. A minority of business men have always turned critical eyes on their own practices—usually in middle age, when success has been won, experience has matured and the need for a sense of spiritual purpose manifests itself, as the psychologist Jung says it does in many practical men of forty or so. It is then that business men begin to try to rationalize what they are doing, and to philosophize. Such philosophizing usually takes a practical turn.

1. THE SENSE OF MISSION

Business men in the nineteenth century had few fears that their work, which they felt was one of the most beneficial activities in the community, would draw them away from living a balanced and mentally healthy—what they would have called a godly and upright—life. It is clear, however, that from early in the industrial revolution, the problem of reconciling life with Christian duty has faced devout business men. The large number of Quaker business families indicates that this has been done to the satisfaction of those who tried, although a strict Quaker like Woolman found that he had to advise people to buy or prefer things which were less profitable for him to sell, and he had to give up business.[2] Few Quakers, however, were quite as pessimistic as this. Banking, said Samuel Gurney, was 'an agreeable business, bringing with it a pleasant intercourse with various kinds of people, and giving the opportunity of very much and most important good to be effected'. For most of the nineteenth century organized religion blessed industry, and many men set out to prove that trade was not the exclusive occupation of Mr Worldly Wiseman, but an instrument of God's will. Such a one, to take one example of many, was William Powell who traded in hardware in Australia and whose achievements inspired his biographer to rhapsodize:

> What a noble thing is trade, when conducted by a noble man, in a noble way and for noble ends! What a sphere does it throw open to intelligence, energy and Christian virtue! What a fine pursuit is commerce—business—money-making in the hands of a sensible, conscientious and believing man![3]

In Mr Powell's rise to the top the hand of God was found at every turn of a career that Samuel Smiles could hardly have improved on:

> . . . the sedulous boy-clerk, in high-toned health, abandoning his forest freedom, and chained by a generous purpose to his desk, in a dim and dingy office; the ailing young man, with shattered constitution and small salary devoting himself steadily to his master's interest, slaving, saving . . .; the young husband, resolved to make one bold but well-considered effort for the independence and comfort of his wife and children, spending all his savings to secure what he saw was his only chance of success—a connexion with a first-class firm on the other side of the globe; the singlehanded storekeeper in a crude township, straining all his energies till inundated with an unimaginable influx of custom through the rush to the goldfields; the large importer, selecting and trading and attaching to his interest agents to whom he could quietly confide his interest, while he made himself master of the mystery of trading; the London merchant, *the city man*, the principal of a large mercantile establishment, conducting its widespread and multifarious details, vigorously, honourably and successfully, yet, with head and heart above the world, living in the region of unseen and eternal realities, putting the interest of Christ's kingdom in the forefront of commercial calculation . . . such a man vindicates the nobility and sanctity of trade![4]

It would be foolish to deny that Mr Powell was unusual—and uncharitable to maintain that his type has entirely died out today; there is evidence to the contrary—though other business men find it an uncomfortable type to deal with.

As the nineteenth century wore on official Christianity became critical of business and has remained so. The righteous merchant was one thing, picking and choosing where he made his profits; but from business in general the Churches began to demand answers to moral questions about wages and welfare and about the social responsibility which the Benthamites deemed individual capitalists could not and should not bother about, and began to impugn *laisser-faire* as the negation of Christianity. The Churches lost their first enthusiasm for economic laws, and especially for Ricardo's Wages Fund, and even began to insist on the direct social responsibilities of business and business men, over and above what was required of them by laws which had to be made to deal with the evils generated by their activities, whether innocently or culpable. As *Fortune* has said, by the end of the nineteenth century God was no longer in business in any real sense.[5]

The new evangelical attitude of the Church to business may have helped to create the philanthropic school of business men, who sought to establish a new relationship between themselves and their workers. They looked round them and, economic verities notwithstanding, conscience pricked them. It was no longer enough to say, as J. J. Colman, the upright mustard manufacturer, said, 'If a living can't be got by selling a good article I am sure it can't by a bad one.'[6]—because it could be and it was every day. There came a moment when here and there a business man would write to his partners, as Sir James Reckitt did:

> Whilst I and my family are living in beautiful houses, surrounded by lovely gardens and fine scenery, the workpeople we employ are, many of them, living in squalor, and all of them without gardens, in narrow streets and alleys. It seems to me the time has come, either alone or in conjunction with some members of the board, to establish a garden village. . . .[7]

From such an impulse sprang the new industrial communities of Lever, Cadbury, Hartley and others, which carried on, sixty years or more later, some of the work of Robert Owen. The garden-city builders who actually sought to create new physical surroundings were few; more put money into religious charities and temperance work, while others found their ideal formula in profit-sharing. Their influence was circumscribed, not so much because they did not affect their workpeople but because they converted so few of their fellow-employers; many of whom indeed retorted that workpeople prefer to spend the 'wages fund' themselves, rather than have part of it spent for them.

Philanthropy has, of course, become one of the proper purposes of a millionaire's life. It is favoured by high taxation, and it enables a business man to continue to exercise influence and power—though there are severe pitfalls in trying to make Oxford University take technology seriously before it is ready to do so even by the most lavish benefactions. University dons are adept in stripping the well-found business man of his money without letting him have much say in how it is spent (although he may be able to draw the line at endowing the classics).

Philanthropy may make restitution; it does not of itself reform the process of money-getting. Later generations of business idealists have felt this without, perhaps, also feeling the urge to achieve personal salvation in the process of building a business, or to create a suburban Utopia clustered round their factory chimney as the medieval village clustered round the castle or abbey. Instead they have turned for their inspiration to professional ethics, and have sought to create a 'code' of business conduct which should turn business men into the professional peers of doctors or lawyers. They have in effect agreed with socialists, such as Tawney, that:

> It is as feasible to turn building into an organized profession with a relatively high code of public honour, as it was to do the same for medicine or teaching.[8]

They propose to do this not, like the socialists, by replacing profits by State service, but by codifying the ways in which profits might be made and by laying down rules to make the firm prosperous, to avoid deceit and to fit men for the right jobs. This discussion of professional ethics in business should be distinguished from the advocates of 'fair business practice'. Of the latter it is well to remember Munby's warning in *Christianity and Economic Problems* that:

> When business men talk ethics, it is time for the public to be suspicious. 'Business ethics' usually means a conspiracy against the public to keep in existence high-cost producers and give more handsome protection to the efficient low-cost firms.

Business men as a body are no longer formally religious but they tend to adopt a High Moral Tone if their motives are impugned by the Monopolies Commission or the British Standards Institution. It has indeed struck us that artists must endure severe criticism of works of art into which they have poured their life's blood; statesmen will—

and must—accept uncomplainingly blistering attacks on acts of policy which they took in the knowledge of facts which their critics are blissfully ignorant of; scientists, scholars, sportsmen live under the burning-glass of criticism. But business men become apoplectic when the mildest criticism is levelled in print against the design or quality of the wares they advertise. 'Libel', goes up the cry; 'slander of goods', 'defamation of reputation', and the telephones in their lawyers' offices are set merrily ringing.

The business man's sense of mission shows itself in other ways, such as a fascination with paper organization of firms in a 'scientific plan'. This can have an immense attraction for leading business men with a mystical turn of mind. They even bring out books on the subject at their own expense, often illustrated with diagrams, and full of such high-sounding statements as:

> The object of the commercial profession is to translate into practice the ideals of the age so far as they require embodiment in material things.[9]

To the academic economist all such theorizing is mere bosh. He may be unkind, but alas, such books never get down to the horrid problems of whether one should sack men, use power politics in the interests of the beloved efficiency, maximize profits in order to pay high dividends to attract fresh capital, make take-over bids, ruthlessly close redundant plant, meet competition when opportunity arises and so forth. The truth is that a professional code can at best govern the day-to-day activities of an established business running on a fairly even keel. It is impossible to relate it to that 'creative gale of destruction', that constant dynamic upheaval, that *élan vital* which is the essential contribution of enterprise as distinct from management, whatever the designation of the human being, or team of human beings, that throw it up. The boss who is a routine manager in disguise can, at a pinch, model himself on the professional man. The boss who is a Schumpeterean hero must look for his philosophy, if he feels the need of one, rather to the Nietzschean Overman. Some do; a certain managing director told a group of other business people at a discussion on spiritual values in industry, in the hearing of one of the authors, that 'profit-making is a God-given activity'.

Nevertheless, the idea of a 'professional' business man is, as we have noted, permanently beguiling. It has become important to some

British business men, in search of a 'new basis' for business life and purpose, and to academic observers, searching for a new rationale of business organization. Much of it flows from the post-war belief of some business men that joint consultation is the answer, an attitude by managers to workers which involves

> recognition of the dignity of man: a relationship in which he feels that he is, in a fundamental sense, a *full partner* in industry, and not for so many man hours every day the *servant* of an employer.[10]

In particular, the idea is growing of a sort of tripartite responsibility of managers to the workpeople for their livelihood, to the shareholders for their capital, and to the customers for service. This idea was stressed by Mr T. T. Paterson in a broadcast when he said:

> To sum up: the change-over from owner-employee to manager-operative has demanded a new managerial philosophy. The manager has a duty: to conduct the enterprise for the total good. That total good will involve the nation, the shareholders, the customers and his men.[11]

Again, the question must be asked, what happens when these interests clash? We know of a business man who got on well with his workpeople until he wanted to take up an export order which involved them in a type of piecework which was slightly less profitable; they refused to let him take the order, and he, in bitterness, went to a London head office and ruled them thereafter by remote control. Workpeople readily appreciate a good manager; but all too easily imagine that he could be still better were it not for the parasitic shareholders and the entrepreneurial board of directors.

Managers may develop the attitudes and something of the ethics of a profession, but the men at the top take refuge in vague idealism while —probably to the greatest advantage of the greatest number—continuing the strategy of business. 'Service, and not exploitation, must be the inspiration of business men,' said Samuel Courtauld, '. . . and I believe that this is a religious inspiration.' 'The world is ripe for a new philosophy,' said Selfridge, 'we are hungry for higher ideals, higher aspirations, standards beyond those man has thus far conceived.' Business men will nod their heads gravely at such sentiments and feel vaguely uplifted, but as they are human will go on being moulded by their environment. What is the environment of business? What effect does it have on the business man? To these questions we shall now turn.

2. THE ATMOSPHERE OF BUSINESS

There was a time when close contact with money was considered to be naturally bad for the character; Montesquieu said that when financiers were given honour all was lost. The respectability of money-making, and the respect accorded to money, do not exclude the feeling that something disreputable clings to business. All through the nineteenth century, the reconciliation of *laisser-faire* with honesty and fairness in business was a major theme. The professions were held, and still are held, in higher esteem, though not always rightly, and it was Sir Ernest Benn who spoke provocatively of 'the clean air, the honest atmosphere of commerce: an atmosphere cleaner, brighter and more honest than any other atmosphere I know'.[12]

The importance of greater honesty in business, as a means of recommending private enterprise as a system to the public was shown in Marshall's remark early in this century: 'the marvellous growth in recent times of a spirit of honesty and uprightness in commercial matters'.[13] What was permissible, if sharpish, practice in the City in 1880 would carry a prison sentence today; what was honesty then would today be inability to adhere to specifications or to required tolerances of weight, size or composition.

Today there are some who will say that business men are the most honest of a generation that is rapidly losing its moral standards. A recent survey[14] of moral standards in Britain showed that the average standard was very low. 'The average customer is dishonest,' said a canteen manager; and a youth leader summed up the attitude of the young in the words 'I see, I want, I take'. The middle class, it was held, was losing its present probity. In contrast to this survey the Bribery and Secret Commissions Prevention League declared that there is no corruption in British commercial life,[15] and quoted an accountant as saying:

> The standard of honesty in business in Great Britain is higher than in any foreign country of which I have personal experience. In high financial circles in London the standard is extremely high. . . . In London and other southern cities a tremendous amount of business is done purely on the basis of a gentleman's agreement, but in the big

industrial cities of the Midlands and the North there is some evidence of the idea that sharp practice in business is legitimate and even clever, provided it does not go outside the limits of the law.

The Report of the Bank Rate Leak Tribunal in 1958 fully bore out this judgment of British business honesty.

Why, then, does the idea that business life is often shady persist? The reason almost certainly lies in the difference between formal honesty and strict adherence to contract which is almost universally practised, on the one hand, and the struggle for power and blatant advertising chicanery which is no less obviously standard business practice, on the other. A firm which acts towards its customers with the most scrupulous honesty, instantly replacing faulty goods or paying compensation for faulty service, will suddenly act on the very crudest ethics of 'caveat emptor' when it comes to buying someone else's *firm*. Values are relative. Strict honesty is good business towards the multitude with whom one's reputation is one's stock-in-trade; but to do down Mr So-and-so is also good business, since he is involved in a single transaction.

Everything depends on who the customer is, when the ethics of business behaviour are in question. Six firms may sell glass bottles, labels, corks, china clay, bottling machinery, odoriferous essences, respectively, to a seventh firm, and behave with the utmost scrupulousness, especially in their claims for the goods they supply. The seventh will describe the assembled result as a nourishing skin food compounded in new and scientific ways to preserve youth into middle age (however sour one's thoughts or discontented one's expression), at a price which leaves a margin of profit which it would never tolerate from its suppliers. A firm which is proud of its reputation for machinery will gladly join with others in a secret ring to control output markets and prices. Integrity in business is, in fact, a very complex thing. A man may be the soul of integrity in half his dealings and a cheap jack in the other half; honest with customers, considerate with his workpeople, but disloyal to his colleagues and ruthless to his suppliers, or the other way about. A reputation for honesty is an asset in business; but this may be acquired in more than one way and for more than one purpose. Frequently a business must go far beyond the law in scrupulousness if it is to possess a reputation at all; sometimes it must merely make sure that it is not transgressing a law which does not impose any niceties of conduct. The public knows this perfectly well; it concludes that business is a jungle where success may at any time depend on doing someone down.

Many business men, however, are humanly unaware of inconsistencies in their behaviour. Those who take it out of the public think in terms of their excellent relations with their business friends, and say, 'I only supply a market; they don't have to buy.' Those that steal other firms' ideas or property say, 'Business men can look after themselves. *My* first duty is to my customers; and my prices show that I do it.'

Probably the most important moral influence today is advertising. A hundred years ago adulteration of goods by small tradesmen was common; but advertising was relatively honest in its crudity. Today it is unnecessary to adulterate goods; it is only necessary to bring out a branded product and advertise it through national media—the popular press and television—to achieve similar advantages; but such an operation is now necessarily big business. The ethics of modern advertising is a subject for a trained casuist; it poses a problem as knotty as that of the popular press with which it lives in a symbiotic relation— the problem when freedom of the press becomes a freedom exercised to debase. Advertisers may truly claim that the news and editorial pages are more untruthful and sensational than the ads, but for this advertising is largely responsible since newspapers (or at least those 'at the gayer and more successful end of the business', as Mr Cecil King described them)[16] are written down to their moronic level in order to gain the circulation to attract the mass advertising.

At one end of the scale advertising is clearly a necessary service; at the other it reaches lengths which the moralist (if not the economist) will condemn without hesitation. Before it became riveted round their necks, business men in the nineteenth century did condemn it from time to time:

> ... It is disgusting to read the barefaced lies in some advertisements. ... The majority of tradesmen still think the art of salesmanship consists in persuading the buyer to buy what he does not want or more than he wants.

said one in 1878.[17]

Such criticisms of advertising are still true, although they are often skilfully dismissed as 'old hat' by the professionals interested, as if that disposed of the matter. Today, though the excesses of advertising are the butt of humorists, there is no suggestion that it could be curbed; and indeed it now plays to private businesses the role that competitive armaments plays to national states.

Advertising can of course be defended. There is, indeed, a general agreement that 'taste' in advertising is steadily improving but that is a defence based on aesthetics—of a limited kind—and not on morals. Here, however, it is only necessary to note that advertising does affect the atmosphere in which a large part of the business community works; for a great many business men, though by no means all, advertising is a first preoccupation. The medieval distrust of business finds an echo in the lower status, so surprising to the American business man, given in Europe to business men who deal with the consumer. The reason is, it may be suggested, the closer contact with mass-advertising. The selling of machinery, transport or other producers' equipment needs the aid of advertising; but it is comparatively honest, informative, straightforward trade advertising—a class of business which, significantly, hardly interests the big agencies. The world of half-lies, fractional truths and ceaseless fuss about trivia in which the advertiser lives is that of consumer advertising, and it is futile to suppose that either the business or the public's mind can be unaffected by it. In proportion as the business man lays claim to some education and philosophy his attitude to his advertising tends to become one of mingled shame and defiance; of distaste for his product or contempt for his clientele. If he has none of these feelings he is either a cynic or quite simply a plain, pure, bloodlessly professional entrepreneur, to whom the selling of a product, good or bad, by any means, is merely an exercise in the maximization of net profit.

The effect of advertising on business men is, almost certainly, to distort their vision; it is something which they have to justify because they are committed to it, or which they delegate to someone else if it has to be too untruthful or embarrassing to handle directly: but which in either case causes them to burk the issue. The operations of the advertising industry itself has attracted the novelists almost more than any other, just because it is so shady and lends itself so directly to satirizing the commercial spirit of the time. Social and satirical novels about advertising leave no doubt that the atmosphere is corrupt because of the enormous prizes to be won, and memoirs by business men are sometimes almost as candid. One of them wrote bitterly:

> Most advertisements, whether of things to eat, cure, wear or use, consist of a fragment of truth, stretched, twisted, distorted and perverted to the utmost limit of the criminal law . . . just short of the point where the sponsor of them could be arrested for obtaining money on false pretences.[18]

The unhappiness of a thoughtful business man making consumer goods can be detected in Courtauld's observation: 'We [industrialists] hold different views about advertising; some think it is beneficient in principle, some do not'—adding that business men in general do *not* like the press, meaning, of course, the popular press which provides the mass market media.

The justification of advertising practices to which the business man naturally clings is that they increase production and efficiency. As the previous chapter showed, the business man takes a simple pride in production and expansion; and these are dependent on the limitless expansion of human wants. The business man is under constant pressure to take a completely material view of life; human progress is presented to him as the growth of human needs. What business offers to the customer has mainly been comfort, a point first made by Disraeil, who, perhaps, did not give industrialism credit for delivering health as well. The fear of business men is that some end to human desire, some point of saturation might be reached; this fear is very real in America. Unless this season's cars catch on, there may be a slump, and slump might mean the end of Western civilization. In Britain, the business man's problem may be to make people as restlessly convinced as the Americans are that the pursuit of happiness is the pursuit of more durable consumer goods. Without this ceaselessly expanding market expansion is threatened, and the pleasures of modern business with it. Anything in advertising, therefore, can be excused—even motivation research—because it keeps the wheels turning and, it may be piously added, prevents a slump from taking place.

To these influences on the business man's thinking must be added the effects of large-scale organization—which helps to explain why the values of the small business man tend to differ in some ways from those of the big boss. There seem to be no enforced limits on size; and economists have discovered that costs never increase with the size of the unit of control, that so far from costs increasing where the unit of control exceeds a certain 'optimum size', it is the largest firms which have the lowest costs.[19] Size may not itself produce cheapness; the causal sequence may more probably run from cheapness through competitive superiority to size; but whatever limits exist are those of business ability itself and display themselves rather in the rare if sensational bankruptcy of the over-ambitious than in chronic 'diseconomies of scale'. The strength of the large organization is undeniable; and large organization means that the men at the top are increasingly remote both from customers and from workpeople; indeed they are remote from anyone but other top industrialists or bankers and a relatively small group of top managers in their own companies. There is evidence that this depersonalizes business men quite as much as it depersonalizes the employee in the mammoth plant. They may avoid the crude arrogance of the soap-king, Evan Llewellyn Evans, who said, 'somehow I always think of people in the ten thousand a year bracket [£2,500] and under like they was animals'.[20] Yet their attitudes may only be a rather more sophisticated version of the same pride.

The small business man does something tangible, which his neighbours understand, whether they like or dislike it. The big business man lives more and more apart from any close human contacts. He even begins to achieve 'the unique rationalization and impersonalization of action and outlook that seem to differentiate the men in American business management', and which are said to be 'due to freedom from unquestioned custom . . . their geographic mobility . . . independent of the past . . .'[21] But it is just in custom and the sense of the past that ethics are rooted. It is impersonality, and an omniscience based on streams of statistical reports which causes men to confuse means and ends, to set into operation actions which they would not, as individuals, care to execute. This remoteness is a relief, perhaps; it can free the top directors from concrete thought and provide them with simple abstract criteria of action for 'the good of the firm'. They find it difficult, for instance, to understand why workmen should object to moving their homes from one part of the country to another, if efficient production dictates this. Yet if anyone were to suggest that rootlessness is productive of other evils—delinquency, for example—they can only shrug their shoulders. This is not their concern.

3. THE REVOLUTIONARY

When business men are reproached for adding to the vulgarities or evils of the age, they sometimes defend themselves by saying that they simply give the public what it wants; although they will also agree that they create markets even more than they respond to them. Business, in fact, creates its customers; it does not take them as it finds them. The customer, said Casson grimly, must be taught, trained, drilled. By creating is meant the creation of new standards of wants; new appetites; new desires; new dislikes; new standards of taste and propriety; a new environment, physical as well as mental, of work, as well as of play. By selling to the public, and by employing the public in factories and offices, the business man profoundly interferes with basic attitudes and traditions. In doing so, he performs a revolutionary role. He was of course the revolutionary of the industrial revolution. Nor has he ceased to be one, for he is changing society today as furiously as when he bought child-labour from the parish poorhouse.

This revolutionary role has a number of implications. One is that there is a continual pressure for expansion with all the social effects that go with it. Keeping the machine running at top efficiency becomes an end in itself. To run efficiently, to expand capacity, unit costs must be continually brought down; therefore people must buy more; to buy more they must have an incentive—the incentive to buy the things in the shops. To business men, as to most economists, the most disastrous choice that common people can make is to choose leisure with their money instead of things. This is the ruination of business, of course, in remote and primitive areas, where the 'backward' natives, after working a few days, and finding that they have earned enough to satisfy their traditional needs for subsistence, give up the irksomeness of attending at the mine. Unfortunately for British business, what is true of New Guinea is still sometimes true of Newport. Absenteeism not only means inefficiency, higher overheads, and lost output, but also fewer people than there might be 'creating demand' in the shops. To make such people discontented with their possessions is the only answer, though it must of course be geared to a decision to work harder, not to mere organization to get higher pay for the same (or less) work.

Business men can be heard to complain that in Britain working-class wives do not hound their husbands to earn enough to buy a washing-machine or a small car; or a better house. They are too inured to men hanging about doing nothing, accepting existence. The business man is (or should be) a keen leveller. The primitive Briton is not pulling his weight—and the cultured classes are choosing all the wrong things when *they* spend what is left to them after tax. The business man's ideal citizen is almost exactly the same as the Labour Party's: the well-off artisan or lower-middle-class office worker—heavily in debt on H.P., and insatiably convinced that rising in the world is achieved by the accretion of material things—deep freezes after fridges; colour after monochrome TV, modern kitchens as well as quik-foods in cans, radiograms, tape-recorders, electric toasters, mixers, shavers, washing-up machines, dryers, cleaners—the home must become, to adapt the famous observation of the Pasha to Kinglake: 'Whizz! Whizz! all by wheels! Whirr! Whirr! all by miniature electric motors!'

'If we are to remain a great power,' said Mr. George Meier, the Managing Director of Truberised (G.B.) Ltd., when introducing a new type of guts collar and stitching machine, 'the home consumer must show interest in new things. Instead of clinging to the old because it was good enough for Grandad, he must put the support and encouragement of new ideas high on his list of good causes. Years of research have been spent on these innovations and the money they will earn will help to finance more research.'[22]

The public is responding. In its review of business in 1956, the *Manchester Guardian* reported that the 'crust' of the old primitive society was breaking.

> . . . the Americanization of popular taste has worked wonders. People have got to have durable goods now, and they work long and hard to pay for them.

It is the building of a general attitude of divine discontent, however, which matters. This is well summed up by the vice-president of Westinghouse who told stockholders in 1958 that 10,800 dissatisfied Americans were born daily. 'What's more, they're going to be dissatisfied every day of their lives. Whatever they have they are going to want more. . . 190 million dissatisfied Americans by 1965.'

From such observations as these, the business man's ideal citizen can be reconstructed. Man or woman, he has an insatiable desire for things. But he does not want much that is custom-made and lasting. He wants things as advertised in stock sizes and the standard range of colours which minimizes cost of production. He is guided by advertising in all media; his taste and intellectual level is that of commercial TV, mass-production newspapers and pulp magazines. His education warms him to funny brand-names, which he asks for in the shops. He never buys raw materials unwrapped, unhygienic, without a cellophane* cover, but, like the child who liked his milk from a nice clean bottle, not a dirty cow, he wants his goods in plastic covers. He accepts the suggestion that these goods will make him happy, successful, beautiful, handsome, popular, healthy. These are the only virtues he seeks to acquire. He will judge food by its appearance, not its taste. He will be ceaselessly and expensively occupied during his leisure; on Sunday mornings, for example, either out in his car, or involved in some hobby, like cine-photography, which consumes a lot of costly material; any culture he takes in he would prefer punctuated by advertising plugs.

* Properly, not to give offence, Cellophane.

Having a good time will involve paying an entrance fee somewhere. Courting a girl will involve expensive courses of self-improvement, lotions, unguents, apparel, and so forth—as it will involve the girl in even more; marital happiness will be ensured by a continual exchange of large presents, which will no doubt reach their apogee at Christmas —but other occasions, anniversaries, etc., will be similarly commemorated. A baby will set off a vast cycle of consumer capital investment, precisely plotted by the market research department. Old things will be ruthlessly discarded; the purchase of new things will be high on the list of good causes. While sitting about and doing nothing is not excluded, it must be done in a hotel, holiday camp or cruise liner far from home. What has no future from the commercial point of view is bird-watching or country walks. The business man can only admire the decision made in *Brave New World* to set up a conditioned reflex against love of country walks when it was found that this left transport and organized sport under-utilized and uneconomic.

To obtain the purchasing power to acquire and discard these possessions at a high rate of turnover, the business man's ideal citizen will work hard, probably on piece-work, and welcome any aid to this provided at the machine or office desk by the time-and-motion study engineer. He will feel intense loyalty to his firm, never more than when it installs new machines; and will cheerfully leave Coventry for Aberdeen at a few weeks' notice if more efficient production can take place there. The ideal citizen will be, like his boss, highly mobile. His demands for higher wages will be strictly related to his increase in productivity. He will double his standard of living at least every twenty-five years—if he lives long enough. With such people for workers and customers, any big business could expect to more than double its size in less than twenty-five years—an enthralling organizational task or challenge. The top managers, being British and not American, would not necessarily live in quite this way, or expect their children to do so. However, this would probably be the main (perhaps the only) point of disagreement between them and an enlightened Labour Party.

The business man in his emphasis on ever-expanding material wants must be opposed to those who stress the relative unimportance of possessions in living the Good Life. This opposition is a necessary part of his function if it is to be successfully performed, even though a few business men may be firm believers in such a Good Life. He must therefore be wary of education, just as he is wary of religion. Education of a practical kind is necessary to produce a modern customer, worker, technician or manager, but it must not unfit either workers or managers for living an industrial life nor should it teach them how to enjoy their leisure inexpensively.

The business man must scent danger, too, in a theoretical socialism which says:

> What gives its meaning to any activity which is not purely automatic is its purpose. It is because the purpose of industry, which is the conquest of nature for the service of man, is neither adequately expressed in its organization nor present to the minds of those engaged in it, because it is not regarded as a function but as an opportunity for personal gain or advancement or display, that the economic life of modern societies is in a perpetual state of morbid irritation,[23]

even if he feels it will not go very far in practice, just as, when practical political socialists proclaim that living standards must be increased more or less without limit, he can feel that the business spirit has conquered socialism. The publicity given to eager shopping in the big stores by visitors from the other side of the iron curtain, especially when one of them finds the wares so irresistible as to try and make off with them without paying, is pure gain to him. *They* may have the sputniks; *we* have C & A Modes.

Not all business men would formulate their social philosophy as precisely as we have done in this section; but something of the kind is implicit in any business philosophy that goes beyond the Victorian age. There are, of course, large numbers of rather old-fashioned business men in Britain, who have not examined the full logic of their ideas, and some, at least, of their actions. Enough has perhaps been said, however, to suggest that business men, as a collective force, mould the people, change the national character and even set an impress on the spirit of the age—not less than any revolutionary party seeks to do.

4. THE PUBLIC'S REACTION

Recognizing their revolutionary role, the business men should sometimes reflect on the public reaction to them as individuals, which is (as the psychologists would say) an ambivalent one; a mixture of hostility and approval. The business man can claim that there is general consent to change and 'progress', of which he is the prime mover, and of which the corps of professional managers are the N.C.O.s; but there is resentment none the less. People want to go to heaven without doing good deeds; people want the fruits of a dynamic society without changing their ways when that hurts. As customers, the public show their appreciation of variety and novelty, and display in the mass an infinite capacity to be taken in; but they also firmly believe that businesses profiteer when they can.* But though people like the flow of new things and sensations, at a deeper level the demonic quality of capitalism disturbs the mind. They are disposed to think ill of the Father Christmas who pours the cornucopia over the store counters. At any moment the business man may, they feel, produce the insane unemployment for which he is thought secretly to hanker.

The public is suspicious of the business man—a suspicion which may well be a transfer of the resentment it feels at his revolutionary role. It is willing to believe that a group of downtrodden inventors are really responsible for progress, and would be responsible for more if it did not suit the big business men to buy up patents and suppress new ideas, even though the Swann Committee formally disposed of this Shavian myth in 1950. The public in its vague way makes the decisive division between boss and manager—and favours the official against the moving spirit. The boss is seen as a man who, tax him how you will, lives on expense accounts—and lives pretty grossly. Because he is thought to be slick, everyone justifies slickness—'everybody does it'. Any business scandal is confirmation that 'financial types' are always 'up to something'. An example of the depth of suspicion is afforded by the firm which investigated what its apprentices thought about its management, and discovered that most believed that, after wages and material had been paid for, the rest of the money was taken by the directors and shareholders; and when some of the lads were taken through the accounts to show what the real size of the profit was, they flatly declared that the accounts were cooked.[24]

In spite of the evidence of the public's suspicion it may be thought remarkable how well business men come out of it. There are not very many popularity polls for business men, and the attitude to them is entwined in people's political views. One was taken by the industrial magazine *Future* in 1950, the period of reaction from socialist adminis-

* From the economist's point of view the buying public is disappointing in its preference for branded goods and fixed prices. It upsets his scheme of things when women shoppers actually think it 'unfair' if shops are free to vary prices of well-known nationally advertised articles (because it takes so much longer to shop round to find the cheapest). This behaviour would be readily understood by a psychologist.

tration when free enterprise was rising in popular esteem. The majority
—though not an absolute majority, 47 per cent—stated that they
preferred to work for a private employer; 58 per cent thought that
people who are efficient got on in private industry compared with 11
per cent who thought dishonesty the main quality of men headed for
success; but being out for yourself, efficiently or dishonestly, was
regarded as the sovereign formula. Sixty-one per cent of those who were
asked thought business men earned too much, half thought profits
too high and wages too low, and less than half approved it—which
was a good score, seeing that two-thirds thought big business was
working for itself purely as against one-third that conceded it worked for
the country's good.

There is little in all this to suggest that the public has grasped the
business man as, in sentimental moments, he likes to see himself—the
servant of society, the man who is poorly rewarded for his superhuman
efforts to bring technical progress into practical reality. Twenty-five
years and more since progressive business men stopped talking about
laisser-faire and proclaimed the professional (if necessarily profitable)
ideal of service, the British public remains grudging and suspicious,
still more than half-convinced that the business man is exactly what
the economists say he is (or regret he isn't): a selfish go-getter. Yet, in
an ironic sense, the business man *is* the servant of the public, and far
more slavishly so than he dreamed of becoming between the wars;
less of a leader, more of a subordinate.

The obverse of a chapter dealing with what the business man expects
from the public is what the public expects from the business man.
From the modern business man's point of view the public can be seen
as a very exacting taskmaster. This will not apply to the small coterie
making millions in the old way—from take-over bids, from government
disposals, from antique-dealing rings, from football pools and so forth
—but it will apply to the general run of industrialists and top commercial brass.

NOTES

1. *The Director*, October, 1954.
2. Childs, M. W. and Carter, D., *Ethics in a Business Society*, New York, New
   American Library, 1954, p. 84.
3. Gregory, B., *The Thorough Business Man: Memoirs of Walter Powell*, Strahan,
   1872.

4. Ibid.
5. Quoted in Childs, M. W. and Carter, D., *Ethics in a Business Society*, op. cit., p. 86.
6. Rees, J. A., *The English Tradition*, London, Muller, 1934, p. 251.
7. Reckitt, Basil M., op. cit., p. 60 and cf. Crittall, F. H. & Crittall, Ellen, *Fifty Years of Work and Play*, Constable, 1934, p. 118 ff.
8. Tawney, R. H., *The Acquisitive Society*, London, Bell, 1930, p. 195.
9. Creedy, F., *Human Nature in Business*, London, Benn, 1927, p. 207.
10. Walpole, G. S., *Management and Men: a study of the theory and practice of Joint Consultation at all levels*, London, Cape, 1944, p. 169.
11. Paterson, T. T., 'The New Profession of Management', *The Listener*, 6 December 1956.
12. Benn, Sir Ernest, *Confessions of a Capitalist*, op. cit., p. 40.
13. Marshall, Alfred, *Principles of Economics*, op. cit., Ch. XII, §5.
14. Rowntree, B. Seebohm and Lavers, G. R., *Life and Leisure*, London, Longmans, 1951, pp. 219–23.
15. Quoted in Rowntree, B. S. and Lavers, G. R., op. cit.
16. *Manchester Guardian*, 31 May 1956.
17. Platt, J., *Business*, Simpkin Marshall, 1878, pp. 156–7.
18. Lister, Stephen, *Savoy Grill at One*, Peter Davies, 1939.
19. Wiles, P. J. D., op. cit. See also Florence Sargant, P., *Logic of British and American Industry*, op. cit.
20. Wakeman, Frederic, *The Hucksters*, Heinmann, 1948.
21. Warner, Lloyd and Abegglen, James, *Big Business Leaders in America*, op. cit., p. 194.
22. *Scope*, March 1955.
23. Tawney, R. H., *The Acquisitive Society*, op. cit., p. 223.
24. *The Director*, January 1957.

CHAPTER VIII

'England Expects . . .'

'Be ye therefore perfect.'

MATTHEW, v, 48

*'It is high time the City raised its voice. Subservience to weakness
and vacillation in Westminster and Whitehall will bring us certain
ruin. . . . The real producers and creators of wealth must have
freedom to conduct the businesses which they know and which are
essential to the nation and the world. There must be stern discipline for the lazy and the slackers. Unions must be put in their
place. . . .'*

MR GIBSON JARVIE, *to the shareholders
of the United Dominions Trust,* 1956

IN THEIR COLLECTIVE ENDEAVOUR to mould the nation to an avidly
consuming pattern, to make it a nation of shoppers as well as shopkeepers, business men have been in some respects almost too successful.
The nation has now become conditioned to expect a steady rise in the
standard of living in regular annual instalments, more or less as a
matter of natural right. When Mr Butler said that the standard of
living could be doubled in twenty-five years, any trifling conditions he
may have attached to the achievement were quickly forgotten, and the
brains of the Labour Party were quick to demonstrate that Mr Butler
could not claim any credit for proposing to do something which was as
inevitable as spring next year.[1] If this simply meant that the demand
for branded goods was to be doubled, business men, or at least a
good many business men, might look forward to the future with
exhilaration, for there is nothing they like better than the certainty of
an expanding market. British business men will readily endorse Peter
Drucker's view that 'a business enterprise can exist only in an expanding
economy, or at least in one which considers change both natural and
desirable. And business is the specific organ of growth, expansion and
change.'[2]

162

1. THE BOSS'S STINT

But it is not so simple. The nation does not merely expect the business man to deliver more and more canned and frozen foods, television sets, motor-cars, refrigerators, deep freezes, reheats, building estates, and so forth; it also expects him—as most business men who have read the previous chapter may be aching to point out—to earn the nation's living. In other words, to keep up exports. The Empire, dominion over palm and pine, the imperial preference which goes with it, are being cast away; the great international banking business centred on London seems threatened with bankruptcy; but British business is expected to find export markets just as readily as when Britain, equipped with a stable currency, an empire that covered a quarter of the earth, overseas investments worth £4,000 million and no burden of sterling debts, was the world's leading trader and financier. In fact, the business community is expected to find extra markets to make good the losses incurred in war, and the inability of the national-ized coal industry to contribute to the export drive. A rising standard of life means rising imports; and it is the job of British business to pay for them.

Not only must more be produced and exported; it must be produced in prescribed ways. In the first place, Whitehall must nowadays be consulted at almost every step, beginning with any attempt to raise capital on the market in excess of a mere £10,000. To set out the list of government restrictions would be tedious and supererogatory in this book; it may suffice to present a single case-history, as given in a learned publication by Mr R. H. Fry, city editor of the *Manchester Guardian*:

> Having gone through patent and trade-mark protection, market research, finance required, etc., his next set of questions was whether he would get a government permit to start up a new business. This is often strongly opposed by the Trade Association, which usually argues that 'the firms now in the trade are kept short of raw materials and are forbidden to sell more than "x per cent" in the home market; if there is any more raw material available it should first go to existing firms to give them a fair chance'. By making out a case that he would be able to export his produce he got a licence to enter the trade. Then he had to get some assurance that he would get raw materials, fuel, machinery, etc. allocated. . . . Then he had to find a place where he would be allowed to buy or build a factory. Quite apart from the economics of location which he has to decide for himself, the pro-

posed site must be 'zoned for industry', and even for the particular
section of industry, under the Town and Country Planning Act. . . .
For any factory of more than 5,000 square feet, permission must be
specially obtained from the Board of Trade under the Location of
Industries Act by which new plants are to be driven away from the
big cities and, if possible, into the development area. . . . The particular
firm that tells this story did not build at first but bought a factory
and got started. 'Very quickly, however, the national export drive
began and as the factory was situated in the silk-producing area, we
were asked by the authorities to move away in order to release labour
for the silk manufacturers, who had at that time a large export
market; so we had to hunt for a new factory.' They finally got established in another area, and waited for the main portion of their plant
which still had not been delivered. Suddenly the makers of this
particular machinery were told by the government that they must
increase their export proportion, and the delivery promised to our
friends was put off many months. They had plenty of ideas and could
have used all the tools they had to make something different, but
'Your permit to manufacture is in terms of the number of items
you may manufacture in a period, or of the amount of key
raw material allocation to you in a period', etc. etc.—with the result
that they could not change much. Then the machinery began to
arrive and their steel allocation was cut down. They turned to alu-
minium which upset their costing. They coped with that by other
economies. They introduced shift work to make fuller use of equipment but, under the new Factory Act, a factory inspector came and
prohibited all shift work for women. And they had been employing
women for many jobs. Still, finally the factory was in full production
with new tools and new lines of products; home market business was
magnificent—the 'future assured'. Suddenly the April 1948 budget
imposed a purchase-tax of $66\frac{2}{3}$ per cent on the whole range of their
products except one; 95 per cent of existing orders were cancelled.
After 'urgent representations' the Government reduced the tax to
$33\frac{1}{3}$ per cent and they were saved.[3]

The endless phone calls, conferences, explanations, filling in of forms
and so on, must be read between the lines of this story; it may or may
not be typical but it explains why the heads of so many businesses large
and even small spend so much of their time dealing with government
departments—getting more and more remote and impersonal along
with the civil servants they soon begin to resemble—instead of being
matey with the managers and the men. It may explain too, the demand
for office space in London, for as fast as the government puts up a
block for a Ministry, business must duplicate them to maintain contact.
Indeed some of them find it advisable to set up Departments of Government Relations.[4] The number of businesses that need no London

Office is dwindling, and the 'London type' of business man, as opposed to the provincial type, is correspondingly increasing. No doubt there has been a Tory 'bonfire of controls' since the last entry in Mr Fry's case-book,* but the business man has moved on to fresh problems; besides he must maintain his London office against the time a Labour administration returns. His state of mind is distinctly pleasing to the left; Socialists have noted complacently:

> It is not unusual to hear the business man, caught up in these restrictions, complain 'I can no longer call my business my own', as indeed he cannot. Ownership no longer gives him the exclusive right to do what he pleases with what he owns.[5]

Providing the goods for home and export over the hurdle-race of State controls is not however all his duty; the business man is also expected to improve the atmosphere of industry (though not of commerce). This demand comes both from the government and from the trade unions. Sir Walter Monckton, for example, told the Institute of Personnel Management in 1955 that 'good human relationships must be established in the individual firm' and called industrialists—it is hardly the job of personnel managers—to 'lift from the workers a mood of resentment which springs from a sense of inferiority, boredom or fatigue, and lift from management a mood of impatience and defeatism'.[6] The T.U.C. general council points out that 'increases in dividends are bound to act as a continual irritant ... the decision where increased investment should be made, should not be left to competing business men'.[7] The T.U.C., added Sir Tom O'Brien, knew more about industry than many directors.

Higher wages, shorter hours, more fringe benefits, which already add considerably to the wage-bill; no interference with the customs of the trade, consultation with shop stewards; 'a great increase in the number of employers who set out to treat people as persons'[8]—all these are conditions of doing business. If the business man complains, is it not an indication that secretly he hankers for the unemployment which made his labour problems so easy between the wars?

The industrialist may reflect that he is not likely to need Professor Jewkes' warning that he must recognize

> that he is very carefully watched, and that he is not likely to be able to engage in practices which are inconsistent with his own rationale.

* Including, as this book goes to press. the C.I.C. Control itself.

He cannot for instance pass off restrictive practices as part of a free economy. . . . He should be prepared to put his own house in order before someone burns it down in the mistaken belief that it is derelict.[9]

His house is forcibly being put in order, in many more ways than Professor Jewkes, with his academic preoccupation with monopolist practices, ever thought of; even so, unless he delivers far more than a standard of life measured in terms of items in a cost-of-living index, this house will be declared derelict, himself a failure. As he sees it the consumer must have goods and services cheaply, the employee must be treated like a prince or princess while producing them, the government must be obeyed while having full liberty to indulge in inflation—or bouts of deflation—to throw markets to the winds, to annoy customers abroad, and promise the earth to customers at home.

> Upon the king! Let us our lives, our souls,
> Our debts, our careful wives,
> Our children, and our sins lay on the king!
> We must bear all.

2. O HARD CONDITION!

The idea that business men could be set such a task, as workpeople are set their stint, and that the penalty for non-fulfilment might be dismissal would have been incredible to the Gradgrinds or Halifaxes of a century ago. Subsequent generations of Levers, Liptons and Monds accepted, if under protest, increasing interference with their freedom, but the possibility that a time might come when they would be set targets for production, be allocated materials in proportion to their success in overseas sales, and be apportioned finance as the government decided, would have dumbfounded them. They were familiar with penalty clauses in contracts; but at least they controlled the conditions which determined performance of their side of the contract. They did not sign contracts which not only imposed penalties for non-delivery, but also contained elaborate stipulations about the way the contract was to be carried out in their own workshops.

Business men have made it as clear as they can that the job, in these terms cannot be done; though they have not resigned. Higher pro-

ductivity, they retort to the politicians, is not automatic at all. Behind
the figures, they say, lies the sweat of the unfortunate business man,
and he can only sweat to some purpose if he is not frustrated. But he is
frustrated—by governments and by trade unions; by trade union
stupidity in particular and by national unreason at large. Sometimes,
more rarely, business men even complain of their own workers, or of the
follies of other business men. Having put their faith in the consumer,
in progress, in a steady growth in material welfare, they now find that
they are very critical of those whose appetite they have stimulated.
Why can't people be sensible about saving and investing, as well as
about spending? Thus Sir Robert Shone:

> Britain of all the great nations of Western Europe, Russia and
> America is choosing to invest the smallest proportion and to consume
> the largest proportion of its income. It is the country losing ground
> most rapidly in the progress towards improved material standards.
> That would not matter if we were content to lose ground . . . but . . .
> the great majority of people through parliamentary votes or trade
> unions are constantly pressing for advances in real incomes.[10]

True; but then Sir Robert did not mention the indiscriminate appeal
of the advertising industry, which never coins such slogans as 'It's
worth working that extra hour of overtime, cheerfully and willingly,
to be able to buy a pair of Silki sox', or 'Get the new Highlift Corselet—
after you've bought three Savings Certificates'. There is no word of the
need for capital on the hoardings. Nor does Mr Harold Wincott
mention this when he points out, most justly, in the pages of the
Financial Times, that

> You can't run capitalism without capital. The only question ulti-
> mately is whether you get your capital by persuasion or by force. . . .
> If the rest of the world is made fit for capitalists, and this country
> reverts to its former vendetta against capital, we shall in the long run
> have only one export left to us. Our population.[11]

The average chairman, when he speaks of national policy at all,
agrees with such sentiments. High taxation and rampant inflation are
to him the bane of business. He sees taxation as the first cause of
inflation because government spending is so high, and his specific is
not a swingeing bank-rate, hire purchase restrictions and tighter credit
but Mr Gladstone's: retrenchment. 'The Government constantly
exhort manufacturers to improve their efficiency but by fettering

restrictions make it impossible for them to procure modern equipment,' declares Mr Gibson Jarvie, in his annual attacks on 'our swollen and hampering bureaucracy'.[12] 'If the government were to reduce its top-heavy departments, cut out waste and put its house in order,' said another typical chairman, 'there would no longer be any necessity to continually penalize companies by raising the rate of profits tax.' But when this was lowered business men remained unsatisfied. 'Your Company,' Sir Claude Gibb told his shareholders, 'will pay eight times the amount of the dividend in taxation on the year's results.'[13] And Lord Brabazon thundered:

> Such madness has never been equalled in the field of economics since the world began. History shows repeated examples of peoples rising, monarchs being overthrown and governments swept away by the injustices of taxation. Yet political parties have sunk to such depths of craven fear over the next election results that not a thing is done. In the end, I have no fear of prophesying, the system will stifle the heart of a great race. Imagination, enterprise and enthusiasm have made us the envy of other countries in the past; and we have become one of the leading producing nations in the world. Today we are the same race, we still have all the drive and divine inspiration and initiative; but the Treasury thinks this is a terrible thing and stops it.[14]

Yet business men in the aircraft industry may feel that it is a still more terrible thing if, in order to keep the taxes down, the government fails to back projects like the V-1000—every business man knows an item of government expenditure which *is* important.

To be expected to run capitalism without capital, taxed to the rims, is bad enough; to be continuously criticized for contriving to do so is even more irritating. Horror was expressed when Trinidad Leaseholds, the British oil firm, was sold to an American oil company: our patrimony was being cast away; the empire being neglected. Yet the plain fact was that the firm in question could not get the money from the British public to develop the patrimony, like many other British businesses abroad who found that they could not sit on concessions indefinitely without doing anything about them. They became ripe for American take-over bids. The British public wanted goods at home; not savings abroad; more council houses not more Commonwealth development.

In the past thirty years all British governments, of whatever party . . . have been anti-capitalist. Taxation, not only on individuals in the form of income tax, surtax and death duties but also on companies in the form of income tax and profits tax, has steadily risen. The result is that companies now find themselves—in spite of many years of apparent prosperity—with insufficient financial resources to develop their properties. . . . If, as a result of following false doctrines, we British find ourselves unable to maintain and develop our properties overseas, it is very difficult to see how we can resist offers from business men in other countries who have the will and the financial resources to do it for us.[15]

One way, of course, to attract the necessary finance is to pay high dividends and offer prospects of capital appreciation—but that way, too, is regarded as anti-social. The business man is always wrong, Mr Harold Wincott declared bitterly.

If you limit dividends and plough back substantial profits in the businesses you direct, the discrepancy between share prices and the assets they represent . . . will eventually attract the take-over bidder. If you increase dividends you will be accused, among other things, of insufficient investment and of fostering inflation.[16]

To find the capital required to meet the demand for a higher output consonant with a rising standard of living the business man needs to make and to keep large profits—just at the time when one of the reasons advanced for putting forward new wage claims is the increase in profits. Not just dividends, but profits before tax; thus, for example, the directors of a firm which reported gross earnings of £100,000 heard a 'thoughtful and by no means left-wing' mechanic say, '£100,000 and they can't give me another 10s a week.'[17] In another firm the cryptic words appeared on the notice-board 'Lest We Forget—£1,580,000'— i.e. the firm's last profit announcement.[18] In adversity, the business man complains, he is accused of mismanagement and improvidence; in prosperity he is accused of robbing the workpeople of their fair share.

You get wage claims if you pay no dividends—as on the railways and in the coalmines. You get them if you freeze your dividends as Standards have done. You get them if you raise your dividends.[19]

3. RECIPE FOR INSOMNIA

Next to high taxation, the cussedness of labour is the business man's greatest grievance. The vigour of the complaint varies from industry to industry; and indeed, from company to company. The thoughtful British industrialist nowadays accepts high wages; he realizes that his workman is also his customer; he knows that 'the new class' of wealthy artisan[20] is above all the class which puts buoyancy behind consumer demand and keeps the flywheel of business activity spinning: this class is the nearest thing yet to the ideal citizen which the advertising industry is trying to create. But it is less than ideal in its attitude *qua* employee. As the business man sees it, labour expects the annual increase in the standard of living as advertised, but will make no real contribution to get it; even when trade union leaders have agreed to link wage increases to productivity, these promises are not fulfilled. Sir Tom O'Brien may say 'Other countries do not owe the British working man a living ... we are facing the fiercest competition from every country under the sun,'[21] but to the business man that is exactly what the average unionist thinks, and if there is competition, if there are any difficulties—well, what is the boss paid for? This is exasperating, and not all chairmen keep their heads down.

> 'The welfare state has taken much of the pride out of craftsmanship,' declares Mr Gibson Jarvie. 'It has made people mercenary—workers who seek the maximum in money for the shortest in hours and the overtime resulting from shorter hours. There is an almost complete lack of interest in work. How could it be otherwise when good workers are sacked because they are good?'[22]

'The task of achieving the Butler target,' Sir Walter Puckey told a meeting of managers in Margate in 1956, 'will create more opportunities for managers and men to expand their efficiencies, jobs and opportunities. The "situations vacant" columns will continue to expand and, as prosperity is indivisible, so the variety of new and better jobs open is very great.' This seems obvious to the business man who cannot understand why these opportunities should be so limited by labour's immobility, disinterest and positive sadism when one of their number works hard.

When unions who know that there is a shortage of their members' skills maintain their scarcity by restricting apprenticeship or entry to the trade, business men do not see in this a shrewd, business-like spirit; they see it as the wanton throwing of a spanner in the works. They remember that even in the worst of the war the engineers opposed trainees and made their training difficult even after 'dilution' had been accepted by their leaders; they point to the injustice that a man in a dying craft—such as textiles—cannot change his skilled work, but must go to unskilled, or semi-skilled, work.

To business men the most outstanding example of the cussedness of labour was the Cammell Laird strike—two unions calling out their men because they could not agree whether driving a screw was wood-workers' or metalworkers' work. To illustrate further the unreasonable-ness of labour,* they point to the newspaper strike of 1954, brought about because craft unions and industrial unions disagreed about the proper differential between the wages of skilled and unskilled workers; and to the Standard strike—which to them seemed to show men striking against redundancy caused by automation when other industries were crying out for the labour laid off. Even when men accept redundancy as necessary, some may strike, the business men say, from sheer cussed-ness. 'It wasn't the dismissals, it was the manner of making them that was wrong . . . it was so *impolite*,'[23] said a striker when the workpeople of Austins came out in 1956. As Mr McCaffrey, then president of International Harvester, was quoted earlier as saying, it is the cussedness of human beings which keeps the boss awake at night.

On the whole, business men take care not to criticize their own workers, however much they may criticize the spirit of the times. For instance, the chairman of the Brush Group said in 1955 that

> Industry as a whole lost more working days during 1954 than in any post-war year, and your board feels that the absence of any major dispute in your factories is major evidence of the good team-spirit. . . . This reflects the level-headed and responsible attitude taken by your management at various levels and by the representatives of the employees. . . .[24]

Perhaps some indication of business gossip about labour behind the scenes is furnished by the remark 'probably half those engaged in industry are redundant; they do not work, they are merely employed. . . . I heard recently that a certain large and famous engineering enter-prise could function more efficiently if it were able to send half its employees away on permanent holiday with full pay'. Every now and then an irritated chairman, while carefully saying that most of the firms' workers are first-rate, etc., will tell a little moral tale.

* The examples that follow are given from the point of view of the business men, hence no attempt is made here to present trade union and other views on these issues.

171

A few weeks ago we took on one or two new employees. They came on Monday but on Tuesday one went to his foreman and said, 'I'd like my cards at lunch-time'. 'Why," asked the foreman, 'don't you like the job?' 'I like the job all right, and my mates are decent fellows but they work too fast here and if I stayed too long I'd get into the habit myself, so I'm quitting.'[25]

There was a general feeling among the bosses that the cat had at last been let out of the bag—to use *The Times* phrase—when Mr Norman Dodds, a Labour M.P., declared after watching municipal workers lay a cable, 'I have never in my life seen men taking things as easily as that. They were robbing the people.'[26] Mr H. J. Randall, chairman of the London Electricity Board, gave further details of these robberies:

> Six men are sometimes sent to carry out a simple job which can comfortably be carried out by two men, and the cost is correspondingly high; but this procedure is imposed on us by the unions concerned and we have no option but to accept it . . . those with least zeal are frequently loudest in demanding wage increases.[27]

Labour relations, company directors often feel, begin at that point, not with the axiom that 'The industrialist must make his employees happy if he is to get maximum production,'[29] If they know something of social research they may cite in their support some recent studies which suggest that happy workers are not necessarily the most efficient.[29]

4. EXPORT OR ELSE

The business man thinks naturally of Britain on the analogy of a company without limited liability which pays its workers (the whole population) and makes its profits (the annual investment programme) on the margin between buying in raw materials and selling exports: on, in fact, conversion processes. Frustration seizes him when he finds that this simple analogy is not properly taught to school children and grasped by the politicians, union leaders and civil servants who run the country, and from time to time set him 'export targets'. (In fact the practice under the Labour government of setting annual export targets was abandoned when it was found that the industrialists overfulfilled 'the plan' and dropped nasty remarks about the experts.)

Industrialists see little sign that exporting is regarded as the vital, as well as praiseworthy, process in the nation's life which they think it. Sir Claude Gibb, for example, told his shareholders:

> Industry appears to be regarded by successive governments as the milch cow which will never need feeding or go dry. Must we become completely uncompetitive in world markets before hard facts are recognized? Without continuous retooling and improvements in production techniques, the present reduction in export orders will continue at an accelerating rate and give rise to greatly increased home market prices as well as unemployment.[30]

Though the exporting business man is accorded a certain special status in many people's minds, there is little disposition to think of the country as a whole as in the export business. On the contrary, sustaining the national balance of payments is seen as something which business men are very well paid to do for the country; the worries are theirs. Indeed, there is a widespread idea among the public that British business men do less than their plain duty as exporters; that they could take exports off the nation's list of anxieties if they really cared to put their backs into the job of proper merchandising and selling 'in the way that the Germans or the Japanese do'. Empire preference, imperial traditions, and Crown Agent contracts, are sometimes held to have given the British exporter advantages which make him at once lazy and greedy; he will not go out and get the small business which added up makes big business, as the German bagman does; and he demands larger margins than bagmen of other nations require. The great export princes live in gilded splendour; they preside over British supermarkets in which the customer must come and take what is for sale. When the Kariba dam contract is lost, and Sir Richard Costain complains that in some inexplicable way British contractors should have got it even if their tenders were not the lowest, and Sir Robert Renwick and others call for special tax rebates on exports, this impression that the British business man is not earning his money is liable to be reinforced.

Newspapers (which are not in the export business) are ready to record great export successes—the sale of a power station or a great dam—much as in the imperial era they would have acclaimed the annexation of a minor province; but they also give ceaseless publicity to the failings of the British manufacturer. Casson's remark that millions of pounds' worth of good business is lost because British business men are too conservative and too dignified to cater to local whims continues to be repeated to this very day. Remorselessly the business men's noses are rubbed in their alleged 'take it or leave it' type of salesmanship;[31] their unwillingness to take the trouble to sell abroad because of the risks[32] or even just the paper work involved;[33] the catalogues that are *still* printed only in English and prices expressed only in sterling;[34] the solecism of packs for China wrapped in white instead of red paper, the poor styling;[35] the failure of British salesmen to visit their foreign customers and ask them what they want improved;[36] the shortness of British firms' credit terms; the length of their deliveries;[37] the well-known, but perhaps overworked, fact that the British motor industry makes too many models;[38] and the machine-tool industry too few; the attitude of some business men that exports are just too much trouble for the money to be made on them;[39] the bad after sales service;[40] the sheer incompetence, in short, of the British business man faced with a tougher customer than the gullible British lower-middle-class housewife —which has all somehow added up to the increase of British exports in volume by 83 per cent from 1947 to 1957.

It is this sense of being unappreciated which some business men find exasperating. It would be bad enough to put up with the State's frustrations, made still worse by the credit squeeze, even if the public realized that successful business required effort; that profits did not multiply of themselves. But the public does not—at least not to the extent that business men would wish. Socialists, in particular, tend rather to think of the business man as cashing in on a process which more worthy people have organized for him—the inventors, the research departments, the managerial brains of industry and trade, and above all the political planners who set the conditions in which business thrives (as they see it). The economists who talk so glibly of percentage increases in the national income, sourly observes the business man, do not themselves produce anything but words or organize anything but their study tables; the job has to be done round the boardroom table, which risks millions of pounds at each decision. Large firms, even whole industries, can miss their opportunities: the British motor industry could have had the volkswagen, for example.[41] If the nationalized industries fail to make their contribution, by not producing enough coal or extra power which will be needed in the years ahead, private industries will have to step into the breach. The business man certainly feels that when nationalized industries get the lion's share of new capital investment or grant inflationary rounds of wage increases, private industry must pay the cost. He sees nothing automatic about the agreeable process by which Britain is to become as rich as America, but without necessarily becoming as adaptable and enterprising as Americans.

5. LEADERSHIP?

This problem of making the public see the business point of view remains. Sir Frederic Hooper, echoing Filene and Drucker, sets it out simply and persuasively:

> The aims of the ordinary man and woman have a lot in common . with the aims of the business firm. They have to earn a living and spend it economically. They have to do something useful and feel it is appreciated, they want to feel that they belong. . . . Each of these personal goals can be realised in the working communities of industry, and some of them can be realised nowhere else. The business firm is the most significant social institution of our times . . . managers should be aware of themselves as leaders in our present way of life, with more influence over their fellows than most of the people with important labels. . . .[42]

The problem, however, remains to persuade public and workers that there are not 'two sides' in industry, that everybody is 'in it'; that in short, the board is on the same side as the workers. It may be true, as Drucker says, that the emergence of management is a 'pivotal event' in human history; but the idea that the boss gets most out of it and puts in least has still a wide currency.

In practice, business men leave to their general and departmental managers, the hard job of persuading people that their interests and those of the firm are identical. Such professionals are paid to introduce better ways of handling human relations in business organizations; to introduce the wide range of measures which are generically called 'joint consultation', and to make them work. As the board often sees it, it is management's job to make workers feel that their humanity is recognized, to give their individual worth its due, to consult them about changes, to encourage them to express their opinions, to listen patiently while these, however inchoate, are expounded, to set up for them a ladder of promotion (but only to promote those good enough), to be immensely considerate, and to be seen to be considerate; and thus to put into operation the one formula which, psychologists say, will get more work out of workpeople than any material incentives scheme. All this is deputed to *management*; it is thought an essential element of management expertise, even if many, perhaps most, boards of directors still do not demand it; or demand it only from the personnel officers, the paid specialists in human relations.

However convenient this may be it hardly meets the business man's need: for people may well get the idea that *management* is reasonable and humane, but that the more line management does its job, the less clear is that that those at the top have a job to do. It came as a shock to the miners when after nationalization the colliery managers refused to sit opposite to their representatives in negotiations, but insisted on sitting on their side of the table; they had always been the 'bosses'. This confusion of thought may pass.*

It is not at all certain that good management will provide the ethical justification for private business, and the *raison d'être* of business men, as opposed to the State system. 'We want something,' Lord Chandos said very truly, 'which shows that the consumer gets the widest choice and that the capital requirements of industry on the whole are better determined that way than by planning.'[43] To put more widely into practice the precepts of hundreds of books on leadership and teamwork in industry will not necessarily prove that point. Those at the top remain isolated, their objectives often not understood, their motives often suspect; their job is policy, and policy is hard if not impossible to explain. Despite the high repute of directors generally, the undercurrent of criticism remains. Are they really worth their money? Are they really working single-mindedly to deliver what England expects? Are they as active and enterprising as they could be? Could they, indeed, be a great deal more like the go-getting American business men?

NOTES

1. Crosland, C. A. R., *The Future of Socialism*, London, Cape, 1956, p. 383, 5, 7.
2. Drucker, P., *The Practice of Management*, op. cit., p. 32.
3. Fry, R. H., op. cit.
4. Cf. Richards, D. S., *The Organisation of Management in Relation to the Requirements of Government*, lecture to British Institute of Management, Autumn Conference, 1952.
5. Socialist Union, op. cit. p. 127.
6. *The Times*, 12 October 1955.

  * See below Chapter XI, p. 231.

7. *The Times*, 24 August 1955.

8. *The Times*, 12 October 1955.

9. Jewkes, J., *Ordeal by Planning*, London, Macmillan, 1948.

10. *The Times*, 5 July 1956.

11. *The Financial Times*, 16 March 1954.

12. *The Times*, 15 August 1956.

13. *The Times*, 26 May 1956.

14. Lord Brabazon of Tara, *The Brabazon Story*, London, Heinemann, 1955, p. 155.

15. Letter in *The Times*, 12 June 1956.

16. *The Financial Times*, 14 February 1956.

17. *The Times*, 8 September 1955.

18. *The Director*, December 1952.

19. *The Financial Times*, 4 February 1956.

20. Cf. Middleton, Drew, *The British*, London, Secker, 1957, p. 118 ff.

21. *Tribune*, 20 November 1955.

22. *The Times*, 15 August 1956.

23. *The Sunday Times*, 29 July 1956.

24. *The Times*, 13 October 1955.

25. *The Times*, 20 December 1956.

26. *The Times*, 7 October 1955.

27. *The Times*, loc. cit.

28. Taylor, G. Rattray, *Are Workers Human?*, Falcon Press, 1950, p. 37.

29. Studies by Michigan University Institute of Social Research : Survey Research Centre.

30. *The Times*, 28 May 1956.

31. *The Times*, 15 April 1954; *Daily Telegraph*, 27 May 1954; *Sunday Times*, 10 November 1957.

32. *The Times*, 20 May 1955.

33. *The Times*, 15 March 1956; *Financial Times*, 27 May 1954; *Sunday Times*, 3 November 1957.

34. *The Daily Telegraph*, 22 March 1956; *Sunday Times*, 1 December 1957.

35. *The Times*, 6 May 1954.

36. *The Daily Telegraph*, 15 March 1956; *Financial Times*, 29 February 1956; *The Times*, 10 September 1953.

37. *The Times*, 23 May 1954.

38. Cf. *The Sunday Times*, 13 November 1955, 7 March 1955.

39. *The Manchester Guardian Review of Industry, Finance and Trade*, 1957.

40. *The Sunday Times*, 1 December 1957.

41. *The Economist*, 24 October 1953; cf Fedden, Sir Roy, *Britain's Air Survival*, Cassell, 1957.

42. Hooper, Sir Frederic, 'What's Wrong with British Management', *The Manager*, September 1953.

43. *The Director*, November 1954.

CHAPTER IX
Continental Style

'I will restore to you the years that the locust hath eaten.'

JOEL, 11, 25

'The average European hasn't the faintest frog's idea of what an exciting game American big business life can be, and you are just wasting your breath trying to get it across to him. Incidentally, he is not worth it. He will often stoop to things that the American (I don't speak of crooks) have long given up as bad practice.'

NEGLEY FARSON

IT IS NOT, HOWEVER, the British business man alone who is being urged to emulate the American. On the continent too the business man, troubled with an unaccustomed and uncomfortable feeling that he has a problem of public relations, is beginning to look more carefully at the transatlantic business scene and to find in it features to admire. He is even beginning to wonder whether American business civilization is what he really needs in Europe; for his own attitudes are evidently inadequate. *Fortune* found that the European business man was, in contrast to the American, *lonely* in society; and therefore '. . . so long as he is carrying out the unpopular game of business, he is resolved to pile up the chips; for inwardly he knows of only one justification for being in industry at all, namely, to get out of it . . . by accumulating as fast and decisively as possible the sort of wealth that establishes *status*—the status that is conferred by government service, scholarship or the fine art of relaxation. 'It is their credo,' added Fortune crushingly but sweepingly, 'and the ultimate explanation of the sad failures of continental capitalism that the sole mission of business is to enrich the business man.'[1]

Not even Belgian business men will swallow that verdict entire; but it is true that the continental business man is newly aware of American business achievements, and not simply in terms of managerial efficiency. From Marshall Aid to the Common Market his thinking has moved along American lines: to justify himself and his works before workers and consumers. Nowhere has this happened more noticeably than in Germany. The German business man is now probably as keenly conscious of American business philosophy, and is certainly importing American business methods as easily as his British counterpart; indeed it is quite likely that at the moment he is rather more Americanophile. There are sound reasons for this; yet the background of German business experience could hardly stand in greater contrast to American. If the Germans decide to model themselves on the Americans, there certainly would seem to be prospects of converting the rest of Europe to a healthier attitude.

1. RISE OF THE GERMAN BUSINESS MAN

The growth of capitalism in Germany was affected, to a far greater extent than in Britain or France, by a rigid structure of class and status; and the German business men arose therefore out of a social background utterly at variance with Anglo-American experience either in colonial days or afterwards in the cities; they had lost ground in the religious wars, besides being completely cut off from the wider perspectives of the new world which had stirred up and liberalized French and English (if not Spanish) society. They lost touch with practicalities at the same time. Although printing, the first of the mass-production consumer processes, came from Germany in the fifteenth century, by the eighteenth the country was lagging far behind Britain, America and France in technical progress. Germany was the land of music and philosophy—and of rigid social discipline.[2] The only towns through which a freer air circulated were the ancient Hanse cities, which still traded with the world, though they had lost most of the spirit which inspired a merchant of Lubeck to carve over his lintel the basic tenet of the true merchant-adventurer: '*navigare necesse est: vivere non necesse.*'

Capitalism, technology and business came to Germany in various ways; but so strong was the structure of a society based on status—and still divided between Catholic and Protestant states—that it had to shape itself largely to the form of that society, rather than (as in Britain) transforming it relatively swiftly. The Napoleonic wars supplied one impulse. The intellectuals among the middle classes began to pine for emancipation, for a more open society; the rulers began to need munitions; the philosophers began to think about the practical uses of natural science. When the continental blockade cut off English wares from Germany, the house of Krupp founded its fortunes on making a substitute for English cast steel, a substitute which presently proved better than the original.

Frederick the Great of Prussia had the sense to realize that his country could not be a military power without industry; yet he lacked industrialists and repudiated the freedom which enabled entrepreneurs to flourish in England and America. He therefore started industries (such as the Silesian coal mines) as a branch of the state bureaucracy. Elsewhere, a few members of the middle classes rose in the civil service, became ennobled, and bought up ancient estates where they introduced new methods and even industries; thus, by one means or another, it became possible for the entrepreneur to begin the transformation and industrialization of German life by the second quarter of the nineteenth century. The business men were not much liked by the intellectuals, because of their behaviour. To them, as to Sombart later on, 'the entrepreneur, cool and calculating, is of a non-erotic type and unsentimental nature'[3]; for 'work implies saving, love implies spending'. But liberalism was able to make only temporary use of social discontent when it seemed to sweep all Germany in the revolution of 1848. It was defeated politically; and the field was left to the unsentimental business man to whom industrialization was a practical job which could be done within the structure of reimposed authoritarianism. Much of the energies which would have gone into creating a more democratic society, with more permeable class barriers, now went into industry. German business put on a Prussian uniform.

Bismarck made the mould into which German business was poured in the last half of the nineteenth century. He broke the out-of-date medievalism of the junker (land-owning) squires while maintaining the autocracy of their King (and later Emperor). He released the creative and revolutionary forces of business, and arranged for the commercial classes to intermarry with the hereditary ruling class which thus was devalued; but in so doing top business men did not find themselves, as they did in England, at the apex of society. Status remained decisive, and the army retained its caste privileges. The successful business man might in time be allowed to put 'von' in front of his name, but he could not aspire to become a full part of the nobility; the purchase of a great estate did not (as it did in England) provide his children with a springboard into the ruling circles. Nor had the German business man the social life and culture to which the French bourgeois, on retirement, might turn with his millions, and thus enter a European society of the spirit. Finance and banking did not achieve the same supremacy in German business or in German social life that they did in France and England; the German stock exchanges had none of the social cachet of the City or the Bourse; and this further circumscribed the German business point of view. The German bankers were mainly Jews, and suffered from social stigma. German industry was even more anxious than British to keep out of the hands of the bankers, just because they were generally Jews. Industrial expansion proceded more out of retained profits than in any other country, and when the Ruhr industry felt the need for credit institutions, they often created their own. Nothing like 'The City' or 'Wall Street' ever arose in Germany, important as banking, including the great Jewish merchant banks, became.

Nor had the German business man any of the frontier-spirit which imbued the American (indeed he often emigrated in search of it). To some extent a horizon of expansion was supplied to him by first the Zollverein of the German states and then by Bismarck's full political unification of Germany. This created a basis on which big business could operate; the German industrialists unified Germany by railways. But Bismarck fought both socialism, parliamentarism and British 'Manchesterism'; he gave the German business man a secure and protected basis from which to operate, and to conquer the world by trade. From this grew two important tendencies in German business: the first, to seek to keep down political socialism by paternalism and workers' welfare in the plant; the second, to emphasize export trade. The German business man did not seek to impose any economic philosophy on the State, beyond occasionally grumbling, in the words of Treitsche, that the army and the bureaucracy were parasites on the merchant and manufacturer. In politics he collaborated with authority; his personal energies he concentrated on business and on that assault on world markets which began at last to frighten the arrogant British exporter in the early twentieth century (and still does).

2. GERMAN BUSINESS CHARACTER

The prototype of the German big business man, as well as the most famous of his breed, was Alfred Krupp. This was perhaps unfortunate for Germany later on, because Krupp, interested in steel guns and armour, did a great deal to foster the international arms race, though there is no reason to suppose it would not have taken place without him. The fortunes of the firm were built on railway equipment, and it became the greatest industrial complex in the Ruhr before the fatal Anglo-German naval race began. It was built on parsimony, willpower and technical know-how; Krupp's greatest grief was when he had to have recourse to the banks in the depression of the seventies. The leitmotive of his life was his love-hate relation with the Prussian state— at once a ceaseless battle with the bureaucracy for the recognition of the quality of his gun-barrels and a ceaseless courtship of the Prussian ruler for favours and, at times, capital. Krupp thought of himself as a loyal servant of the state; yet he was still a liberal business man in the English sense, ready to defend his right to sell guns to all-comers. He was patriotic yet internationalist; individualist yet rigidly conservative; paternal to his workmen, to whom he offered higher wages than ruled in the market, security and some plant social services; he was yet tyrannical to his family and even forbade his son to study at the university, thinking his own plant and his own example a complete education. A tiresome self-made bourgeois, contemptuous of all culture, he was yet personally and resourcefully interested in technology at a time when few British industrialists realized its importance (or had forgotten it). He

> 'had faith in himself, his enterprise and the soundness of the world in which he lived, holding that faith with the simplicity of his generation. He considered that he possessed the key to the secret of life. . . . Only one preliminary condition needed to be fulfilled. Everyone must do what *he* wanted. . . . And as his strength of will far exceeded that of those who worked for him, he succeeded in creating something out of nothing, and out of that something the greatest armament industry in the world'.[4]

This could be a broad picture of the achievement of German business men as a whole in the last half of the nineteenth and first decade of the twentieth century. Stumm came from the same mould:

> 'I demand and I expect complete confidence in me. I refuse to discuss any unjustified demands. I shall, as I have always done, try to meet any justified demands before they are formulated even, and I therefore ask everyone who does not wish to accept this, to give notice as soon as possible, so as to avoid my giving them notice, and so leave the establishment in a lawful and orderly manner to make room for others, as I can assure them I mean to remain master in my own house and on my own soil.'[5]

In the early years of the twentieth century, however, the great Ruhr industrial autocrats like the Krupps and Stumms were reinforced by German business men with a remarkable technological flair in many fields, but all deriving an immense advantage from German technical education. Siemens, for example, learned engineering in the Berlin war academy from Ohm, and turned from gun-cotton to wireless telegraphy;[6] Diesel studied engineering at Augsburg technical high school, and from inventing refrigeration by means of ammonia turned to its use as fuel for light engines;[7] Duisberg went from his chemistry studies in Gottingen to Bayer & Co.;[8] Emil Rathenau was an electrical engineer; Heinkel's career began when, as a poor student, he saw a Zeppelin burn out and decided to devote his life to the heavier-than-air craft.[9] The top German business men set a tradition of giving control to scientists rather than accountants. Coming late to industrialization, they were able to lay-out their plants more advantageously than the British. Thorstein Veblen noted that

'The German adventurers in the field of business, being captains of industry rather than finance, were also free to choose their associates and staff with a view to their industrial insight and capacity rather than their astuteness in ambushing the community's loose change.'[10]

Young men who went into German industry early found themselves part of a research *team*; for example, in 1908 Bosch worked with Haber on synthetic nitrogen, and built his march to the top on this technical success.

The discipline of the Prussian army, and the different but just as exacting discipline of science, shaped German industry on a particular pattern. It made possible precision in management as well as in engineering. An American observer, even before the first world war, noted that:

'As modern capitalism develops, it assumes more and more the aspect of a system in which the individuality of men is sacrificed. The operation of a large manufacturing plant approximates more and more to the routine of the army; with the perfection of machinery, the human labour comes to resemble the drill of the soldier, monotonous and mechanical. Patient toil, endurance and obedience are the qualities fostered in the army and utilized in industry. The capitalist could scarcely ask for a better training school for his employees.'[11]

This discipline has its disadvantages. Because German workers tended to be obedient, and not to complain about conditions in the factory any more than they did of those in the army, production was often inefficient. The smoothness of German administration astonished everybody; but the art of industrial efficiency, and above all of work study, was born in the far less disciplined society of America (though the Germans took it up in the 'rationalisierung' movement after the first world war). Heel-clicking and subservience in the management hierarchy also meant that German executives often lacked the self-criticism that was so healthy in America. Krupp left detailed—and quickly outdated—instructions for his management; it was years before his son was able to escape from the strait-jacket which they imposed on the organization and its higher control.

Order, regulation and system were and remain characteristic of German business because they were characteristic (as they still are) of the German business man. From this grew the cartels and other producers' price agreements which have always been a marked feature of German industry. Cartels were legalized in Germany when the United States was busy with the legalized sport of trust-busting. Even the British business man found that he was totally incompetent to restrict competition in the same disciplined degree as the Germans (to the deep relief of British economists). To the Germans competition spelt disorder and muddle; it did not seem to them a mechanism, as delicately adjusted as a watch-movement, for achieving market equilibrium. They regarded it as the rudimentary, chaotic stage of capitalist development, to be eliminated as it moved towards a collective orderliness.[12] This feeling was emphasized by the importance of status in Germany; cartels were aimed at defending the position of existing businesses, and workpeople and trade unions approved of them as a defence of employment and wage-rates. The idea that a great firm could be thrown off balance or even destroyed by an upstart was repugnant to a type of mind which was schooled to put the aristocracy above the bourgeoisie, defer to the king and army, and to dress its own ranks in a comparable hierarchy of wealth and prestige.

The creation of the great German industrial complexes proceeded from similar motives, quite as much as from a scientific appraisal of the advantages of vertical organization. The German industrialist, imbued with a lust for security, fearful of conditions which he did not control, always had a tendency to seek to buy the sources of his own raw material, the means of transporting them to his factory, and hence the power to price every intermediate state of manufacture. The Englishman instinctively felt it was cheapest to 'buy out' his materials, because he thought that competition would keep their prices down *to him*; the German feared that if he did not have control, he would be *deprived* of his needs. Thus the great Ruhr industrialists from steel-making went to mining, and hence to shipbuilding and machine-construction. They sought to be the producers of their products and even the users of them; the only thing they had not got (and thought the British had, or could have) was control of world markets. The tendency was very widespread; Thyssen bought up shipping, locomotives and railcars; Stinnes, starting in mining, went on to electricity and thence to woodpulp and newspapers; even Diesel, once he had made a practicable oil-engine, proceeded to buy Galician oilfields to make sure of his fuel supplies (and lost heavily on them).

To the organization of these great business empires German business men devoted their immense talents for order; and, in the same degree, their compulsive urge to work. In their own way, German business men found, as early as did Americans, that business could be a completely absorbing way of life; indeed, in the abandonment of any other interests, beyond a traditional domesticity, they may have led the way, for the nineteenth-century American business man still preserved a vague idea of getting something out of business, other than business itself. The German, cut off from politics debarred from Society, morally repelled by the conception of a life of culture and leisure, insensitive to art, gave to business organization his entire energy. Business was his estate, and almost nothing but business.

German upbringing has always emphasized the importance of doing a job properly; it emphasizes thoroughness or 'Tuchlichkeit'. In business everywhere, particularly in the scientific era, this was and is the cardinal virtue. It involved a great development of cartels, it is true; but it also yielded an intense devotion to specialized tasks, which paid off well both in applied science and in methodical marketing—more especially abroad. At home, the Germans have never pursued the consumers with blandishments: because they are only Germans. Abroad, the German attitude is just the opposite: nothing is too much trouble. The English often give the reverse impression, though they are now trying to emulate the Germans, and, as the previous chapter suggested, very uncongenial they find it.

It may be significant, however, that these are the virtues of people unsure of themselves; as an American observer puts it, this love of orderliness and passion for detail constitutes a 'protection against the vagueness of their basic emotional drive'.[13] They need the security of order and system; they need to be disciplined; indeed part of German antipathy for the English springs from the lackadaisical self-assurance which the English display (though it may be declining) and which they find hard to forgive in a Teutonic people. For the same reason English and German industrialists and technologists often get on extremely well.

The obsession with system and status prompted German business men to provide remarkably complete welfare services on a plant basis. Krupp was only one of the first to build houses for his workpeople; Fritz Henkel, the washing soda king, provided schools and sanatoria. In 1872 Siemens started a pensions fund for all workpeople, a profits bonus, and priority for re-engagement of staff who had been laid off. Karl Zeiss even introduced the eight-hour day, though most German employers expected their workers to be as ready to work long hours as they were themselves. Good relations on this basis were very common in Germany (and still are); Benz was 'papa Benz' to his employees and Robert Bosch (who had introduced the eight-hour day in 1886) was appalled when his own workpeople joined the revolution in 1919; Ballin committed suicide when it happened in his works.

The minority of enlightened employers among German industrialists often held the opinion—perhaps before it was even developed in the United States—that happy plant relationships based on a paternal care for welfare would contribute to a society without class tensions, or envy of the have-nots for the haves: 'I have always felt it the noblest duty of an industrialist,' said Duisberg, 'to find a solution for the social problem.'[14] Carl Bosch almost echoed Krupp when he said, 'I consider it a much more important moral obligation to assure our 125,000 employees, which we and our subsidiaries employ, a secure livelihood, than to pay dividends based on changing economic conditions'.[15] Men of this stamp were, however, unusually liberal—Bosch, for example, favoured workers' representatives on the Aufsichtsrat.*

---

* In Germany the organization of limited companies (g.m.b.h.) differs some-what from the British or American model. The shareholders elect a 'supervisory board' or Aufsichtsrat, which in turn appoints the executive board, or Vorstand. The functions of the Aufsichtsrat are confined to these appointments and the examination of annual accounts. It must have a minimum of 3 members rising to 15 or more for companies with a capital of over 20 million DM. The important post-war innovation is that one-third of the members of the Aufsichtsrat must be elected by workpeople. Members of the Aufsichtsrat need not be shareholders, but no director of the firm can serve on it. Before the war there was no limit to

To some extent, this policy succeeded. Germany suffered fewer strikes than England or America. German work-people could sense the pride of the boss in being a good employer. In small firms, the relationship was even closer than in Britain, or France; the German felt like the officer of a regiment towards his men: he insisted on work and discipline, but their personal worries were his concern. This tradition has proved very durable and is still continuing. The German business man is therefore able to force a great deal of welfare which they may not really want down his employees' throats; but he is also perfectly capable of sending his car to take his secretary's grandmother to hospital. Toward his colleagues, however, he is more formal: Christian names are used paternally towards workpeople, but towards employees of the same social class formality is practised. German social relationships are not, in fact, secure enough for the American fashion of using Christian names among colleagues to take root there.

3. GERMAN BUSINESS MEN AND POLITICS

German industrialists feared socialism from the middle years of the nineteenth century, thinking it a far more immediate threat to themselves than did the British bosses. They had little standing in politics, and when men like the second Krupp went into the Imperial parliament they generally got little but worry out of it. Afraid of socialism, they distrusted in the main social democracy; opposed to Manchesterism they generally distrusted liberalism also; and they acquiesced readily in the growth of autocracy before the first world war. The war itself took them by surprise. The onset of the second world war was received, if fatalistically, as a disaster by most of them. Between the wars there came a period in which German business men apparently had a chance to influence politics: but they failed and proved as completely subservient to Nazism as they had been (with more excuse) to Kaiserism.

---

the number of appointments to Aufsichtsrats which one man might hold, but to-day it is limited to 10, which makes the previous system of interlocking boards less complete. Shareholders only elect the Aufsichtsrat; they do not meet to receive the directors' report. The Aufsichtsrat must meet twice a year at least, its members serve for 4 years and are paid by tantiemes. The board of directors is directly accountable to the Aufsichtsrat, but is responsible to the shareholders, as is the Aufsichtsrat. Under this system the vital position is chairman of the board, or president who controls the company once the Aufsichtsrat has appointed him.

Their punishment was to be regarded as in large part responsible for German aggression, whereas they had merely supplied an efficient instrument for waging war.

After the first world war, liberal-minded German industrialists looked back to see where they had failed. Many of them became supporters of the Weimar régime;[16] but they also became disillusioned with it when they found that it was powerless to deliver Germany from the toils of reparations, the loss of shipping and colonies, or from internecine war. They emerged as the only winners from the inflation of 1922–23, and some of them emerged as profiteers; for only those with real assets could hope to beat inflation. During the inflation Hugo Stinnes used vast credits, easily raised in physical assets, to buy up other physical assets, while the debts so created melted away in his hands. Many other great fortunes were created at that time. This did not, however, endear the business men to the rest of the community.

Having demonstrated their power to survive, German business men took in hand the rebuilding of the economy. Many became fervent internationalists, both because Germany needed foreign trade, and also because they believed that international cartellization would prevent another war. Robert and Carl Bosch were leaders in this effort, which was paralleled by the efforts of Stresemann to attract the foreign (and mainly American) capital without which reparations could not have been paid. For a time it looked as if 'the miracle of the rentenmark' was succeeding, and that Germany was settling down to life as a mercantilist social democratic state. But when the foreign credits were cut off in 1929, German prosperity collapsed like a house of cards. The depression swept away the prestige of business men along with their hopes, as completely as it did the hopes and prestige of business men elsewhere.

A good many German business men supported the Nazi movement with funds even before the onset of depression in the thirties, because they saw in it a counterpoise to communism. Its crackpot ideas seemed of little real danger; but as a way of putting down red gangsterism it seemed a useful tool. The lack of political prescience and intellectual depth common to the business mind was in Germany added to the business man's political inexperience; the result was fatal. The Nazis on their side learned how to make superficial concessions to win them the big business money the party needed. When Hitler explained away his socialism by an insistence on 'the necessity of private property and of an economic order based upon the profit system, individual initiative, and inequality of wealth and income',[17] many business men were reassured that even if he did achieve power business would rule the roost. Others fell heavily for Germanism: Duisberg, of I. B. Farben, for instance, who declared 'the important thing for industry is a strong state, a mighty and energetic government'.[18] Yet, until the very last minute, many German business men believed that Hitler would never attain power; that he would merely make it possible for a conservative régime under Schleicher or von Papen to take charge and restore stability and confidence.

The business men's attempts to control the politicians miserably failed; just as amateurish attempts by Robert Bosch, the sparking-plugs magnate, in 1932 to get help from the French bankers and business men came to nothing. Once the Nazis were in power, the vast expansion of production which rearmament and state public works produced kept most business men too busy to raise their heads much above their desks to take stock of what was really happening in Germany. Some, who did see and were disgusted, clung to the idea that Nazism 'had at least solved unemployment and eradicated communism', and by burying their heads in their accounts managed not to see too much. The vast proliferation of controls made their lives miserable at times, despite their profits; and they let off steam (fairly safely) by cursing this aspect of the régime which, many of them felt sure, had its days numbered. Heinkel, for example, blamed some of the later defects of the Luftwaffe on government interference at this time—and also upon propaganda about the nature of the coming war, which was to begin and end in Poland and caused him to concentrate on short-range aircraft, effective in Poland but less useful in a global struggle against Britain and Russia.

Liberal-minded German business men detested Nazism from the start. Carl Bosch sought an interview with Hitler in order to persuade him that German nationalism was atavistic and suicidal and to advocate international co-operation at a time when the French and British governments were ready to play ball. Hitler harangued him and had him shown the door. Yet later on when Hitler wanted to collaborate with a group of leading German industrialists, and told them to select one of their number as a plenipotentiary, they elected Bosch, for all his known views, as their representative. Hitler then abandoned the idea; and found other means to reduce the business men to a *Stand* or caste in the corporate Nazi state. Whether they stuck to business or objected to the Nazis, most German business men feel to-day in-

creasingly guiltless of bringing Hitler to power, or even of aiding and
abetting him; and they resent the way in which the Allies gaoled men
like Flick for complicity in war crimes.

Bosch in the end advised his friend Krauch to take a job as adviser
on scientific research to Goering. His state of mind is revealed by his
own comment at the time:

> 'All this party nonsense makes me sick, but I'll have to continue to
> pull the cart, otherwise science and learning will be lost . . . it is even
> more important, however, to save our youth from the Nazis than to
> rescue science'.[19]

Bosch was one of the few business men to feel strongly about the fate
of the Jewish bankers and storekeepers about which no German industrialist could feign ignorance. The typical industrialist's distrust of
financiers, so much stronger in Germany than in most countries,
fatally tempted them to stand aloof while the Jewish merchant banks
were plundered; the small shopkeepers were easily persuaded that they
would be better off when the strong competition of the Jewish department stores was removed. Further, the dependence of German industry on bank credit—'international Jewish finance'—in the depression blinded business men by anti-semitism into failure to realize that
the régime intended to control and even own them also. Even such an
individualist as Heinkel, master of a vital know-how, who fought the
party bureaucracy, and even tore down the swastika when it was first
flown over his works, found himself helpless under political direction.

Once in the grip of the Nazi state, German business served it as a
flexible instrument for world conquest. In return, the Nazis, convinced
that a Herrenvolk must be predatory, gave German big business every
opportunity to extend its network into the conquered territory, and to
use the slaves in factory production. There proved to be nothing inherent in the structure of business to prevent it almost automatically
doing these things.

4. A BUSINESS MAN'S UTOPIA?

Experiences under the Nazi regime have deeply affected the attitude
of German business men in the postwar period. There has been a real
attempt to learn from the past. The first post-war business experience

was, however, of the past repeating itself. Business men emerged as successfully from the currency-reform of 1948 as they had from the inflation of 1923. The reform was economically necessary if Germany was to return to a market economy and to dynamic production; but it divided the population into two parts—those who lost 90 per cent of their savings and working capital, and those who owned industrial and real assets and who lost 90 per cent of their bank balances but retained their real wealth. Once again, business came out on top.

Once again, the allies poured money into the defeated country—and on this occasion refrained from the monumental folly of demanding reparations on any scale. The only punitive line they took towards the German business man (besides trying to hang some war-guilt round his neck) was again to take over his industrial secrets and know-how, to fix a ceiling on certain types of production, and to break up the great concentrations in industry, especially in the Ruhr, in the belief that these great concentrations of power had worked for war and had enabled Hitler to wage it successfully. Possibly the Americans on the Control Commission felt it proper to do some trust-busting, while the British Labour Party, though busy creating nationalized monopolies of its own, was just as ill-disposed to Ruhr cartels, and was indeed meditating the nasty idea of a British Monopolies Commission as a rod for the British business man's back.

In the event, of course, German business men have quickly thrown off these shackles. Krupp von Bohlen, operating at first from Brazil, re-established himself with great secrecy and tact, selling off a great many Krupp interests, as the allies required, but almost always to friends who arranged for him to resume control; two plants were sold to his sister and his nephew. To-day the Krupp empire is almost as large as it previously was, and Flick has been able to create a motor combine overtopping Volkswagen. He himself is said to be worth $200 million. Before the war, eight trusts controlled between them 95 per cent of German crude steel production, 51 per cent of coal output and has a mass of other interests. To-day, eight trusts control 76 per cent of steel and 36 per cent of coal output; six of them have even got their pre-war names. [20] Jejune allied theories were no match for German organizing ability.

The post-war resurgence of Germany, in fact, has drawn paeans of praise from British and American economists—and the envy of British business men has steadily grown. Finance minister Erhart set out to create an economy in which business enterprise could restore prosperity, by cutting or progressively abandoning controls, keeping welfare services down to starvation rations and the rewards for initiative up. Tax concessions in particular were designed to reduce the marginal tax burden, there were reductions for savings and overtime earnings were exempt from tax. 'The strong were given the chance to save themselves in the hope that if they succeeded they would pull the others along.'[21] There was no sellers' market for business men; there was a buyers' market and a chance to make and keep a profit; an incentive to get into business for everybody. The result was a triumph for freedom to business to see what it could do.

To Americans, the encouraging aspect of the German economic resurgence is the closeness with which it follows the American formula, rather than that of the British mixed economy and the post-war history narrated in the previous chapter. Germany has been rebuilt by business men; to Americans that should largely be a sufficient justification of the business way of life. German business men do not wholly see it this way. They are, of course, profoundly interested in American methods, though they have by no means adopted them all. They are now big buyers of American management consultancy. But their espousal of a free market economy is in part motivated by their reaction from the Nazi years of controls, associated in their minds with an absurd war strategy, destruction and defeat. They fear that any development of a British-type welfare state might impair their new freedom; but to them it is also the next thing to the communism which has submerged the bosses in East Germany. They fear the tendency to extremes, which is indeed a German characteristic; and they correspondingly welcome the 'safe' American approach through plant welfare and the conception of the business community as an institution. This seems to accord with the paternalism described earlier of the better type of German firm in the past. German business men have readily submitted to having workers' representatives on the supervisory boards of companies just because they wish to associate the trade unions with capitalism in an intimate way; though whether this will be possible is, to British trade unionists, highly doubtful. Like the Americans (and the directors of British banks) the German bosses yearn for plant unions and company staff associations.

This is not all that German business men have learned from the past, however. They have begun to see that their forbears' isolation from politics was a fatal weakness. Once again the business man has emerged as the real architect of a German renaissance, after the autocrats and generals have failed: the question is, will the business man again abandon the country to false leaders and prophets? There has sprung up in recent years quite a large literature discussing how the entrepreneur (unternehmer) can increase his standing and leadership; liberal, and also Catholic, commentators are urging him to shoulder his responsibilities with more determination. It is pointed out, for example, that every business man is essentially a politician even if he does not go into national politics, by reason of his activities in his firm and his interest in capitalism. Herr Vital Daelen[22] asks 'why do we entrepreneurs take an interest in politics?' and answers, 'in Germany trade and law become subject to politics; we, the entrepreneurs believe in the western democratic state and wish to help form it and defend it'.

The problem—the permanent top business problem—is how? If the Germans had a solution, how gladly business men in every other country would be to learn from them. It is, however, extremely difficult to pin down the elements of a practical programme. Most of Germany's modern business philosophers ask for little more than that German bosses should catch up with American, and sometimes British, ideas. Thus the development of the entrepreneur into a professional manager, with no reputation of capitalist exploitation to live down, is one theme; it appeals to German respect for the 'learned man'.

German business men are as anxious as the more forward-looking British to establish professional status and safety for themselves and like their British confréres, look to the American model, though with interesting German overtones:

> '. . . the basic question is whether the intrinsic appeal of business itself to young men can be increased. Nothing less will suffice than to create a new élite—business management. . . . The crying need is for young business men to make management an élite calling or, to put it differently, to create in their own field a distinction of éliteness. It is up to them to build in their own way a prestige that is built on their own contributions, material and otherwise, to scholarship, to the fine arts and to culture and, even more so, on public admiration for the efficiency and speed with which they consummate the largest transactions. . . . Herein also lies the way to meet the competing appeal of the professions and the government service which, not being so rooted in money-making, and so exposed to its sordid temptations, have been distinguished by a reputation for service.'[23]

It is also urged that the business man should go into politics directly; here the model is Britain rather than America, and perhaps the

Germans are bemused by the number of members of the House of Lords who hold directorships. Herr Robert Pferdemenges, the Cologne banker, told a meeting of the Industrie under Handelskammer in Hanover in 1954:

> 'The thought that "a political song is a dirty song" is generally held, Nevertheless, I want to point out in all seriousness that it is high time that the entrepreneur becomes more conscious of his duties as a member of the state and co-operates more fully in all decisive questions affecting the community.'[24]

Pferdemenges has set an example by going actively into politics himself; his plea is that business men should not try to manipulate parties by donating funds or buying newspapers, but by actively becoming politicians themselves. German political writers have attacked the idea (not exclusive to Germany) that the firm 'can't spare anybody' when political workers, at every level, are wanted.

Perhaps partly under religious influence, German business commentators have called for the cultivation of an entrepreneur's 'personality'; that is, the natural qualities of mind which will cause his leadership to be accepted, at every level, factory, neighbourhood and national, and his achievements to stand out as a conclusive and living demonstration of entrepreneurship—the business way of life, in fact. Besides his technical and commercial qualifications, he must have an 'ethos'.[25] Because he is creative—that is, builds factories, he can have an ethos superior to the mere money-getting which was condemned by the medieval Church; but that ethos must be presented through the man, not a mere system:

> 'The entrepreneur has the greatest influence on his own surroundings in his works, or firm, in his locality, in his town, in his country. The entrepreneur's achievements come through his personality and his personal activity. The German people are longing for personalities. They do not want civil servants, they do not want anonymous representatives of a party, they want a genuine personality who is ready to appear at any time in public.'[26]

There has been quite a search for examples of this type in German business history. Such a man was Wilhelm Oechelhauer, son of a paper manufacturer, who became chairman of the iron and steel association, mayor of Mulheim/Ruhr, and at once an industrialist and a politician interested in social problems as well as founder of the German Shakespeare Society, who said that 'purely human demands can often be well combined with business needs', and proposed workers' representation in 1886. A number of little organizations among business men for studying how they may develop the right type of personality, or image, have grown up.[27]

These stirrings may suggest that Germany is ripe for the development of public relations as a profession. Professor Winshuh has, indeed, frankly told German directors that if they want popularity and favour, they must not only earn it by deeds, but pay for the publicizing of it. But Germany is backward in these arts; even consumer advertising is in its infancy. There survives, rooted in German psychology, the belief that quality is its own advertisement—and that it is up to the home consumer to get out and find out what is for sale. The whole philosophy of branded goods has yet to emerge in Germany.

Whether the search for a business credo will persist in Germany is still uncertain; the very success of German post-war business is bringing forward another set of German traits in German bosses: a feeling that they do not need to justify themselves. Men like Krupp and Flick are again as wealthy and powerful as the Ruhr industrialists in the palmiest days. The smaller business men are developing cartels within the legal limits. The German flair for exporting has reasserted itself; German firms have comfortably ensconced themselves in markets which British politicians have thrown away, like the Middle East, and are finding that they are welcome in the new independent states of the Commonwealth. This is at once upsetting to British business men, and a heady draught for the German ego. Beyond all this, however, lies the enticing prospect of the Common Market, where German talent for organization seems to have a clear run, and the angry British business man is on the wrong side of the door. But to become absorbed in these entrepreneurial adventures may be to neglect the vital task which German commentators place on the business man—the ending of social conflict, the bringing together of both sides of industry, the creation of heroic yet paternal commercial figures whom the German people can admire. When that has been achieved it will, apparently, be time enough for German business men to flaunt their wealth; indeed, it will then be felt that magnificence becomes them. But meantime the acceptance so readily given to the American top executive has still in Germany to be won.

5. LE PATRON AND LE PATRONNAT

The growth of the Common Market will be a great opportunity for some French business men; but it is likely to teach a great many more just what modern business is really about. The first instinct of small French manufacturers was to oppose the Common Market; and it seems a sound one. But it is an indication of the state of French business opinion that when the ubiquitous manufacturers' associations assured their members that it would be a good thing, they quickly changed their minds—especially as the English seemed to be so much against it also—but even if they had not, the treaty would have been signed. French big business was content, and French governments were convinced that the Common Market was sound political policy. The mere fact that the majority of French businesses are small, high-cost, uncompetitive, and largely unaware of modern American efficiency methods has been overlooked. Perhaps naturally, as so many French business men and economists are unaware of it.

Business in France remained *infra dig* much longer than in Britain; as in Britain the nobility and ruling circle were ready to intermarry with rich banking families, and the very largest and wealthiest of manufacturers who were personally acceptable more or less in proportion to the distance of their business from the consumer and shopkeeper; mining was about as respectable as land-owning. The small provincial family business remained, even more than in Britain, a family business which stayed in the family. It remained *petit bourgeois*. Even the wealthiest business families could not be received by the ancient nobility—the 'Verdurins'—in the nineteenth century; but they did become part of the '500 families' which, by virtue of wealth and connections, were supposed to rule France; 'Le duc de la Roche-Qui-Mouse will never mix with le duc de l'Industrie', it was said, but contacts were made quite high up. Whereas in Britain the advance of business men into Society was, after the turn of the century, achieved on a broad front, in France relatively few broke through into the wealthiest top French circles. Furthermore, once they had broken through, they tended to abandon their business interests, which existed to support the way of life to which they had graduated. In Britain, the successful business man bought land and set up as a country gentleman; in France, to achieve a chateau or even a small estate was seen as largely incompatible with remaining wholeheartedly in business.[28] Nor did the sons of the *arriviste* business man go into the business to refresh it with new ideas and youthful ambitions. It has always been a hazard of a rising British provincial family that the family firm will lose a member in every generation to the arts, as well as to the services, armed or civil. In France it was often rare for *any* of the younger generation to bother with the business at all. They had more amusing things to do. Only if the business remained small did the sons continue to run it, much as they did a family farm.

French big business is generally extremely efficient. It has produced a string of big names: Schneider, Michelin, Renault, Coty, Boussac. It has had to stand up to the competition of big business everywhere, when it has been engaged in international trade. It has many links with German, and some with British and American big business, especially in oil and steel. Used to co-operating with international cartels, and experienced during the Vichy years in dealing with the Germans, it expects to organize an opportunity for secure profits in the Common Market. French big business men are still recruited in large part through the remaining family interests in the big firm, although the career official has arrived too; but as yet the French are little interested in specific training for the management bureaucracy. Their training is mostly in law and political economy (rather than theoretical economics), and for the rest it is done in the firm by attachment and understudying. French big business men live the life of big business everywhere, working the same long hours insulated in the intricate problems of their own organizations and negotiating with their government through a mass of employers' organizations, *syndicats* and *fédérations*. It is, however, unique to France that when they do raise their eyes from their papers, they seek to get into touch with the trend of affairs in the world in rather different ways than the Americans or English. There is, for example, no parallel elsewhere to the 'Conseil de Synthèse' which provides French top executives with permanently retained advisers of the highest intellectual calibre and width of experience of men and affairs beyond business, to visit them regularly and *tell* them, in hours of skilled conversation and disquisition, what is going on. It is not sufficient for the top Frenchman to discover that he has no time for reading. He is not proud of it, as the British business man may be; he refuses to be cut off from developments by the tiresome inefficiency of the printed medium as a rapid conductor of ideas. The British panjandrum may sometimes hire a broken-down intellectual to read the press for him and tell him of anything of importance while he changes in his office for dinner at the Ritz; he would hardly retain a bishop, an ex-Cabinet minister or a traveller of world renown, for two or three days a month,* to make him *au courant* with the trends of the times.[29]

In France, perhaps even more than in other European countries, big business and banking is a world of its own, walled behind a certain social exclusiveness even when it realizes that it is not, in the artists' sense, really creative and *important*. Big business apart, the average French business remains very much a part of the middle-class household. The business man is paternalist and autocratic, treating his employees as *mes enfants*, as much part of his *maison* as his own children and domestics. This has not only led, in an age of rapid technological change, to discontent among the children, but to a failure to modernize. The business tends to be conducted like a good household—care is taken not to contract debts, to live well within one's means, to use equipment as long as it holds together. Profit in these mental blinkers is seen as the largest possible margin on any given turnover. Prices are kept as high as possible, and the maximum protection from competition is sought. Above all, the family is determined to keep unfettered control; most business men have peasant origins, and bring to their businesses the peasant attitude to land which is totally incompatible with 'playing the business game' as Americans have developed it. The French business man would rather not expand or modernize his business if to do so means bringing in outside capital which might—and probably would—seek to gain control of the family patrimony. Bank credit is shunned; and the banks are themselves generally unenterprising about industrial credits. Expansion therefore can only come out of accumulated profits—or family thrift. There is thus always a tug-of-war between the family's desire to spend, and father's wish to plough back his profits, and in a period of technical development, there are never enough profits in a small business to modernize it.

It is an old story that if a Frenchman extends his factory to be able to accept a larger order, he is either a Jew or an Alsatian. Werner Sombart said that French capitalism displayed only half of the capitalistic virtues—thrift, care and hard work—and lacked the other half— the dynamic drive of enterprise, the readiness to take big risks for the sake of big results. France is still largely a country of small individualistic firms, with here and there a giant to break the skyline. Capital-

* The worship of University professors has not gone as far in France as elsewhere.

intensive industries must be on a large scale; but the mass of small French industries are formed round the luxury trades which are French specialities. Their owners are ignorant and often opinionated; they look to the State to support them, and their ideas of cost control, for example, are primitive, while the French system of distribution is the most uneconomic in Europe. They rely for protection on a network of trade associations. Their labour relations are also prejudiced; and even French big business lacks 'industrial relations sense'. The British business man may be open to criticism on these grounds too; for example, in the early 1920s, the mass of British employers wrecked the hopes of those who first set up the Federation of British Industries with the aim of sponsoring a great industrial charter which would guarantee minimum wages, grant generous severance pay, and provide fringe benefits; all of which have now been or are being adopted by or forced on British industry.[30] But to the Frenchman, British employers seem to have accepted and adapted the role of the trade unions in a masterly manner, which has produced a moderate Labour Party. In France the dogged, anti-Labour attitude of the business man has ended not only with businesses paying for social welfare out of their own pockets directly, but also with an irreconcilably bitter anti-capitalist feeling among the workpeople, who vote communist often for that reason and no other. To some thoughtful French business men, American business ideals and classlessness in industry really begin when he crosses the Channel.

The French business man does not find in business a way of life, like the American or German, and, increasingly, the English. He may, and usually does, work very hard in his office; but he is not always thinking of expansion. He has not copied the British post-war pastime of the take-over bid, though, of course, amalgamation in French industry does occur. A French business man once said to an American: 'Look here; I have a nice home in Paris and a house on the Riviera; my sons are married and I'm happy. Why should I knock myself out to compete, to sell more and to create a mass market and then die of heart-failure like you Americans?'[31] Another asked, 'Do you mean to tell me that you can respect a man who has become wealthy through the ruin of half a dozen competitors? Such a man is a menace to society!'[32] In Emile Zola's novel, *Le Ventre de Paris*, one of the characters remarks, 'As for making money just to make money and giving yourself so much trouble that you have no time for pleasure later on, good heavens, I'd rather sit back with my arms folded!' This may be civilization, but to an Anglo-Saxon it is not business; and it is not likely to prove good business when up against German competition either. More important, while it has provided the individual French business man with a good life, it has not yet provided the French masses with the cheap houses, household appliances, clothes and amusements made available by business men's frenzies in Anglo-Saxon countries. But it seems as if France is now on the verge of the mass-produced age; and if the French firm will not produce the reasonably-priced motor-bicycles the French artisan wants, or the refrigerator the French housewife reads about increasingly in her magazines, somebody else will. Traditionally in France the income left after buying food and shelter is spent on enjoyment and domestic help. Now French families at all income levels are demanding to have their existence eased by the conveniences common elsewhere. The art of advertisement is developing more rapidly in France than in Germany; both are on the verge of TV indoctrination. What has yet to be created in France is the mass-market, the admass mind, and the specialized low-cost production of consumer durables and the wide selling by brand names which can create an expanding economy. The French employer has fought unions, only to be driven to agreeing to such innovations as the forty-hour week, at the political level at which, indeed, like all business men he is quite lost. Despairing of altering public hostility he tends to adopt the attitude of 'the public be damned'.[33] He has entirely failed to see the chance of doing the job the other way round—the American way—and developing the affluent society earlier described, in which, if individuality, taste and beauty become less important the purveying of comfort and pleasure might give him the status and acceptance he craves. To this point we shall return in the last chapter.

NOTES

1. Schlamm, W. S. 'European Business is Different, *Fortune*, February 1960.

2. Kohn-Branstedt, E., *Aristocracy and Middle Classes in Germany*, 1830–1900, London, P. S. King, 1937, Ch. 1., *passim.*

3. *Ibid.*

4. Von Klass, G., *Krupps: the story of an industrial Empire*, London, Sidgwick & Jackson, 1954, pp. 5–7.

5. Stein, G. and others, *Unternehmen in der Politik*, Düsseldorf, Econ. Verlag, 1954.

6. Von Siemens, Werner, *Lebenserinnerungen*, Munich, Simhart & Co., 1956 (16th edition).

7. Diesel, E., *Diesel, der Mensch, das Werk, das Schicksal*, Stuttgart, Reclam-Verlag, 1950.

8. Duisberg, C., ed. ven Puttkamer, J., *Meine Lebenserinnerungen*, Leipsig, Philipp Reclam jun., 1933.

9. Heinkel, E., ed. Thorwald, J., *Sturmisches Leben*, Stuttgart, Mundus Verlag.

10. Veblen, T., *Imperial Germany and the Industrial Revolution*, New York, Macmillan, 1915, p. 190.

11. Howard, Earl D., *The Cause and Extent of the Recent Industrial Progress of Germany*, New York, Howard Mifflin, 1907, p. 82.

12. Wallich, Henry C., *Mainsprings of the German Revival*. New Haven, Yale University Press, 1955, p. 114.

13. Ibid, p. 336.

14. Duisberg, op. cit.

15. Holdermann, Karl, *Im Banne der Chemie; Carl Bosch*, Düsseldorf, Econ. Verlag, 1954.

16. Huess, Theodore, *Robert Bosch, Leben und Leistung*, Rainer Wunderlich Verlag, 1948.

17. Sweezy, Maxine, *The Structure of the Nazi Economy*, Cambridge, Harvard University Press, 1941, p. 26.

18. Duisberg, op, cit.

19. Bosch, op. cit.

20. The Manchester Guardian, 9 May, 1958.

21. Wallich, op. cit.

22. Stein, op. cit.

23. Winschuh, Joseph, Young Business men and Germany's Future, *Harvard Business Review*, May 1951.

24. Stein, op. cit.

25. Hoffner, J., *Das Ethes des Unternehmers*, Cologne, Verlag, J. B. Bachem, 1956.

26. Stein, op. cit., p. 23.

27. Winschuh, Josef, Das Unternehmerbild, Frankfort, Verlag, August, Lutzeyer, 1955, p. 140.

28. Cf. Landes, David, S., 'French Business and the Business Man'—a social and cultural analysis in *Modern France*, ed. E. M. Earle, Princeton, 1951; John E. Sawyer, 'The Entrepreneur and the Social Order,' in *Men in Business*, ed. Wm. Miller, Harvard, 1952.

29. Cf. Cahiers du Centre de Recherches et d'Études des Chefs d'Entreprise, esp. no. III, 'La Fonction de Responsibilité dans l'Entreprise' rapport de M. Paul Huvelin; Andre Gros, *La Reconstruction de L'Homme*, Plon, 1956.

30. Tennyson, Sir Charles, *Stars and Markets*, op. cit., p. 149.

31. Phillips, Warren, 'Notes from Europe', *Wall Street Journal* 6 August, 1953.

32. Sawyer, J. E. 'Strains in the Social Structure of Modern France,' in *Modern France*, op. cit.

33. Ehrmann, M. W. *Organised Industry in France*, Princeton Univ. Press, 1957, p. 34.

CHAPTER X

The Shining Example?

'No doubt but ye are the people, Wisdom shall die with you.'
JOB, xii, 2.

'In all the foundries visited it was apparent that the management had a good knowledge of every aspect of the work and were alive to their shortcomings. They were active and were a shining example to all who worked with them . . .'
Grey Ironfounding Productivity Team Report.

AMERICAN MANAGERS CAN ONLY feel smug when they read the reports on their attitude and productivity made by teams sent to the States by the Anglo-American Council on Productivity. This Council, which was set up by a Labour government, sent, between 1949 and 1952, sixty-five teams of business men, technicians and trade unionists to visit America. These teams reported an unanimously favourable impression of the American manager.

1. AMERICAN COMPARISONS

One of the most remarkable things about their reports is the importance they attached to the American *attitude* to productivity. That the reports should describe the types of machines and the plant layout was to be expected, but that they should speculate on the attitude of the American towards his work shows an interest to be looked for from psychologists, but not from hard-bitten managers, technicians and trade unionists. Typical of their enthusiasm for the American manager are the following comments:

> Every member of the Team was deeply impressed by the knowledge, enthusiasm and interest displayed by all sections of American management in every department of their business.[1]

> Amongst the top executives we met, we encountered a freshness and breadth of outlook which manifested itself in many ways, from an

interest in economic and political affairs to a readiness to encourage
and pass on knowledge to juniors.[2]

Top management in America is conditioned by a dynamic expan-
sionist outlook and is prepared to experiment and apply the best
methods of getting the maximum production at the lowest cost, and
to pass on part of the savings to the consumer. This influence per-
vades and colours the thinking of production staffs at all levels.[3]

This comparison with America is not a new thing: what is new is the
widespread publicizing of it. For a long time a general feeling has been
growing in Britain that British business has much to learn from America
and that British business men are culpably slow in learning it. At first
confined to a few exponents of scientific management it has broadened
and spread to the rest of the community, so that even those Labour
politicians who are opposed to private enterprise on principle, feel a
grievance that they are missing material advantages because of the
stick-in-the-mud attitudes of the business men of whom they disap-
prove. (This new grievance gives them great pleasure, of course; not
only is private enterprise wrong and oppressive, but it is also insuffi-
ciently enterprising and therefore still more wrong.)

Sixty or seventy years ago American business methods were considered neither efficient nor worthy of emulation. What has changed
the British view of it is basically the way in which the American economy
has far outstripped the British in production and in the material standard of life which it delivers to its customers. Economists as well as
business men had perceived long before the Second World War that
American economic growth was outstripping everyone else; Professor
Rostas first reduced this general observation to statistical measurement
in 1944. The war further demonstrated the colossal capacity of American industry to produce.

British business men murmured that the Americans had 'bigger
resources' and 'a larger and more hard-working population'; but
every investigation has inexorably shown that America's advantages
are by no means overwhelming and have inexorably pointed to the
main culprit—the British business man himself. The management
experts and the economists have hastened to give chapter and verse.
The alliance between the management experts and economists is however a pretty loose one, and they frequently and bitterly disagree with
each other. In general the economists believe that it is monopolies and
restrictive practices which make British business men inefficient, and

contrast with them America's anti-trust laws. The management experts consider that it was the failure of British business men to *manage* which made them inefficient and forced them to take refuge behind trade agreements and in trade rings. They ask where the whole of the modern idea of management comes from. Is it not America? From F. W. Taylor onwards nearly all the practical experimenting has been American; the British have slowly copied. The work on management education has come from America, too; and even now Britain has only the palest copies of the Harvard Business School. Finally, industrial consultancy in its protean forms, as applied increasingly in Britain, is imported from, and is continually developed and nourished from American models.

The business men themselves took the productivity reports fairly badly—and in one or two instances actively tried to suppress them. Many industrialists defensively insisted that even the Americans admitted that Britain had plants that bore comparison with any of theirs—forgetting, perhaps, that what counts is the average, not the exceptions. The British public, which seems to be increasingly envious of American success and touchy at America's lengthening lead over Britain, had further evidence from a report on the Fawley Refinery that its business men were letting it down. There, American management, using British labour, and accepting British conditions, did a construction job at American speed. The public perhaps did not reflect that a refinery is a specialized type of plant, and did not know that most American firms which have set up plants in Britain declare that they find little difference in their workpeople's performance either side of the Atlantic. Something about the breeziness, informality and lack of class consciousness of the American managers at Fawley caught British imagination. It reinforced a strong tendency to think that what this country wants is not a lot of hard rethinking of its basic problems, but some American business leadership, breezy, egalitarian, and fizzing with ideas. It is indeed significant how consistently British economists, management experts and business men have for forty years measured Britain against America rather than against the performance of European countries. (Now, alas, *both* comparisons are adverse.)

The conclusion seems to be that the British business man should become more like the American business man in every way, or nearly every way. There are already many similarities. We have drawn fairly heavily on American sources to illustrate business tendencies in Britain, and this can be done just because in many respects the tendency is for

British business to follow American business. But to contrast the differences may help to throw more light on the British business man to-day, and perhaps show some of the ways in which he is developing—and some in which he is unlikely to develop. It may also help to show the effect on the quality of British business life if it becomes more like the American. The productivity teams found most of the reasons for greater efficiency in the attitude of American managers and in the American Way of Life. The latter gives the American business man a supreme, and probably unexportable advantage, for—

2. 'THE BUSINESS OF AMERICA IS BUSINESS.'[4]

Unlike his European counterparts the American business man has a philosophy of life, an understanding public and high prestige. He lives in an atmosphere of public approval and interest which encourages him to think highly of his function in society. Hence Americans can take business seriously; for them it is a worthy pursuit for the whole of a man's life; whereas the British business man, lacking the support of public opinion, tends to regard it either as only one aspect of his life, or as 'a rather distasteful way of acquiring the wherewithal to conduct their real life, their private life, according to the civilized and serious ritual which expresses the values that are considered really important.'[5] At best he is accorded a grudging acceptance for performing a necessary but, in countries with an aristocratic tradition, what is thought to be a rather unworthy task, the making of money. The enthusiasm and vigour, even the idealism, which the Englishman in the past gave to the armed services, to politics, to the colonial service and the Foreign Office, the American has devoted to business. The American business man is, therefore, much more part of the main stream of American life—indeed he is the parent river. He mixes with, and often interchanges with diplomats, defence chiefs and professors. An interchange which is comparatively rare in Britain.

Because the Americans like business they like reading about it too, in much the same spirit that English people like reading about the gentry. It has often been noticed that there is nothing in Britain to compare with papers like *Fortune* or *Harvard Business Review*. The former was reported to be read by 38 per cent of top executives in 1957, and the latter by 24 per cent.[6] The British business man is more likely to read *The Economist* or the *Financial Times* for general news—and turn to *The Tatler, Country Life* or the *Illustrated London News* for information about personalities.

American business men can feel that American business has lived down its crude nineteenth-century past—its Rockefellers, Jay Goulds, Morgans; its monopolists, cornerers and trust-mongers; today it has become a social institution solidly embedded in American civilization. Even the past can be excused because at least the Vanderbilts and Carnegies opened up the country. With the management-philosophers on the one hand and the fear of communist ideas on the other, the American business bureaucrat can feel reasonably secure. There could hardly be a greater contrast with the atmosphere in which the British business man has worked.

The business man in America is presented by the press as the embodiment of the success which the average American would like to achieve. Mr. Graham Hutton has noted with approval:

> Every perceptive European visitor to America perceives that, in a society lacking Europe's aristocratic and medieval distinctions the captain of industry is a hero-type for adult men and women.[7]

According to Mr. Sigmund Diamond, in *The Reputation of the American Business Man*[8], a change has taken place in the public portrayal of the business man as hero. In the nineteenth century personal success was first attributed to personal *virtues*: thrift, industry, frugality and diligence, while later the emphasis shifted to personal *abilities*. Typical of the nineteenth century was the book by Walter R. Houghton, published in Chicago in 1889, called

> Kings of fortune, or the triumphs and achievements of noble, self-made men, whose brilliant careers have honoured their calling, blessed humanity, and whose lives furnish instruction for the young, entertainment for the old, and valuable lessons for the aspirants of fortune,

and that by James Burnley published in Philadelphia in 1901:

> Millionaires and kings of enterprise; the marvellous careers of some Americans who by pluck, foresight and energy have made themselves masters in the fields of industry and finance.

In the twentieth century the business man is portrayed not only as possessing personal virtues and abilities which have led to his success, but also as embodying the values of American society. According to Mr. Diamond:

> The simple, democratic, human entrepreneur, the entrepreneur as father, husband, grandfather, hobbyist, churchgoer—embodying common qualities to an uncommon degree and performing functions associated with all social levels—becomes then, a characteristic of twentieth-century discussion. The individualism of the entrepreneur, which once meant his personal uniqueness, now means his conformity with qualities possessed by all.[9]

This change in business ideology is in accord with the democratic spirit of the age. Indeed, there is a striking similarity to the change in the public portrayal of the Royal Family; both are now presented as 'embodying common qualities to an uncommon degree'.

3. THE AMERICAN BUSINESS CREED

The central activity in a society will be supported by a philosophy which explains its *raison d'être*. A philosophy which has not only its original writers, but also its host of enthusiastic exponents. Both are to be found in American business society but not in the European. All the 'philosophy of management' comes from America, from Ford to Burnham and from Filene to Drucker. The British have their philosophers of government and of imperialism, but the British business man has not inspired a single philosopher in over a hundred years.

The change that has taken place in the outlook of the American business man has been far greater than the change in any other country. The opening up of a new continent offered unprecedented opportunities, in an industrial age, for business men to operate on a grand scale, first as railway promoters and land speculators, then as commodity cornerers, monopoly builders and in massive share speculation. The whole emphasis in most of the nineteenth century was on freedom to amass as much wealth as you could and to spend it as flamboyantly as possible. The doctrine then was strictly business is business, and, as Vanderbilt said, 'the public be damned'. In the last year of the century Henry Havemeyer, President, of the American Sugar Refining Company could still say, when questioned before the Industrial Commission: 'I do not care two cents for your ethics. I do not know enough of them to apply them.' When asked next whether one of his practices was right as a business proposition, he replied: 'As a business proposition, it is right to get all out of business that you possibly can. If you get too much of a profit, you get somebody in competition.'[10]

Competition was the great defence, but as a defence it had the weakness that the public began to take it too seriously. By the early 1900s. the public was no longer willing to be the passive recipient of eulogies about the virtues of competition, but wanted to make certain that these virtues were upheld. Thus started the long history of anti-trust regulation and the attack on *big* business.

The public's attitude to business was changing and becoming much more critical. Flamboyant riches were no longer socially acceptable— at least for business men; an exception was made for film stars. As the centre of society the American business man has been more susceptible than the European to public opinion. Hence, in the last twenty years, he has wanted, more than any other business man, to be respectable. Dr. Beard, writing in the late 1930s, noticed that he was in search of a creed.[11] This he has now found in the doctrine of social responsibility.

To the European the most striking characteristic of American business philosophy to-day is this emphasis on social responsibility. It is most often expressed in the idea of management as a trustee; for instance:

> Today, most managements, in fact, operate as trustees in recognition of the claims of employees, investors, consumers, and government. The task is to keep these forces in balance, and to see that each gets a fair share of industry's rewards.[12]

Such an attitude is heralded as both morally right and as essential for the preservation of capitalism. Senator Ralph E. Flanders put the reason for accepting social responsibility rather more crudely than usual when he said:

> In this age of management, in which the manager enjoys power, material reward, and a feeling of satisfaction in excercising his experience and abilities, the preservation of his position must be to him and to his class a matter of serious consideration. That preservation can only come as a result of the sensitiveness of the members of the management class to their responsibilities as trustees for stockholders, for suppliers, for employees, and for their customers.[13]

So strong is this stress on social responsibility that it has even aroused a protest. Theodore Levitt, writing in the *Harvard Business*

Review on 'The Danger of Social Responsibility', urged business men to return to the (European) idea that their primary function was making a profit, and stated provocatively that:

> 'Altruism, self-denial, charity, and similar values are vital in certain walks of our life—areas which, because of that fact, are more important to the long-run future than management. But for the most part these virtues are alien to competitive economics."[14]

He argued that individual liberties were safer in a plural society in which each individual leads many different lives, as a manager, a husband, father, member of a church and leader of a boys' camp, than they were in a monolithic society in which one institution embraces the complete lives of its members. The danger he saw was that the corporation might become a modern equivalent of the medieval Church. Such a criticism would rarely apply in Europe, because business men there are, perhaps surprisingly, much more strictly *business* men. In general, they consider that their main task is to make money, rather than to concern themselves with community affairs. This contrast is partly due to a less exalted view of business, reflecting the place of business in public esteem, and partly to a greater concern for the individual's separate identity as a private citizen. British directors, when asked whether they should take an active part in community activities, still tend to stress that this is a personal matter, to be decided by one's view of one's responsibilities as a citizen rather than as a director.

The American business man thinks ardently of his function in society and, apparently, provides a continuing market for articles on the philosophy of business with titles like 'Search for a Managerial Philosophy', 'Faith in Creative Society', and 'A Businessman's Philosophy for Foreign Affairs'. It is the moral earnestness of so many of the articles which most strikes the European reader:

> In my judgment we shall win or lose the Age of Abundance to the degree that the business man exhibits two basic virtues. The first is honesty—downright old-fashioned truth-telling. The second is that business men must have clear convictions about the kind of society, the kind of system they want, and they must be willing to stand up and fight for those convictions.[15]

> The real issue is not only who can deliver the greatest amount of end products, but whether the *way* we accomplish this end result and the

human values we develop in the *process* of production are not worth preserving; whether in the long run our concept of the individual is not also more creative and efficient. Our business philosophy, essentially a by-product of our enterprise, may yet prove to be our most valuable product line.[16]

Indeed, to many Americans, business is not merely a philosophy, it is also a religion, therefore, they have a missionary desire that others should hear the glad tidings. Typical of such preaching is Clarence B. Randall's faith:

> I am convinced that business men must write as well as speak, in order that we may bring to people everywhere the exciting and confident message of our faith in the free enterprise way of life. . . . What a change would come in this struggle for men's minds if suddenly there could pour out from the world of American business a torrent of intelligent, forward-looking thinking.[17]

The American belief in the essential rightness of the 'free enterprise way of life' is centred on its greater capacity to produce than any other system. It is a way of life, not merely an economic system. For this reason Russian technological achievements shocked American public opinion more than European. In Europe the Western ideals rest on a broad conception of Western culture and not so narrowly on purely economic achievements.

4. CRITICS ON THE HEARTH

This creed of social responsibility, however genuine, is also a defence, for though the American business man may be, as Graham Hutton has suggested, a hero type, he is not without his critics. Indeed, Professor J. D. Glover, analysing 'The Attack on Big Business', remarked that:

> The widespread hostility, suspicion, and just plain unfriendliness manifested by this criticism is an important element of the environment *all* business operates in. As such, and properly understood, it has a claim to be taken into account. In fact, often it is not. Principally this seems to be because many business men do not understand this part of the reality about them as well as they do other parts.*[18]

However, one of the greatest contrasts between the American business community and the European is that criticisms of business in America

* A statement which is even more true of British business men.

are concerned with reformation rather than replacement. In America most critics accept capitalism as a desirable way of life, but seek to modify current trends to bring it still nearer to the good life. In Europe the critics either seek, like the socialists, to abolish private enterprise, or like such business men as John Spedan Lewis, founder of the John Lewis Partnership and author of *Fairer Shares*, or George Goyder, author of *Future of Private Enterprise*, to transform it.

Recent criticisms of American business take two main forms. The first, represented by Professor Galbraith and Mr Lewis Mumford, is concerned with the effects of business on the American way of life, arguing that it encourages an over-emphasis on production and fosters wants which are unimportant, at the price of neglecting those elements of the good life which need communal provision. The second, represented by such writers as William H. Whyte, C. Wright Mills, Erich Fromm, David Riesman and Chris Argyris, maintains that big corporations and mass production are generating a way of life which is harmful to the individual manager or worker.

Professor Galbraith in *The Affluent Society* launched a biting and witty attack on the American emphasis on production:

> 'In the autumn of 1954, during the Congressional elections of that year, the Republicans replied to Democratic attacks on their stewardship by arguing that this was the second best year in history . . . no person in either party showed the slightest disposition to challenge the standard by which it is decided that one year is better than another. Nor was it felt that any explanation was required. . . . Second best could only mean one thing—that the production of goods was the second highest in history. There had been a year in which production was higher and which hence was better.'[19]

He emphasized that 'no one questions the superior position of the business man in American society. But no one should doubt that it depends on the continuing preoccupation with production'. His book is a fundamental attack on the American business creed that people want material goods, that the more they are produced the better will be the country's way of life, and that the satisfaction of these wants, even if they are artificially created, is deserving of the highest praise. Such an attack could be more dangerous than that of socialism to the prestige of business men, for few socialists have denied the great importance of production. They have been concerned with the ownership and organization of industry, they have not questioned its aims of maximizing production; rather they have argued that nationalized industry would produce more, and without fluctuations.

While the European business man is seeking a sense of belonging, the Americans are being warned that too great an emphasis on together-ness may be a threat to the freedom of the individual. A theme running through some of the recent criticisms of American business is that of the danger of a pressure to conformity, or, as Galbraith has put it, of the 'bland leading the bland'. The best known of these criticisms by Whyte has added to the English language, on both sides of the Atlantic, the term 'organization man';[20] though this discovery, rather naturally, has aroused no excitement in Germany. This is the man who seeks to identify himself with the organization and who conforms to group values and behaviour. Whyte sees him as a threat to innovation and individual creation. Even in Britain, where individuality is still prized, within limits, as a social asset, a few top managers of the largest com-panies are wondering uneasily whether organisation men may reign in the next generation—they, of course, are still definite individuals, but will their successors be? Professor Galbraith and William H. Whyte have been mainly read in Britain for their picture of America, rather than for their relevance to Britain: neither affluence nor the organization man are yet pressing worries in Europe.[21]

Another group of American critics, such as Chris Argyris, O. A. Ohmann and Daniel Bell, are concerned with the effect of modern industrialism on the worker, arguing that large-scale production fails to provide the necessary satisfaction and meaning in work, without which the worker must be frustrated and bored. Argyris thinks that the authoritarian organization of industry, and its division of tasks, are only tolerable to those who abandon emotional maturity in favour of apathy and dependence.

These criticisms are far more stringent than anything that has been published in Britain since the war. Before the war the British critics were concerned with the evils of capitalism; evils which were to be abolished by nationalization. A few have continued to believe in the panacea of nationalization as the solution to problems of human relations, but most critics of social conditions have been disillusioned, cynical or indifferent to the problems of happiness in large-scale organization, and have turned their attention elsewhere, to the promo-tion of greater equality, both of opportunity and of income. In America, by contrast, the critics have worried about the evils of industrialism itself and especially those of large-scale industry; they have displayed through this century a continuing concern with *bigness*, although the form of the concern has shifted from the economic to the social. Many of the problems, such as the alienation of the workers, which in Europe have been attributed to private ownership of the means of production and distribution, in America have been ascribed to size. In Britain, economists, like Professor Sargant Florence, found that size did not produce inefficiency, and that was assumed, by many, to be the answer to all criticism.

Such recent American attacks as those on the Organization Man or the Power Elite reflect the much greater interest in, and knowledge of, business displayed by American intellectuals. They are in themselves evidence of the high esteem in which business is held. The close contacts which exist between industry and the universities is fruitful for both; an American professor in the social sciences may well earn much of his income as a part-time consultant in industry. European intellectuals are uninterested in business; a few may concern themselves with the working of the economic system, but they display no curiosity about those who run the system. Most European intellectuals, if they think of business men at all, only see the economists' entrepreneur calculating his marginal costs, or the wicked capitalist.

The American business man may know his critics and even pay well for their advice, much as he will pay fees when advised an unpleasant treatment by a doctor. In Britain, however, even friendly criticism is likely to be labelled socialist and untrue. Some British business men bitterly complain, for example, that the conservatives are really socialists and that reform-minded 'young Tories' are redder still. No journal in Britain written for the business community contains articles as severe as those published in *Fortune*, which attack certain aspects of the business way of life. Such criticism was not labelled Un-American, even at the height of the attacks on Un-American activities; this would astonish many British business men if they ever read *Fortune* with a critical mind.

Both the importance of the business man in American life, and the ways in which he is being transformed, also find their reflection in American novels, plays and films. Traditionally the American novelist, unlike the social scientist, has looked at the big business man with hostile or contemptuous eyes. At the beginning of the century, when James Burnley was writing of the marvellous careers of the Kings of Enterprise, Frank Norris in *The Pit: A Story of Chicago*, presented a very different portrait:

Ah, these men of the city, what could women ever know of them, of their lives, of that other existence through which—freed from the influence of wife or mother, or daughter or sister—they passed every day from nine o'clock till evening? It was a life in which women had no part and in which, should they enter it, they would no longer recognize son or husband, or father or brother. The gentle-mannered fellow, clean-minded, of the breakfast or supper table was one man. The other, who and what was he? Down there in the murk and grime of the business district raged the Battle of the Street, and therein he was a being transformed, case-hardened, supremely selfish, asking no quarter; no, nor giving any. Fouled with the clutchings and grapplings of the attack, besmirched with the elbowing of low associates and obscure allies, he set his feet toward conquest, and mingled with the marchings of an army that surged forever forward and back; now in merciless assault, beating the fallen enemy under foot, now in repulse, equally merciless, trampling down the auxiliaries of the day before, in a panic dash for safety; always cruel, always selfish, always pitiless.[22]

The style of business has changed from the days of the robber barons and so has the novel of protest. Today the attack is a more subtle one, as in J. P. Marquand's portrayal of 'Willis Wayde':

For a second Willis dominated the scene, modestly and sincerely. His ease was the best thing about him. You could not tell, Steve was thinking, how much of his cordiality was real. There was no way of gauging the depth of his sincerity. It might very well have been that he did have a soft spot in his heart, and that he had honestly meant what he had said about loyalty, and been deeply sorry. On the other hand he might have no heart at all. Authority and success had made him strangely impervious, since success had smoothed down all his edges, turning him into a type interchangeable with any photograph on the financial page of the *New York Times*. It was hard to tell about these people, who had all been processed in the same way, but he was essentially an American type.[23]

Fortune has expressed anxiety at the way college graduates are fed on a diet of great American literature which consistently paints the business man as a scoundrel or worse; and *Life* has sought to encourage a more adulatory approach to the business hero. Although the novelists have on the whole remained unrepentant, a stream of unfavourable portraits from Charlie Anderson to Babbitt has not made any noticeable effect on American youth. They have swallowed both the success books and the novels of protest, and gone on to business school. The public image of the business man seems little affected by the novelist. Business remains, by and large, the American way of life and private enterprise the right system for God's own country.

5. BUSINESS AS A WAY OF LIFE

We have already abundantly seen that to the American business man, business is a way of life; he lives business far more than does his average European counterpart as yet. This is still the great contrast, and the one which makes Europeans most uneasy: can they import American know-how and the American attitude to productivity without making business the centre of society? An American's business is not just an occupation for his office hours, however long, but something which permeates the whole of his life—where he lives, how he dresses, what he owns or buys on the instalment plan, whom he knows, what he does, and, if he is prescient, whom he marries. Like the squire in the English village the American president may go to church to set a good example and because in many communities this will be accepted as one indication that he is a good citizen. The British executive still tends to think of himself as a private citizen who happens to work for the XYZ company. The American executive, the organization man, feels himself to be part of a community called the XYZ company. When he takes part in local activities it is always as a representative of the XYZ company. Because it is 'good business' for its executives to be active in the local community, visibly good American citizens, the truly American corporation pressures its executives to do so. The American executive, instead of reacting in horror at this invasion of his privacy as the British manager would do, tends to exalt a community life centred round the business. Typical of this attitude is the following description from *Great Enterprise*, a study undertaken by *Fortune* into the historical facts and daily behaviour of fifty large corporations:

> When executives talk of 'the company', they refer not to some mental abstraction but to a tangible organic group. It is a group to which a man can become personally attached, and corporation executives are increasingly accustomed to think of themselves and to introduce themselves as company men. Their lives centre more and more in their corporations, even their social life: friends are friends from the company. The corporation meets their money needs, provides legal advice, medical service, loans when necessary, finances advanced

education and travel throughout the world; it usually takes note of the birth of children and may even help the children to get jobs. It looks after the aged and the widowed and frequently stands the expense of burials; its representatives regularly attend funerals. And it increasingly provides—less as yet for the factory worker than for the manager—a sense of being an integral and valuable part of a common effort.[24]

Such an all-pervasive community encourages both security and a deep-seated fear of insecurity; security because of the feeling of common effort, of community participation, insecurity because of the fear that one might cease to be one of the boys and be cast out into the cold. Conversely, the British manager is both more secure and less secure than his American counterpart, more secure because he leads a number of separate lives which are rooted in an old and established culture and is therefore not so committed to the corporation, less secure because he does not have the same feeling of belonging to a community, at a time when that old and established culture is crumbling and changing out of all recognition.

At one time, though the established and the rising American business man thought almost exclusively about business, there was no such all-embracing company approach. But today, this complete identification of all the employees, if possible, and certainly the entire management team, with the company's life and purpose is believed by Americans to be one of the causes of efficiency. The plant, the firm, is described with little exaggeration as management's temple, shrine, place of worship.

> ... it has to carry down the line. The low priests, the altar boys, everyone. There's no place in the temple for the non-believers. Every religion has a curse for the infidels—and this one does too. My father shouted it at me once ... he accused me of *not being a company man*— and he said it as if he had looked into my soul and seen all the devils of hell writhing around in there.[25]

This identification is not, of course, confined solely to industry. Americans increasingly stress, from early education upwards, the value of 'togetherness'. It is an ideal that Europeans find attractive in its greater friendliness and repellent in its infringement of individuality and solitude. Working out of hours on the company's problems and interests goes right down the line. Ambitious young men will be gently asked by their superiors how they spend their spare time. Golfing? Fine. Gardening? Fine, fine. The family, round the TV? Fine, of course, but . . . but oughtn't a young man to be studying a bit in the evenings for his career? Not just on his own job—he's assumed to know that—but on the next one up? When J. G. [the boss] comes round next time that's the sort of question he will ask—not what you're doing, but what the other man is doing, to see if you could be pushed up one, made more useful. . . .

The firm may very well go further in its demands on its managers' life. An increasing number of American companies pay considerable attention to their executives' wives. According to *Fortune*, half of all the companies on which they had data made wife-screening a regular practice; and the application of many an otherwise suitable candidate for an executive post had been turned down because of his wife. The corporation knows exactly what kind of a wife it wants:

> With a remarkable degree of uniformity of phrasing, corporation officials all over the country sketch the ideal. In her simplest terms, she is a wife who is (1) highly adaptable, (2) highly gregarious, (3) realizes her husband belongs to the corporation.[26]

One company is adding wife training to wife selection by starting courses on 'how to help your husband get on'. Even in Britain a few firms are concerned with their rising executives' choice of a helpmate since, particularly for those who are promoted from the bottom, it by no means follows that as they grow with their job their wives grow with them. It sometimes happens, in Britain, that a man changes his wife when the boardroom comes within measuring distance . . . and firms operating abroad may exercise the right to remove, recall or dismiss a man who makes the 'wrong sort of marriage'. But the British approach is piecemeal—and the high proportion of men in large companies who, by reason of their social origin, have the 'right sort of background' ensures that wives are not—or not yet—a serious problem.

6. SUCCESS: AMERICAN STYLE

The pressure to succeed in American business is also greater than in Europe. This is partly because American society places a higher premium on success than a European one; but also because, business being a way of life—not an aspect of life—success for the American can only be in business and not in some outside avocation. This pressure

shows itself in many ways, such as the emphasis on work, the popularity of success books, and the competition to hold and improve your
job which becomes more intense the higher up you go, whilst in Britain
competition frequently becomes less intense once a certain degree of
seniority has been reached. The American works hard and wholeheartedly at his business career all the way up and is critical of the
British business man for not working in the same spirit. This contrast
is seen not merely in the hours he works—it is possible that many
British top executives work fully the 57 to 60 hours a week of the
American ones*—but in many other ways as well. Lunch to the British
business man is usually a social occasion to be enjoyed with his colleagues in the relative privacy and peace of the managers' or directors'
dining-room, or more elaborately with cocktails and wine at his club or
in an expensive restaurant. The American, when he is not entertaining
is inclined to regard lunch merely as a rather unfortunate break for
refuelling which, to be most beneficial, should consist of a light snack
and no alcohol, so that the senses shall not be dulled and affect the
afternoon's work. The president too may take his snack in the common
canteen to save time, or have a sandwich at his desk.

Success books have had a long-standing popularity, ranging from
books like A. McCurdy's

> *Win Who Will*, or, *The Young Man's Key to Fortune*. Being a practical
> treatise on money-getting, the mystery of accumulation, and causes
> of failure. Including many autobiographical sketches of distinguished
> and famous men showing how they became wealthy

published in Philadelphia in 1872, to their modern equivalents, with
titles such as *How to Win Success before Forty*, and the famous *How
to Win Friends and Influence People*, which cover the tables in American
bookshops. Benjamin Franklin was one of the first Americans to write
such a success book and took as his model still earlier calls to men of
business to a serious, strenuous and ordered life.

One result of this American emphasis upon success is the frustration
of those who don't get to the top and who usually cannot, unlike their
British counterpart, sublimate their disappointment by growing prize
carnations or breeding Pekinese. Senior American managers are becoming worried about the problem of the middle manager who realizes
that he is not going to get any further and who is bitter or crushed at

* See figures given on p. 130.

what he feels to be his failure. The American Army too is reported to be trying to convince colonels that they are not failures merely because they have not become generals.[27] Europeans are better protected against feelings of insecurity. If they have come from the working, or even the middle classes, they can blame the class structure and, in the past, the lack of educational opportunities, for their failure to succeed. If they come from the upper classes their connections will usually ensure them a reasonable position, and their education and social set will give them other interests. Failing these they can fall back on the comforting explanation that things are not what they were.

The anxiety of those who do not reach the top in America is made all the more intense because of the popular myth that success depends on you; that anybody can get to the top provided he works hard enough and cultivates the necessary virtues; that even if there are psychological barriers or deficiencies, psychology can remove them. Hundreds of books have been written to support this myth. One published in New York as recently as 1948 declared, for instance, that:

> Profound study of the records of America's most successful men thirty years ago and then again today reveals that patience, perseverance, stick-to-it-iveness, unflagging courage are requisites.
>
> Neither birth nor education, neither nationality nor religion, neither heredity nor environment are passports or obstacles to the highest success in this land of democracy. . . . Worth alone counts.[28]

The carefully documented studies which show how over-optimistic this myth is will probably not stop the flood of books on 'Success is up to you' and 'Noble—self-made men'. But, according·to Lloyd Warner and James Abegglen, who studied the background of more than 8,000 business men:

> The men who hold the top positions in American business today are in most cases from the higher levels of American society. Slightly over half are sons of owners or executives of business firms and 14 per cent the sons of professional men—sons of doctors, engineers, ministers, lawyers, teachers or men in other professional occupations. Thus two of every three leaders of American business come from families whose economic and social positions were well above the average of the nation.[29]

A comparison between the Warner-Abegglen study and the Acton Society Trust's analysis of over 3,000 British managers suggests that although there is no such bench-to-boardroom myth in Britain, the opportunities for rising from the bottom are only slightly better in America than in Britain.[30]

Business considered as a game has been developed far more seriously in America than in Britain, and the rules have been more scientifically worked out. Adaptability, mobility and sociability are three of the most important for success when the game is played the American way. A successful business man must always appear to be 'a regular guy' and his wife must always be 'one of the girls'. They must not seem to be different, neither too fashionable nor too clever. They must do what their neighbours do; live in the same type of house, wear the same clothes, enjoy the same amusements, and bring up their children in the same permissive way. According to *Fortune* one rule transcends all others:

> Don't be too good. Keeping up with the Joneses is still important; but where in pushier and more primitive times it implied going substantially ahead of the Joneses, today keeping up means just that: keeping up. One can move ahead, yes—but slightly, and the timing must be exquisite. 'We will have a grand piano' says one wife 'when we are ready for it'—which is quite different from 'when we can afford it'.[31]

A successful business man and his wife must also be mobile; they must be willing to move their neighbourhood and to change their friends when promotion requires it. According to Warner and Abbegglen, mobility is one of the key characteristics of the big business leaders. They describe these mobile men as being able 'to a singular degree, to devote all their available energies to the solution of immediate and practical goals', together with a capacity for keeping a substantial emotional distance from people which permits them to detach themselves and move on.[32]

One of the factors in success in any country is knowing the right people, but this assumes special importance in the U.S.A. because business is so closely integrated into the community. An ambitious man anywhere should cultivate useful acquaintances, but when work and leisure are separate a man can have what friends he likes. Where his friends tend also to be colleagues, he is likely to be judged by the company he keeps, and must therefore be more circumscribed in his social life. The importance attached to useful friends in American business is illustrated by an advertisement of the United States Lines in 1956:

> There are great advantages to be reaped by British business men if
> they travel by United States Lines . . . most important, a fresh con-
> tact is more easily made under sociable conditions aboard ship than
> over an office desk: the people the business man meets may turn out
> to be more than just good friends—they may be *useful* friends.

It is interesting that this advertisement which ran for a long time in
British papers was later changed by dropping the last part of the
sentence.

Great emphasis is placed in American companies, indeed in American
society generally, on easy human relations. The American business
man must appear both friendly and accessible, qualities which are
symbolized by the universal use of first names—Hi ya Bill to the
president—and by the ever-open office door. The British business man
will normally keep his office door shut, but in most American companies the office door must be left open to show that you are always
accessible.* This holds true no matter how great the din outside, nor
how disturbing constant interruption may be. No wonder some
American business men come to their office before everyone else or
work at home as well, for otherwise they would have no opportunity
to think. In a British company the secretary is the watchdog who
guards her manager's privacy and with whom all arrangements must
be made before the sanctum can be penetrated. But in many American
companies you can walk straight in through the boss's open door.
One large company, which is a particularly ardent supporter of the
ever-open door policy, found that the occupants of the executive suite,
all of whose rooms opened on to a central hall, were too often inter-
rupted. Their solution was not to shut the door or to have a secretary
arrange appointments, but to take the names off the doors so that
callers who did not know their man by sight would be baffled.

The friendly relations which Americans practise within the company
are similar to their relations with managers in other companies. An
American giving his impressions of British business pointed out that
it would be almost inconceivable for an American firm to print on its
headed notepaper 'Please address all communications to the secretary'.[33]
British business relations are often anonymous relations between
businesses instead of between individuals.

* The ever-open door policy may be one explanation of the popularity of golf
in business circles since it provides an alternative opportunity for business intrigue
without the danger of being overheard.

7. OPTIMISM

We suggested in Chapter V that two of the most essential qualities for success in business were optimism and self-confidence. The American manager, as we have seen, although he is criticized, remains the key figure in American society and there is no real threat from within to his position. In fact he has every encouragement to be optimistic. His European counterpart, threatened with nationalization, restricted, heavily taxed and often regarded as pursuing an unworthy occupation, is bound to be more cautious and pessimistic.

This American optimism shows itself in the attitude to problems; the British manager may perhaps see a problem, but he is liable to think that nothing can be done about it, especially if it is a problem of human relations. The American manager, on the other hand, constitutionally thinks no problem insoluble; if he cannot find a solution himself he will buy one ready-made from a consultant. One rather curious aspect of this optimistic approach to problems is that the American is easily persuaded by a current fad into believing that there is a problem in, say, to quote two recent crazes, management development or creativity, and into buying a solution to it, at a high enough price to make him feel that it must be worthwhile. Such a solution, to sell well, should be elaborate and lengthy. Profiting from the recent fad for management development, many consultants have produced elaborate manuals describing how it should be done, a tailor-made one for each company's needs, the results of two years' intensive—and highly paid—work. It is perhaps not surprising that these manuals bear remarkably close resemblances to each other. One company, which had a particularly fat manual, decided to abandon it after some years, because it found both that there was still a shortage of good managers, which the manual was supposed to prevent, and that its managers had recently made a gross mistake which cost the company $2 million.

The consultant provides a packaged programme for the latest problem; to ensure consumers' appeal any programme will include an attractive array of gimmicks. One popular gimmick, for instance, in management development was the replacement chart, which superimposed on an organization chart an array of different-coloured boxes to show a man's degree of readiness for promotion, and lots of cryptic letters such as $x^1 x^2$ to show who was the first or second replacement for each job. The top boys had great fun with these, spreading vast charts on the floor and colouring them by hand because nobody, except the inner circle, must know what colour belonged to whom. Jones must not find out that his name was surrounded by yellow to show that he was considered 'ready for promotion after training'—he might slack if he did—nor must Brown discover that his name was red, 'has reached his limit', because it might stop him running after the imaginary carrot. Neither must Smith know that he is green, 'ready now', for fear that he would chafe at any delay. But like all gimmicks, the popularity of replacement charts waned, to be succeeded by fresh gimmicks just as lucrative.

The British business man often exhibits a sturdy, some would say a foolhardy, independence and belief in the value of his own opinions and in his judgment of others. Hence, in British industry, the psychologist is only on the periphery, if he is present at all. In American business the psychologist may be found at the very centre acting as father confessor and guide to top management. In one company for instance, all top managers spend an hour a week with the psychological consultant, who helps to relieve them of their guilt feelings, of their sense of isolation and of not being understood.

The commonest use of psychologists is for personality testing, to tell management who shall be promoted and who shall be recruited. Some American managements have relegated the essential business of assessing people's capacities to the psychologist who will, for a suitable fee, produce a beautifully coloured profile of each manager showing, for instance, that Jones rates 35 per cent on neighbourliness and 80 per cent on aggressiveness, in comparison with Smith's profile, which bulges in other places, as he ranks 90 per cent on neighbourliness but only 20 per cent on aggressiveness. To see a man's character so precisely charted exercises a fascination even on those who may have read that personality tests have not been properly validated. In spite of scepticism, if tests are used it becomes almost impossible not to believe that Smith is not much more neighbourly than Jones.

The American business man's strength is that he takes everything absolutely seriously. If this lets him in for coloured charts, patent systems, psychology, success books and executive self-criticism to a degree that the British business man still finds slightly *infra dig*, and the German business man has not yet fully caught up with, it also makes sure that he overlooks little that makes for his own and his firm's success.

NOTES

1. *Meat Packaging and Processing Team Report*, Anglo-American Council on Productivity, 1951.
2. *Hosiery and Knitwear Team Report*, Anglo-American Council on Productivity, 1951.
3. *Materials Handling Team Report*, Anglo-American Council on Productivity, 1950.
4. President Coolidge, in a message to the Nation, 1924.
5. *The Director*, September 1954.
6. 'New Dimensions in Top Executive Reading', Harvard Business Review, Sept./Oct. 1957.
7. Hutton, Graham, *We Too Can Prosper*, London, Allen & Unwin, 1953, p. 40.
8. Cf. Diamond, Sigmund, *The Reputation of the American Business Man, Mass., Harvard University Press*, 1955.
9. Ibid., pp. 180–1.
10. Quoted in Glover, J. D., *The Attack on Big Business*, Boston, 1954, pp. 356–7.
11. Beard, Miriam, op, cit., p. 764.
12. Clarence, Francis, Chairman of General Foods Corporation, address at Annual Conference of Harvard Business School Alumni Association, 12 June, 1948.
13. 'The Function of Management in American Life', Graduate School of Business, Stanford University, 1958.
14. Levitt, Theodore, 'The Danger of Social Responsibility', Harvard Business Review, Sept./Oct. 1958.
15. Luce, Henry R., 'The Character of the Businessman', *Fortune*, August 1957. An address to an international business conference held in Paris in 1957.
16. Ohmann, O. A., 'Search for a Managerial Philosophy', Harvard Business Review, Sept./Oct. 1957.
17. Randall, Clarence B., *A Creed for Free Enterprise*, Boston, Atlantic-Little Brown, 1952, pp. 3, 5.
18. Glover, J. D., *The Attack on Big Business*, Boston, 1954, p. xi.
19. Galbraith, John Kenneth, *The Affluent Society*, London, Hamish Hamilton, 1958.
20. Whyte, William H., *The Organization Man*, Jonathan Cape, 1957.
21. Cf. Lowenthal, Richard, 'The Tyranny of Means: Not *yet* that *affluent*', The Twentieth Century, January 1959.
22. Norris, Frank, *The Pit: A Story of Chicago*, London, Grant Richards, 1903.
23. Marquand, J. P., *Sincerely Willis Wayde*, op, cit.
24. Maurer Herrymon, Great Enterprise: Growth and Behaviour of the Big Corporation, New York, Macmillan, 1955, pp. 150–1.
25. Hawley, Cameron, *Cash McCall*, op. cit.
26. *Fortune*, 'The Wives of Management', October 1951, p. 86.
27. American Management Association, *Management Education in American Business. General Summary*, Lyndall F. Urwick, op. cit.

28. Forbes, B. C., ed. *America's Fifty Foremost Business Leaders*, New York, B.C. Forbes & Sons, 1948.

29. Warner, Lloyd and Abbegglen, James, *Big Business Leaders in America*, op. cit., p. 14.

30. Duncan-Jones, Paul and Stewart Rosemary *Educational Background and Career History of British Managers, with some American Comparisons*, Explorations in Entrepreneurial History, Vol. 9. No.2.

31. *Fortune*, 'The Wives of Management', op, cit., p. 88.

32. Warner and Abegglen, op. cit., especially pp. 69 and 81.

33. *The Director*, September and October, 1954.

CHAPTER XI
The Rate for the Job

'Who planteth a Vineyard and eateth not of the fruit thereof?'
I CORINTHIANS, i, 7

'Ah! Make the most of what we yet may spend!'
OMAR KHAYYÁM

'Many of the best professional and business brains in the country are heavily employed in making the best arrangements possible so far as taxation is concerned.'

Memorandum of the Law Society to the
Royal Commission on Taxation

NOTWITHSTANDING ALL THE MOTIVES which may be ascribed to business men, the love of money remains extremely potent. There is, perhaps, some slight danger that the reaction against the economists' picture of enlightened greed as the prime mover of society may be carried too far. Studies of management are now made in which the financial incentive is never mentioned at all. The assessment of desirable qualities in up-and-coming managers, referred to in Chapter IV, entirely omits 'love of money'. Psychologists and sociologists increasingly discuss the requirements of 'industrial leadership' without ever referring to a keen eye for the profit-and-loss account. Despite our avowed sympathy for the view that the behaviour of business men, in all their variety, is a great deal more complex, and their influence a great deal more potent, than can be explained simply by the desire to get rich, the time has come to reiterate that there is little or no business without a heightened consciousness of the value of money, and a marked desire to get it; as we have said, it is this which distinguishes the business man *par excellence* from managers, accountants, engineers, or other kinds of 'organization men', such as generals, civil servants, secret policemen, etc. It is this which makes it so difficult to *suppress business* even as a matter of State policy, if you desire to do so: a point to which we shall finally return.

226

1. A WORLD UNSAFE FOR MILLIONAIRES

The time has long gone by when in Britain the business man could make a fortune limited only by his commercial ability, his acquisitive capacity and his bodily strength. The number of millionaires is now fairly small. In 1880, when money was more valuable, it was reckoned in terms of dollars that France contained 75 millionaires, Germany and Austria 100, America 100, India and Russia 50 apiece, England 200. [1] It is, as we have seen, still possible to make a million. Into the interesting question whether it is possible not to lose it—whether capital appreciation and anti-tax arrangements in fact still outrun the heavy but irregular impact of death duties—we shall not enquire. It is perfectly clear that there remain very large numbers of rich business men, and that it is possible, whatever people may say, to become extremely rich. At least one firm of lawyers specializing in testamentary work limits its operations to estates of £100,000 and over, and even so is hard put to it to keep up with the demands on the firm. It may be that the larger fortunes are still inherited rather than accumulated; certainly the far larger top fortunes ($50 million and over) of the United States seem mainly to be inherited or got from oil. [2] The cleverest business men of all choose their own parents, even in our day.

Income, of course, is another matter. In the past, a business man could not only make money, he could save, reinvest and have left an income large enough for what Veblen, watching the 'Moguls' live, came to call 'conspicuous spending'. Taxes were few; social obligations were few, because they did not exist under the theory of *laisser-faire*; but food, housing and above all personal services were extremely cheap. Riches could not only be possessed on paper—they could be enjoyed. It was possible to make a fortune in the creation of a great business in a fairly short time; to live extremely well on the income, and to pass on the capital practically intact, and the full control of it to one's sons. This was indeed one of the great incentives. 'The family and the family home,' Schumpeter pointed out, 'used to be the mainspring of the typically bourgeois kind of profit motive', and he added that the results of the efforts of men who are building for what they hope will be a long line of descendants is apt to be different from the work of those who can hope neither to take it with them nor to pass it on at death. [3]

Today, not only is the usufruct of a great business fortune much

227

smaller, but it can no longer buy the personal service that equivalent incomes bought thirty years ago. It is, as we have pointed out, still possible to make a sizeable fortune by various means in British business today—but it is to make a sum which at most yields an income adequate to confer a rather higher-than-average standard of living. The idea of building by savings a capital asset that will yield a man a spendable income of £50,000 a year is an absurd ambition under present-day taxation. To live at the *rate* of £50,000 a year in income equivalent is, theoretically impossible. At £15,000 a year net income after tax is £6,000,* and thereafter every £1,000 of income represents £137 of disposable income. To obtain from business a £10,000 or even a £30,000 a year *standard of living* is, as we shall see, by no means impossible; but it has to be done in ways that would appal the Victorian business man. The really wealthy man in Britain today, the man who can live in the degree of magnificence of Sir Ernest Cassel, who, when told a certain industrialist had £200,000 a year, replied, 'I don't call that rich' —such a man is not an Englishman; he is an American, or, more likely, a Greek shipowner. For him are reserved the very particular attentions which the really magnificent rich can expect in Britain.

The importance of this, of course, is that it is today possible to rise into the effectively rich class from the resources of a far smaller enterprise than was possible even before World War II. When to earn £10,000 a year after tax requires an income of nearly 50,000, it may be attainable with a firm employing perhaps 200 or 300 people, a capital of under a million; it is not necessary to create a Lipton's Tea. It is not true that the bosses of small firms can quite lord it with the panjandrums of the biggest City firms; but they almost can with the directors of the great manufacturing combines; and certainly can outshine the chairmen of the nationalized boards. One of the effects of steeply progressive taxation, of an egalitarian ideal, is that a man can get almost as much out of a small firm making a gimmick with a big mass market, as a man guiding the policy of a shipping line, a bank, or a plantation that controls the economic life of a whole colony. From the point of view of being as well off as the law permits, Britain is the land of the backyard industry.

An illustration of this is provided by the denationalization of road haulage. Road haulage was eminently the field of the small and middle-sized business—competitive but remunerative. When, after the Labour Party had take it over, the Tory government tried to sell it back to

---

* For a married business man in 1960 with two children and not taking other allowances (dependants, insurance, etc.) into consideration—approximately.

private hands, everyone was surprised at the difficulty they encountered. While men were glad enough to come forward to buy lots of five to fifteen trucks—especially of specialized types—nobody came forward in a hurry to take back the former undertakings that had operated hundreds of trucks. The former owners, it is true, had mostly already invested their—very handsome—compensation elsewhere. But one important reason was that in present conditions very good money indeed can be made from a small fleet, relatively easy to operate and control, but the headaches involved in running a large fleet efficiently does not give a commensurate return to anyone, either an individual or a group; in fact it only gives, for harder work and greater risks, much the same disposable income for the men at the top as would a small business. Building up a truck fleet and servicing its customers was a slow and an individualistic business. When the owners were dispossessed they realized, after the first shock to their pride, how much they had been doing for how little. Some of them found out what mugs they had been when they put their compensation to work in other industries. The State was left with the B.R.S. trunk routes.

Business men have not been slow to point out what a terrible drag on the enterprise of people like themselves the present taxation system in Britain exerts. What incentive is there to make a fortune, they ask, when you cannot enjoy a higher standard of life from it, and you cannot pass much of it on to your descendants? The reply is that it is still enough to make business men eager to make fortunes, despite all deductions and exactions, if they can. In the Middle Ages, after all, the risks of toiling in vain were just as great, and probably greater, yet as fast as merchants fell to bankruptcy or—more often—to disease, others took their places. Money is always worth having.

Nevertheless the effect of high taxation had sufficiently alarmed Tory Chancellors of the Exchequer after 1957, for them to meet some of the business man's plaints. Between 1957 and 1959 the standard rate of tax was reduced by 1s. 3d., which (Socialists were indignant to discover) gave back far more money to the rich than to the middle classes. Further, in the 1957 budget personal allowances and childrens' allowances were taken into account in surtax; but this relief was described by *The British Manufacturer* as only 'added incentive to industry's middle ranks' which might slow down the emigration of much-needed technologists[4]; in 1960 *The Director* resumed the demand for a much higher starting point for surtax. The halting of inflation after 1957 has done most to ease the position of salaried men between the upper millstone of surtax and the nether millstone of soaring prices.

But for the really rich an extra five or six hundred pounds was almost negligible in terms of the incentive to live less on the expense account or to make a more productive effort. Such relief would hardly be sufficient, for example, to turn a man from selling a business he had built up to a larger concern in order to use the capital appreciation for income purposes; nor would it be enough to enable a man to hope that at last he could build a small into a large business out of the extra savings this relief made possible. The basic effects of high taxation are unchanged. Unchanged, too, is the basic salary and take-home pay structure of British business.

2. THE BOSS'S TAKE-HOME PAY

Though the top range of income which is attainable in the present taxation structure is fairly well defined, no reliable set of statistics of what business men actually earn, either when they have reached the top, or on the way up, exists. The young man entering business on a salaried job cannot, as can the young man entering the civil service, the armed services, and some of the professions, calculate fairly closely what he may hope to make at various levels of achievement. Only the very large firms think in terms of standard increments for particular functions or degrees of responsibility; and even in these promotion is not as of right. In most firms, the majority of executives make individual bargains with the company; 'asking for a rise' is the standard method of testing one's increased value to the firm. Being offered a rise with enhanced responsibility is part of the process of 'making a price' for an executive job. There is sometimes a structure of staff salaries up to about £2,000 a year, but above that there is only a series of carefully kept secrets.

No official salary index for business executives is compiled. When the staff associations of the civil service were giving evidence before the Royal Commission on the Civil Service,[5] and wished to establish some sort of parity of pay between degrees of responsibility in the service and outside it, they found this a great inconvenience. They requested that the Board of Trade should compile such an index—which would mean, of course, taking compulsory power to force employers to reveal the private bargains between them and their executives. So far no attempt of the kind has been made; and even if it were, the results would be open to much question. In fact, the only approximately true comparisons which could be made would be between the large corporations and the civil service and nationalized industry. Salaries in the mass of medium and small firms could not easily be reduced to any average relating pay to function, prospects and responsibility.[6]

It is therefore possible to give only very approximately the salary range for large and medium-sized firms, as they have ranged in the last five or six years. Anything below £1,500 a year is now in most companies a salary for a very junior executive. 'Middle management'— a vague term, which includes specialists as well as those general executives who will never rise to the top, besides those who are winning their way upwards on merit and by methods which have been examined— may expect salaries of between £2,000 to £4,000. Salaries above £4,000 a year go to top managers and working directors (i.e. directors who, besides being on the board, play an executive role). These figures are supported by the evidence of the First Division Civil Servants which said:

> As far as we can discover, large outside organisations do not regard people earning salaries of less than [£2,500 to £3,500] as doing the equivalent of administrative work in the sense that they can take and implement decisions affecting the general policy and wellbeing of their organization.[7]

This description would cover some of middle management, as well as the board, so £4,000 was probably a fair dividing line in 1954. But it is going up; in March 1960 *The Director* calculated that jobs in the £2,000 a year level in 1950–55 had risen to between £2,500 and £4,000; and higher salaried posts in proportion. Broadly speaking, the larger

---

* According to a survey made by the American Management Association into 'executive compensation' the salaries of presidents ranged from $35,600 to $100,000 a year for companies whose profits were $2 million and under; $44,000 to $147,500 for companies with profits of $2 million to $7 million; and companies with profits of over $7 million paid their chief executives between $88,000 and $210,600. Second and third highest paid executives in these ranges were paid between two-thirds and one-half the salary of the president. At $2·80 to the pound, which is not a realistic conversion factor, this means that for the largest and most profitable American companies the chief executive was making between £24,000 and £59,000 a year, while other directors or top managers were getting £15,000 to £37,000. After federal income tax at 1951 rates, chief executives had between £16,000 and £20,000 left, other top executives £16,000 and £9,500. British chief executives on such salaries would in *all* cases be reduced to a dead level of take-home pay of about £5,200 to 5,500 a year. There can thus be little correlation between remuneration and size or showing of firm and British top executives' salaries.

the firm the larger the remuneration of its directors and top executives. In America, indeed, there is a close correlation between top remuneration and company profits.* How high do top business salaries get in Britain? It is not possible to answer positively. The veil between the public and the boardroom was recently torn aside as one result of the schism between Sir Bernard Docker and his fellow-directors of B.S.A.; it transpired that Sir Bernard received £3,500 as chairman's fees, and £20,000 a year as managing director's salary. In addition, he received contributions by the company under his pensions schemes of £9,566 a year, and an expenses allowance of over £11,000.[8] Disregarding for the moment the latter two figures, £20,000 for the managing directorship of a firm of the size of B.S.A. (capital £8 million) is probably competitive for managerial talent. The annual accounts of the larger firms disclose that total emoluments average between £10,000 and £20,000 per director,[9] but some directors are part-time. The other directors of B.S.A. averaged £5,000 each. £25,000 to £30,000 may be taken as a fair figure for the *direct* remuneration for the chief executive of the largest firms in Britain, and £10,000 for the chief executives of their subsidiary companies. £4,000 would be the salary of the managing director of a medium firm employing 400 people, but he would probably have a share in profits and other payments which doubled that sum.

The First Division Civil Servants estimated that in a manufacturing firm of 400 employees the managing director would get about £4,500, and in a shipping firm, £7,000. Men carrying the sort of responsibility that top civil servants carry, they reckoned, got between £5,000 and £10,000 a year (or about twice as much as most civil servants do). The chairman of a nationalized industry now gets from £7,500 to £10,000, with allowances in addition. The full-time members of a nationalized industry board get from £5,000 to £7,500, according to size of board 'no more than is enjoyed by directors of private companies a fraction of the size of the national colossi', according to *The Economist*, which considered that such rates were entirely inadequate to attract business men of the highest calibre.[10]

Even the much higher salaries given by firms a fraction the size of the national colossi, however, are far less than is earned for comparable work in America. The president of General Motors in 1954 received the equivalent of £245,000 a year. The chief executive of du Pont got £200,000 a year, and of Fords, £163,000 a year. Firms like Chrysler, I.B.M. and Republic Steel paid their chairmen or presidents nearly £110,000, a year.[11] These are all large organizations, though none of them as large as the British nationalized industries. The bigger British firms, like I.C.I. or Unilever, can compare with them in size, but even the gross salary of their top executives is probably not half as great as that of the lower range of American top-paying firms. The difference, however, is just as great down the line, though its purchasing power is exaggerated by converting at the rate of $2·80 to the pound. Even before the war a study of the fifty largest American corporations showed that the average for executive salaries was £5,000 a year. The highest paid executive got the equivalent of £18,750, the next highest £15,000. According to *Business Week*, the average for top executives for over 100 major companies was about £50,000 a year.

Not only do American business men earn far more than their British counterparts, but more is left to them after taxation. According to a calculation made by Sir Patrick Hamilton in 1951, an executive earning £3,000 in Britain, married and with one dependant, was left after tax with just over 40 per cent of his gross income, while the American getting $15,000 was left with 75 per cent of it. Of an income of £5,000 the English business man retained 30 per cent. The American getting $25,000 kept 60 per cent of it. The British £10,000 a year man was left with £3,000; the American $50,000 a year man with nearly $25,000.[12] In 1960 *The Director* complained that to raise a director's salary from £6,000 a year to £7,000 only gave him an extra £346 of take-home pay, against an extra £517 in the United States and an extra £574 in Canada.

3. P.A.Y.E. AND SCHEDULE D

Taxation, of course, is the key to the remuneration and the incentives of the business man. On the one hand, high and steeply-progressive taxation curbs his remuneration (whether taken in the form of salary or of profits or of both) down to levels at which considerably less enterprise and effort are expected in other walks of life though, as has been suggested, it is probably an exaggeration to say, as Sir Patrick Hamilton does, that 'the rewards of commercial and industrial enterprise and administrative success have been reduced to levels comparable to those of the civil service; the nationalized industries; the medical and legal professions, and even teaching'. Taxation acts as an increasing disincentive to the man who climbs; Sir Patrick argues that the additional financial rewards above £4,000 a year gross are not sufficient to make for great extra efforts, although as we have argued earlier, the non-financial incentives become increasingly important the higher up you go.[13] On the other hand, there are various ways of supplementing income, avoiding tax and of living at a considerably higher standard of living—or expenditure—than one's gross income at current tax levels permits; and top positions in industry and commerce allow this to a far greater extent than any other walk of life. It is a supremely important incentive, though one that works in grotesque ways at times.

Business circles, understandably, prefer to stress what present-day British taxation does to their gross incomes. Comparisons of the purchasing-power of salaries today and before the war, taking into account both the incidence of taxation and the rise in the cost of living, have become popular and can be made in various ways. According to *The Economist*,[14] in 1956 a man on a pre-war salary of £700 and £1,000 would have needed four times as much simply to maintain his pre-war standard of living. To enjoy the standard of living obtainable from a pre-war salary of £1,200 would in 1956 have required over £4,800. To increase it simply by the average amount by which the country's standards have risen—7 per cent—would require £5,600. Yet this range covers only junior and—in pre-war terms—middle executives. Even before the war, the top executive on a salary expected to earn £3,000 to £7,000 a year. In other words, these figures suggest that the top executive today can only expect to enjoy the standard of living of the junior or middle executive before the war, and the changes in surtax and allowances in the budget of 1957 did not really alter this picture.

The business man at the top naturally compares himself with the pre-war top executives. According to *Business*[15] the senior executive in 1956 who earns £20,000 a year is left by taxes no better off than the man who had £2,190 before the war. The £5,000 a year director of today is no better off than the man with £1,270 before the war—such as an university professor or an assistant secretary in the civil service in those days. *Business* in fact concluded that relatively few executives who earned £1,000 a year in 1938 have in fact doubled their standards of living, whatever additional responsibilities they have shouldered, whatever improvements or inventions they have fathered, or however high they have climbed in the executive hierarchy since then.

Under very high taxation it is, of course, extremely difficult to give men or women who have reached the higher salary ranges any worthwhile increases in their standard of living (as opposed to increases in their gross emolument), to compensate for extra effort or responsibility.

To give a man on £3,000 a year a 20 per cent increase in his purchasing power means that he must receive an extra £1,245 a year; a man on £5,000 a year needs an additional £2,375 a year.[16] To give a managing director an increase of 20 per cent in his purchasing power as a mark of gratitude for his conquest of a new market or his introduction of a new invention means raising his salary by over 60 per cent. It is also extremely difficult for the man on a high salary to keep up with inflation. Between 1938 and 1955 the retail price index rose by over 150 per cent, making an average cumulative rise of 5·3 per cent per annum. Between 1945 and 1951 (the Labour government) prices rose, on the same basis, by 5·7 per cent a year, and between 1951 and 1955, under Tory rule, by 4·9 per cent. According to *Business*, in a period when inflation continues at the rate of 5 per cent a year, the executive should have his purchasing power increased by at least that much, unless such an inflation is to be openly recognized as the basic method of redistributing income in favour of the artisan from all other classes in the community.

The Tory Chancellor of the Exchequer has promised that the nation's standard of living will increase by 100 per cent in twenty-five years. This is possible for the £15 a week artisan, though it may bring him into the present surtax range of income. But the man now earning £3,000 a year would on present tax rates have to receive £140,000 a year in 1980.[17] Evidently, the high salary man is not included in this bright vision. Or, if he is, it is presumed that inflation has now been permanently stopped and taxation rates will be further lowered.

Such figures, which can be endlessly varied, merely reflect the process of redistribution of income in Britain, and the effects of egalitarianism on high salaries. Though it is clear that many members of the upper classes have had their standards of living heavily reduced in the period 1938–56, it does not in fact prove that all members of the middle class have done so, and certainly not all business men. Few men are on the same salaries now as they were in 1938. They are all earning much more; but over the whole period the increments that they have had, and which may look large in absolute figures, are continuously deflated by taxation and inflation. The salaried man over this period has worked hard for fairy gold. If he had £650 a year in 1938 as an up-and-coming young executive, and is now chairman, a young and efficient chairman on £10,000, his actual increase in purchasing power is £1,160 only. His salary has in fact not quite tripled though he has risen to the highest point. On paper he is making a fortune. In fact, he is—if he is wholly dependent on salary—about able to run his own car, live in a five-bedroomed house with one servant and send a brace of boys to public schools. That will be, *on a straight salary*, and in theory the modest reward for success in business from 1938 to 1960. In an appendix to this chapter the (not entirely imaginary) life histories of four types of successful business executive, whose careers may be taken as representative, are given to illustrate what success has brought financially over the last twenty years; and it should be remembered that the big increases in gross salary must be won in these cases by considerable ability in business—they are not to be had by mere promotion as the result of seniority.

All such figures emphasize the well-known fact that the salaried professional, when in the civil service, local government service, education or in business, cannot now expect very greatly to increase his standard of living, however well he does; but, of course, nobody imagines that in such conditions business men submit to such a fleecing. Civil servants may have to; the attraction of business is that it offers almost the only possibility now of escaping from the taxation-inflation squeeze on the middle classes. The younger executives can and do get annual salary increases which more that offset inflation until they get into the surtax class.[18] Simple salary increases are not then enough. The business man at the top has, however, three methods of raising his real emoluments, and even more his effective standard of living, far above the £8,000-a-year ceiling: he has an expense account; he has the opportunity of participating in large capital gains; he has his 'top hat' pension scheme.

4. CAPITAL GAINS

Clearly no business man aware of the effects of taxation and inflation will have omitted to make capital gains, however small the personal capital with which he started his business career. If he has not made money by buying and selling property and shares in the 'great inflation' between the years 1940 and 1955 or 1956, he is no business man in the sense defined in this book. The devoted company official—whether an engineer, lawyer or accountant—may have failed to grasp the opportunities, simply because, though his abilities are invaluable to the company in a subordinate capacity, he lacks the money-making business instincts which are one essential condition of rising to the top. The true entrepreneur can hardly have missed the opportunity presented during

Dr Dalton's reign as Chancellor of the Exchequer or, for example, in the year of Tory freedom, 1955, when an average portfolio of industrial shares appreciated by 35 per cent.

A top executive, with a secretary to do the work, time to follow the market, which he may argue should be part of his normal duties in guiding his firm's destinies, and a sound broker, cannot have failed to make very large capital gains. The very inflation which was eroding his salary made it possible for him to win it back many times over on the Stock Exchange. This possibility, of course, was, and is, open to all of us. But the business man has special advantages. He has, or should have, facilities for judging what firms will do well; he has contacts; he is continually talking with men who are watching markets closely; there are always people who wish to oblige him; and he has, or ought to have, a substantial sum with which to operate. He may also have an additional advantage; he may, as part of his emolument, be given shares in his own firm. Thus, even if he has no gift for playing the markets—and even for business men in times of no inflation this is a tricky pastime—an issue of his own firm's shares to him at par may bring him in a useful capital sum. Though he pays tax on this (just as American executives pay tax on the huge bonuses they receive annually or at other intervals) he stands to gain from subsequent capital appreciation, of the likelihood of which he has inside knowledge. If his firm is amicably taken over in a take-over bid, he has hitherto been eligible for the 'golden handshake'—very large untaxed compensation for loss of office; but from 1960 this, above £5,000, will be taxed. He is not precluded from getting another directorship thereby.

5. PERKS AND ALLOWANCES

How much business men add to their incomes by private dealings is unascertainable: presumably they shared as a class very largely in the rise of Stock Exchange values between 1945 and 1955 of an estimated £9,420 millions. It is also far from ascertainable how much they benefit from their expenses accounts. This is in fact debatable ground constantly fought over between them and the Inland Revenue. In theory allowable expenses do not add to a man's income or enjoyment at all: they are incurred solely to obtain orders or maintain business goodwill. But out of this formula a great deal of personal expenditure can be squeezed, expenditure which, for the professional man or woman must come if at all wholly out of salary. Like the professional practitioner, the business man is permitted to charge such things as a proportion of the expenses of his car, and his entertainment expenses against production of bills.[19] The greater part of the advantage comes from the expenses which he draws through the firm, which is entitled to charge all sorts of expenses to costs; even if it has to pay out of profits it can still place large amenities in the way of its top executives. A firm is required to tell the Revenue on form P11D what benefits it allows the directors. But in practice the estimates of the benefits may often be token amounts. Junior and middle management, if they get anything—and in many large firms they draw little or nothing more in the way of allowable expenses than civil servants—get direct expenses on business trips, part of the running costs of their cars, some entertainment and so forth. They may receive a fixed tax-free expenses payment, though this has to be justified by vouchers and a statement, designed to find out if the business man is getting any personal benefits, in which case an assessment will be issued against him.

A large or medium-size firm can supply its senior executives with a large car, which remains the firm's property, but which is treated by the executive as his own—all running costs and repairs being passed back to the firm. Though the Inspector of Taxes must in theory ask about this, he cannot easily get an answer that he can object to. Alternatively the car, bought by the firm for £1,200 can be sold in a few months to the executive second-hand for £300. The word 'entertainment' can be so interpreted as to cover almost every meal the executive —and often his wife or his mistress—takes; entertainment at home is allowable if given for business purposes. The wives of men in middle management have no such advantages, and not only is their standard of living vastly below that of Mrs Big but is also sadly below that of their husbands if the latter dine out on sales department expenses. The social lives of the mistresses of middle management are, however, more easily put on expenses.

Some firms, though as yet only a limited number, supply their senior executives with a house or flat; and if the firm possesses a house, they can pay for a servant or servants to go with it; these are employees of the firm, like any fitter or machine-minder. This has been a frequent and natural practice among firms overseas—such as oil companies; who, however, usually charge the employee a modest rent. Taxation is causing the idea to be extended to seniors in Britain as a means of giving the top men a trouble-free home environment in which to solve company problems. Dukes may wash up, and thousands of directors no doubt test the new detergents personally; but the necessity can be avoided.

More important, there are holidays; in an egalitarian age the cost of a *good* holiday, away from οἱ πόλλοι is soaring. A holiday far from the mass consumer market, however, can be taken in the guise of business trips abroad, or be innocently tacked on to *bona fide* trips. This overcomes problems of hard currency or travel allowances, as well as that of finding the money for continental and American luxury hotel bills. Business trips have given executives toiling to increase exports for a drab, rationed, post-war Britain changes of air and scene not easily obtained by ordinary mortals, except by means of pull with UNO, UNESCO *et al.* Directors have personally attended to irksome jobs overseas which in the past they would have delegated; or they have felt it necessary to accompany a member of lower management on such a trip to give him full directorial backing. There are now innumerable international conferences, fairs, *concours*, study visits, missions (often government-sponsored) and so forth which, though perhaps not directly productive of results visible in the profit-and-loss account, it is none the less desirable that big business men should attend. Since taxation rose, so has attendance at these important affairs. Nor does this necessarily mean loneliness for the business man. It is a post-war quip that whereas in the past business men abroad were always trying to pass off their secretaries as their wives, nowadays they are always trying to pass off their wives as their secretaries. However, they are sometimes found out, and in one case the judge declared, 'I cannot help feeling that it would be better if the Crown paid more attention to wives who are not genuine business women than to husbands who are genuine business men.'[20] Many firms, as Sir Bernard Docker's story to the B.S.A. shareholders showed, are very willing to send the wife abroad to help the sales campaign along with the managing director.

Finally, the personal benefits of Mr Big's secretarial assistance should not be underestimated. Many top men will have at least two—one to cope with the firm's affairs, another to deal exclusively with the great man's private affairs, so as to give him more time to work for the firm. He may have a social secretary also, who will arrange his tax-free dinners; and also assist his wife in any of her problems.

In America these buttresses to directorial standards of living are called 'fringe benefits'.[21] It is easy to see that on a generous scale they can take care of a large part of a man's living expenses at a very high standard of living. The free use of a large car may be easily worth £700 a year; of a large house or luxury flat in town at least £1,000. A free secretary provides the equivalent of £700 or £750 of service; and free service in the company house or flat almost as much again (and indeed more since servants are not easily obtainable even by those who can afford them). Meals may easily be worth £1,500 a year, and holidays tacked on to business trips another £1,000. This is quite a modest assessment of the worth of such things—yet it totals already £4,700—which is the equivalent, to those who must pay for them from their net earnings, of a gross income of at least £55,000 a year on a basic salary of £8,000 gross. In short, though it may look as if few Britons can have a net income of £10,000 a year on present taxation, in fact it is possible to live on a £10,000 a year basis, and indeed considerably higher, without drawing on capital or being dependent on capital gains.

Nor is it necessary for the business man to live on his expenses in order to save his salary for his old age. There are many types of executive pension schemes. For the senior man these are now particularly attractive because of the very big tax relief which the 'employee's' own contribution attracts. It is thus easy enough under a 'top hat' scheme to save for a pension of half or two-thirds of the salary reached at retirement—which may be £10,000 to £20,000 a year. The premiums will be correspondingly great, and the greater part of them will in fact be paid by the Exchequer, since the firm's share is a cost, and the director's own share, on that part of his income which is taxed at 19s in the £ is negligible—even if the annual premium is two or three thousand pounds a year. Many senior executives in fact prefer to take out an increase in salary when it becomes due by a larger contribution by the firm to the retirement pension.

These fringe benefits vary, of course, from firm to firm. Moreover, they vary in their application to men at different levels. It would be rash to suppose that the larger the firm the larger the fringe benefits. The small firm can generally afford lavish benefits only for its one or two major executives, who commonly hold most of the shareholding anyway. Some of the very largest firms keep almost to civil service rules about cars, lunches and expenses on business trips. Others whet the incentive of the young executive quite early, and their top men do very well indeed. Others, again, keep all 'perks' for the charmed circle of the board. Family firms often simply keep them in the family, just as in the past all the profits came to the family. There are as many arrangements as there are individual circumstances. Clearly the exporting firm, operating largely abroad, is on a better wicket than the small building society or retail store. By and large, what distinguishes business prospects for the successful from prospects in other careers is the scale of the fringe benefits obtainable. (Of course all the self-employed, whether doctors, lawyers, architects or farmers, can transfer a proportion of their living expenses to professional allowable expenses.) In business, there can be little doubt, fringe benefits can at least double the net value of an income; and can perhaps do so from departmental manager level upwards. The business man who wants an adequate return for his talent prefers the type of firm which looks after his interests in this way; and the natural tendency in an egalitarian society is for firms to turn increasingly to this method of giving their executives an adequate incentive and attracting the best brains.

6. INCENTIVE

On the basis of gross salary, therefore, big business may not look very much better than the civil service or the professions in its top rewards. Business men are concerned, in fact, to stress this point of view. Thus Lord Chandos, addressing the Institute of Directors, said:

> An industrial company has, let us say, four plants in England and a head office with an executive chairman in London. Let us suppose that each of these four plants employs about 5,000 or 6,000 men. The managing director of each of these plants, after twenty-five years experience of the industry, will be paid perhaps £10,000 a year. Upon his ability to handle his fellow men, his relations with the work-people who come into the plant, his knowledge of production and selling and marketing, will depend the whole success and harmony of each of these great undertakings.
>
> After doing this job and doing it successfully for a few years, the time comes when one of these men has to be promoted to the first position—managing director or chairman in London, responsible for the policy of the whole of the four. . . . I cannot in my own experience point to an actual occasion when a job of this magnitude has been refused by a selected person but he has on occasion accepted with great reluctance. Why does he accept with reluctance? Because he is fined about £1,500 a year for his promotion. He leaves the production plant; he was probably living nearby in a house with a

few acres of land, where he can raise some chickens and a cow or two. He comes to London where the amenities available to him are much less, where his cost of living is in innumerable ways higher, where he has to entertain more, and has to wrangle with the Inland Revenue over every whisky-and-soda that he gives to a customer. The result of his promotion is to leave him £1,500 a year worse off.[22]

It is certainly a pathetic picture, but it is one applicable only to a spartan company which gives, at most, a small fixed expense allowance to its chairman and branch managing directors. In this case the extra expense of living in London will certainly make raising a subsidiary branch salary of £10,000 to a London salary of £15,000 a wry jest, even after the 1957 budget. But in general things are not done like that; which is no doubt why Lord Chandos confessed he had not heard of any actual occasion when the big job was refused, quite apart from the pleasure of being god in the organization.

These considerations do, however, show that firms which are run purely on a salaried-executive basis have little to offer to the man at the top; and this must lie at the heart of the weakness of the appeal of the nationalized industries. They have drawn to their top management retired generals, trade unionists, technicians and senior civil servants, to whom £10,000 a year and an expense allowance running into a thousand or two is big money. The real business man knows that a far smaller unit of production can pay its chief executive much more in real terms; because the best men are scarce, they are likely to insist that they do get such consideration for their services. And those who do reach the top are in a position to see that they do in fact get a little help over taxation matters.

It is not possible to live in the affluence of the Victorian millionaires in modern industrial Britain; the margin between even the best-off and the average is far narrower than it was fifty years ago, but it is still considerable. Leaving entirely aside what can be done by means of capital gains, we suggest that it is certainly possible to aim at a standard of living of at least £10,000 a year net; and the time has yet to come when British firms, like many American, put an executive plane, as well as a car, at the disposal of directors. The ceiling of £8,000 may apply to the richest of dukes, film actors, successful barristers, and persons living on the unearned income drawn from fortunes made in the past—or more recently in wartime—but not to top business men. Ironically, steeply progressive taxation puts a premium on getting into business which is something every economist thinks desirable for the intelligent young; indeed, it puts a premium on working hard instead of living off unearned income (since there are few perks for those who do that). Admittedly, for those who do not wish to work it puts a premium on living on capital. It is thus not surprising that a fairly wealthy class of business man remains; and so does a powerful incentive to get to the top.

7. SOME SALARY PROFILES

It is usual nowadays to work back from an existing salary and to show what it is worth in terms of 1939 purchasing power as the result of taxation and inflation. This however is only an exact picture for a man who has not changed his job—it might be appropriate for the chairman of a family firm who was taking £10,000 out of the firm in 1939 at the age of fifty and the same at sixty-seven, seventeen years later—in which case his real income would be about £1,800 in pre-war purchasing power. Since 1939 everyone has had promotion in the business and professional worlds, as well as increased responsibilities, both private and on the job. To provide some idea of what has really happened to salaries, therefore, four typical but fictitious business careers are appended, with a comparison with a (fictitious) Inspector of Taxes who becomes, before retirement, Head of the Inland Revenue. These show only the incomes received in the form of salary, and leave out of account the value of expense accounts, payments by the firm in the form of truck (free cars, e.g.), and, of course, income earned outside the firm from capital appreciation. It also leaves the value of pension funds out of account, but takes account of tax allowances for insurance premiums. It should be sufficiently obvious that without assistance of this kind, even the most highly paid of modern business men (a) earn relatively low 'take-home' pay, and (b) those that have risen by their talents since before the war have received, in pay, very small real increases as a reward for their efforts—or an incentive to further efforts.

These examples, however, leave out the few industrialists who are earning fabulous sums in firms that they own, or largely own; but these figures probably, in terms of salaries, are a very fair average of the successful business career built not upon personal service but on professional administration in one or two companies.

1. MR GEORGE WADDELL

Waddell comes of a professional family; his father was a schoolmaster at a minor public school. He got an exhibition to Oxford, second class honours in P.P.E. in 1933. He wanted to be a lawyer, but being without capital in that slump year he got himself taken on, *faute de mieux*, as a trainee at Hans Stores, the upper-class departmental store, in Belgravia. He became an assistant buyer in 1936, and buyer two years later, having then married and insured himself. He did well in the war, rising to major, with a DSO. On his return, he is inveigled back to Hans by an offer of becoming personal assistant to the general manager on £850, with the prospect of promotion and some trips to the Continent; he does very well indeed, becomes the key departmental manager (furnishings and fabrics) in 1948, saves several other departments from disaster thereafter, by 1954 he is assistant general manager—and is now general manager at forty-eight.

Year	Post	Gross Salary	Salary after Tax	Salary after Tax at 1938 prices (rounded off)
		£	£	£
1934	Trainee	175	170	180
1936	Assistant Buyer	300	288	300
1938	Buyer	400	380	380
1940–5	Army			
1945	Personal Assistant to G.M.	850	646	400
1948	Departmental Manager	1,500	1,000	520
1950	Assistant General Manager	2,500	1,750	850
1956	General Manager	4,500	2,675	1,010
1957	,, ,,	4,500	2,925	1,070
1960	,, ,,	6,500	3,765	1280

2. MR WILLIAM BRADSHAW

Bradshaw worked his way up from the floor of an engineering firm in the North. He took his National Certificate in mechanical engineering in his spare time, and duly became an M.I.Mech.E. but not till he was thirty-seven. He then became a senior foreman at £300 a year. The war found the firm making parts for tanks and armoured vehicles; in 1940 Bradshaw became a departmental manager. Three years later he was assistant works manager, and by the end of the war works manager. In this capacity he did a fine reconversion job to agricultural machinery and became general works manager in 1949. Two years later as assistant managing director he joined the Board, and in 1954 he became managing director. He has had one rise in salary in that post. His gross salary is now ten times what it was in 1938, his real salary four times as much for running the firm as it was when he was mere superintendent.

Year	Post	Gross Salary	Salary after Tax	Salary after Tax at 1938 prices (rounded off)
		£	£	£
1938	Factory Supt.	300	300	300
1940	Dept. Manager	600	501	410
1943	Asst. Works Manager	950	646	410
1946	Works Manager	1,500	1,000	590

1949	General Works Manager	2,200	1,536	770
1951	Asst. Managing Director	3,500	2,063	925
1954	Managing Director	6,000	2,914	1,185
1956	,, ,,	7,250	3,254	1,230
1957	,, ,,	7,250	3,626	1,330
1960	,, ,,	9,000	4,527	1,510

3. MR JOHN MONEYMAN, D.SC.(BIRM.)

Moneyman comes of artisan stock and won his way to the University by scholarships. He proved to be a good chemical engineer and joined a medium-size chemical firm, which produces pharmaceuticals (both ethical and proprietory), as well as pesticides, at the age of twenty-five. His starting salary was £8 a week. In two years he became a development engineer at the centre, designing new plant; when the war came the government demanded a big expansion of the drug-making side, as well as certain recherché poisons for M.I.5. Moneyman became assistant chief engineer and then in turn reorganized the three component works of the firm; in 1946 he returned to Head Office to tackle the adaptation of wartime discoveries and techniques to the civil and export markets. He then rose successively to be managing director of the subsidiaries, to technical director, where his grasp of the firm's affairs—and his own skilled manœuvring—made him logical choice for the managing director when the former man (and last member of the family) retired in 1956.

Year	Post	Gross Salary	Salary after Tax	Salary after Tax at 1938 prices (rounded off)
		£	£	£
1936	Research Assistant	400	369	390
1938	Development Engineer (central planning)	600	548	550
1940	Assistant Chief Engineer	850	677	550
1942	Chief Engineer (A Works)	1,200	819	540
1944	Works Manager (B Works)	2,000	1,265	790
1945	,, ,, (C Works)	2,500	1,465	900
1946	Head Office Manager (Development & Planning)	3,500	1,994	1,175
1948	Managing Director, subsidiaries	5,000	·2,660	1,370
1949	Director (Technical)	6,000	2,945	1,475
1951	,, ,,	7,000	3,046	1,370
1952	,, ,,	8,000	3,153	1,340
1954	,, ,,	10,000	3,687	1,500
1956	Managing Director	15,000	4,516	1,700
1957	,, ,,	15,000	5,031	1,850
1960	,, ,,	20,000	6,567	2,190

4. SIR JAMES TYCOON

James Tycoon entered a big steel firm as a young metallurgist with a reputation in 1934; he was twenty-five, 1st Science Tripos, and a D.Sc., and a blue for hockey. Within two years he had invented a new magnesium steel of infinite importance, especially in war, and was made research manager; he then married the daughter of the then chairman of directors. This did not win him immediate promotion; and to everyone's horror, including his wife's, he promptly joined a bigger steel firm, and took over all its armaments' research. This firm lent him to the Admiralty in 1940 but continued to pay him, so with the combined salary his income (exclusive of his wife's) was £2,000. His work saved thousands of men's lives at sea. In 1944 his firm paid him more on his promise not to go to U.S.A. permanently after the war; he was knighted. In 1945 he was back in industry, and became managing director of his firm in 1949. In 1951 he was a major figure in the steel nationalization fight; and by skilful hiving off, saved his firm from being nationalized; he won a seat in the 1951 election as a Conservative. He joined several other boards of smaller steel firms not nationalized. With denationalization his directorships increased to seven.

Year	Post	Gross Salary	Salary after Tax	Salary after Tax at 1938 prices (rounded off)
		£	£	£
1934	Metallurgist in Steel Firm	300	284	300
1936	Research Manager	700	621	650
1938	Joins new firm; Armaments Research Dept.	1,300	1,123	1,123
1940	Lent to Admiralty	2,000	1,435	1,170
1944	Promises to return to firm after war	3,000	1,653	1,030
1945	Research Director	3,500	1,822	1,110
1947	Technical Director of Group	5,000	2,581	1,410
1949	Managing Director of firm	8,000	3,395	1,700
1951	Joins boards of non-nationalized firms	12,000	3,742	1,680
1956	Chairman	20,000	5,044	1,900
1957	,,	20,000	5,561	2,040
1960	,,	20,000	6,620	2,200

5. SIR AUBREY BLOODSUCKER

Sir Aubrey reached his fortieth birthday in 1932. He rose steadily in the service, and by 1947, at fifty-five, was a pillar of the revenue and advised the government on 15 new forms for dealing with expense allowances which netted over £937,000 in extra tax for the Revenue. He has therefore got to the top, where his position may be compared with that of the recipients of the 15 forms.

Year	Post	Gross Salary	Salary after Tax	Salary after Tax at 1938 prices (rounded off)
		£	£	£
1932	Higher Grade Inspector	900	817	850
1936	Senior Inspector	1,020	933	980

1939	„ „	1,100	980 app.	950
1941	Principal	1,200	832	590
1943	„	1,500	999	630
1947	Deputy Chief	2,250	1,460	800
1952	Chief Inspector	2,750	1,753	750
1956	„ „	8,000 (inc. pension of 1,375) }	3,516	1,330
1957	„ „	8,000 inc. pension }	3,919	1,440

NOTES

1. Beard, Miriam, *A History of the Business Man*, op. cit., p. 684.
2. Cf. 'The Bountiful World of Royal Dutch Shell', *Fortune*, September 1957.
3. Schumpeter, J. A., *Capitalism, Socialism and Democracy*, op. cit., p. 160.
4. *The British Manufacturer*, April, 1957.
5. Royal Commission on the Civil Service, *Minutes of Evidence of the Association of First Division Civil Servants* (24 May 1954). H.M.S.O., 1954, p. 182.
6. Cf. Jaques, E., *Measurement of Responsibility*, London, Tavistock Publications, 1956, pp. 123 ff.
7. Royal Commission on the Civil Service, op. cit.
8. *The Times*, 17 June 1956.
9. *Business*, April 1952.
10. *The Economist*, 27 September 1957, and cf. Lord Simon of Wythenshawe, *The Boards of Nationalized Industries*, London, Longmans, Green, 1957, pp. 31, 32.
11. *Financial Times*, 27 January 1956.
12. Hamilton, Sir Patrick, 'Remuneration of Directors', British Institute of Management Conference, Harrogate, November 1951.
13. Ibid.
14. *The Economist*, 28 January 1956.
15. *Business*, January and March 1956.
16. *Business*, April 1955 and March 1956.
17. *Business*, March 1956.
18. Cf. Copeman, George, *Promotion and Pay for Executives*, Batsford, 1957, p. 31.
19. *Financial Times*, 29 August 1956.
20. *Evening Standard*, 16 March 1956.
21. 'Fringe Benefits for Executives', *Management Abstracts*, June 1956.
22. *The Director*, November 1954.

CHAPTER XII

Living With The Business Man

'Seest thou a man diligent in his business? He shall stand before kings.'

PROVERBS, xxii, 29

'Let no man then grudg Marchant's state
Nor wishe him any ill
But pray to God our Queene to saue,
And Marchants state help still.'

The Marchants Avizo, 1589

SOME READERS MAY FEEL at this stage that the composite portrait of the business man which emerges from these pages is an unendearing one. It makes him neither heroic nor lovable; it shows him respectable but not always perfectly straight; efficient but ruthless; a man of foresight, but also a man of tenaciously guarded secrets; an originator, an innovator, even a revolutionary—yet in general a dull dog. A busy man, with less and less time (as Sombart gloomily reported before World War I) for nature, art, literature, politics or friends. A man, often enough, with a high moral tone, even a high sense of mission —but a mission, in the last analysis, to mould other men into a pattern of his own, to force his values, as business life has developed them, on the industrial-commercial-technological society which his kind has done so much to create. A man who, though savagely taxed, contrives to do pretty well for himself, financially and in terms of social esteem. Some top executives may say that such a piece of impressionism is an unrecognizable boardroom portrait in general, as it certainly is of Mr This and Sir That in particular; we readily concede it does less than justice to the variety and even sometimes eccentricity of the individuals who make up the British boardroom élite. We have, however, made some attempt to find out what business men are like, and now the problem is to work out how to live with them. For even those who feel that the business man, the commercial spirit, is an evil, must recognize that he is a necessary evil so long as Britain expects a doubling of its standard of life in twenty-five years.

1. NECESSARY EVIL

Some socialists have not quite grasped this. When in 1956 Mr Gaitskell came out with the scheme for the State to participate in the control of large private businesses by buying up such substantial shareholdings as would enable them to nominate State directors to their boards, the fundamentalists of the party cried out for 'old-fashioned nationalization'; Mr Bevan attacked the new doctrine—now embodied in official party policy—on the grounds that nobody knew how the new State directors would behave, nor where they would come from (fairly sensible doubts). To this wing of the party, the business man's continuing existence betrays the high ideals of socialism by encouraging the acquisitive instinct and hence they feel that, by perpetuating the business man's way of life, they are serving Mammon.

What this dwindling fundamentalist minority failed to realize is that there may be no choice to make. Even if they do not desire to double their own standard of life and could persuade the majority to agree to put spiritual things first and the lure of advertising second—which the 1959 election showed to be impossible—there remains the hard fact that Britain cannot in the foreseeable future opt out of the productivity race. Though man does not live by bread alone, the British people, to an increasing extent, must live by the proceeds of their industry and commerce. A country which grows barely a third of its food (and a far smaller proportion of its bread alone), which has but one major raw material, of which production is tending to fall, which is likely to meet increasingly severe competition for exports, and which is running short of art treasures to hock, must live by honest business.

It is the tragedy of socialists that this truism has become so much more obvious than in the days when the party was founded upon the hope of nationalizing the means of production, distribution and exchange; in those simple, far-off times, Britain *was* an island built on coal and surrounded by fish—and besides had a colossal private income from investments and hardly any debts. Now Britain must live not merely by what it makes and sells to the customer at home but above all to the customer overseas. Moreover, this country's position in the world is such that it must run pretty hard merely to stay in the same place. All British assumptions on becoming yet more opulent, while contributing to the defence of the free world, are based on the proposition that not only will British production continue to be even more vigorously expanded by investment and increased efficiency, but also will continue to compete successfully in world markets: in short, that the nation will continue to be good at business.

Producing efficiently is hard enough, but selling is even more so, for exporting requires not merely competitive prices and quick delivery, not only superior salesmanship and organized after-sales services, but an entrepreneurial capacity to break into new markets, to create new wants in older markets, to bring off skilled deals in a world which does not think it owes the British workman a living. 'We have to be servants where we were the masters,' said one merchant to the authors. 'There's no standing on dignity, either. We've got to go back to the seventeenth century for our examples. If the customer wants candy-floss we've got to supply it, cheaply, quickly and attractively presented, otherwise *we* don't eat dinner.' There must thus be an aggressive and adventurous salesmanship which can persuade the overseas customer that British atomic piles, *et al.*, are the ones he must have. But if business men are to compete successfully abroad, they say, they must be able to try out their ideas at home. They must practise selling their baubles as well as their marine boilers to the home-grown native. The manufacturer in a mass-production industry who is to sell at competitive prices abroad will want a large, and this may mean unrestricted, market at home to help carry his overheads. British business men scout the idea of special-izing exclusively in exports, like the Japanese. If we are to sell well, they say, we must *all* live well, work hard, be thoroughly industrialized and Americanized and export a run-on from domestic lines.

It follows from this argument that whether or not there is an alterna-tive to the exporter and overseas salesman, full of adventurousness, flexibility and aggression and paid the rate for a vitally important job, if any alternative is to be found, it must have these qualities. Further, *if* the business man is to be kept, but merely to be controlled, civilized, made 'accountable' for the results of his demonic energies,[1] the process of reform must not destroy in him these demonic powers. What might at a pinch be possible in America, Russia, China or India is just not possible in Britain. Thoughtful business men have taken comfort from this for a long time.

2. ALTERNATIVES TO THE ENTREPRENEUR

Socialists, too, are beginning to realize it—indeed they seem, at least temporarily, to have abandoned their attempts to find an alternative to the business man—it is the export problem that has become one of the major stumbling-blocks of the socialist ideal. There is now an increasing aversion to saying that anything and everything can be nationalized, partly because it is so plain that the time is rapidly coming when further nationalization would involve the State in the export business. Mr Crosland remarked cogently:

> There is a wealth of difference between selling cars or electrical goods in a highly competitive export market and selling coal or electricity in a monopoly home market; and it is not clear that the routine type of management which appears to be characteristic of centralized public boards, suitable though it may be for the basic utilities, would be flexible and dynamic enough for this quite different task.[2]

This, most exporters will agree, is putting it mildly. But if public enterprise is unsuitable for the really hard jobs, much of the socialist's case for nationalization goes by the board in a hard world of hard-faced foreigners.

It is a far cry now to the prewar days when Lord (then Mr) Attlee could seriously write 'in socialized industry all alike will be animated by a common motive—the public spirit.'[3] Even in 1945 socialists somehow thought that public boards would exceed in wisdom and enterprise the ruck of business men.

> 'They were to be staffed by selfless men of outstanding ability, devoted to the national interest. We assumed that such men were to be found in large numbers; naturally they had no chance to come forward in the degenerate capitalist era in which we were living. We also assumed that the workers in the industries would be transformed ... Thus a combination of selfless management and selfless workers would bring about the brave new world of socialism.[4]

The disillusionment in the years 1945–51 was very heavy, and there were some sad moments when state directors were thought to lack wisdom at critical moments when large national assets abroad were at stake. The State owned just over 50 per cent of Anglo-Iranian's equity but, though nothing can be known for certain, it is widely rumoured among oilmen that the Treasury representation on the board of that concern at the time of the Abadan crisis was the most unrelenting and determined to hang on for unattainable terms; nor has anyone revealed that, before the crisis developed, the Treasury directors vainly begged the business men for a better public relations policy in Tehran, lack of which so greatly contributed to the débâcle.

If business men must be retained for the export side of national economic activity, it is clear that a large part of industry must remain in the 'private sector' and—what will be particularly irritating to socialists—doing the job of jobs that requires a very fat expense account. It is no use trying to get an oil concession out of a visiting Sheikh or an order for three refrigerated ships out of a visiting Latin-American business tycoon on the sort of luncheon vouchers which the Treasury permits higher civil servants; something considerably more *recherché*, requiring an extensive and costly investigation of London's night life will probably be expected. Where State money is massed behind a single new product, such as atomic energy, the advantage gained by the technicians and scientists may seem likely to set off any deficiencies in salesmanship by public enterprise; but it has yet to be seen whether State enterprise will be successful on the sales side. It competes, or it will compete, with the Yanks; there seems every reason to assume that the American business man will take special pleasure in skinning the British nationalized exporting industry. Socialists must face the fact that even when they have abolished their own home-grown capitalists, they will still face the foreign variety: the terrible Zurich bankers, for example, who, every incoming Chancellor of the Exchequer is warned, hold sterling in the hollow of their hands.[5] Until the whole world is socialist, there will be scant respite for the British Labour Party from business efficiency and competition.

The Labour Party's present view seems to be that, valuable though nationalization on the classical model may be, or rather may have been, for particular industries, it provides no general answer to the problem of bringing a socialist way of life to these islands. This disillusionment with nationalization among those who supported it stems from two main causes. The first is simply that, on the facts given above, there is no evidence that nationalized industries can beat the business man at his own game, or yet play it as well, even in the home market—any more than there is any evidence that the co-ops can beat the profit-making departmental stores and chains.[6] The second is really the crueller blow to the idealists: nationalization has not brought with it the social, as opposed to the merely materialistic, advantages on which even greater hopes were pinned. People do not work differently or feel happier because they are working for a public board. Many of those who are doing so in fact would rather work for a wicked capitalist[7] saying that then, at least, they knew who was the boss.

From the worker's point of view there are almost as many disadvantages as advantages to nationalization. Unionists admit that having a trade unionist on the board means having a director who knows a hundred ways of saying No that a man who has spent his life on the management side would never know. Further, the joint machinery set up for negotiation and joint consultation has proved very cumbersome. The burden of trying to be fair to thousands of workers, interpreted usually as providing similar conditions of work, has in fact not only produced long and frustrating delays while requests go through tiers of joint committees, but has also made it hard to meet local wishes when these, though reasonable in themselves, might be used as an argument for a national claim.

The disillusionment with nationalization is one reason for the change in Labour Party policy. Another is the feeling among socialist intellectuals that the sting has already been withdrawn from the capitalists' tail. Mr Roy Jenkins, for example, has said:

> A classical Marxist clash is not possible in a situation in which, before it takes place, the President of the National Union of Mineworkers is already more powerful than any six capitalists.[8]

This realization has at the same time further weakened in the minds of many socialists the appeal of 'workers' control' as an alternative to boards of directors of the present type.* Syndicalist ideas linger in the minds of some of the rank and file. There is still a minority of younger fundamentalists in the party who would remove the 'insiders' from the boards both of nationalized and of big private industry, without much consideration, whether or not a board elected by the workpeople could run them successfully.[9]

An alternative to nationalization is State shareholding, the emphasis shifting to participation in capital appreciation rather than control. Profits are morally wrong; but not when the State participates in them. Business men have proved highly antipathetic to this. Yet if a State shareholding in their companies makes profits respectable at last, they should be extremely thankful to have it, for they are always complaining that socialist misunderstanding of the nature of profit makes for endless trouble between the two sides of industry. The Labour Party has even agreed that the State should not actually appoint

---

* The boards of the nationalized industries are appointed by the Minister and are not representative of any particular interest although one member is chosen for his trade union experience. The T.U.C. decided as long ago as 1944 that direct representation would jeopardize their independence for they would, for instance, then find it hard to quarrel with the Board's policy on wages.

directors in the firms it buys shares in, but it should follow the example of the big insurance companies which do not interfere with the direction or management except when their interests as shareholders are threatened. This may simply mean that the State as shareholders will be interested in profits and little else, which Mr Gaitskell would be the first to condemn, but which business men will find quite normal.

Thoughtful business men in Britain are now much less alarmed by the prospect of State shareholding than they used to be, or than their opposite numbers would be in America. They have noticed that in Germany something like 37 per cent of the share capital of industry was state owned by 1952,[10] yet the top German business men seem as little inhibited in their business decisions, or in their affluent way of life, by this state shareholding as by the fact that a third of the Aufsichtsrat which appoints them formally consist of workers' representatives. The State can no more participate in day-to-day executive decisions than the workers; and those who make the executive decisions will always enjoy the real power—especially as the object of policy in large concerns is almost invariably expansion which equally suits the State as rentier and the worker as drawer of wages and beneficiary of fringe-benefits.

The great mistake socialists perpetrate—and seem likely to continue doing so by the very nature of their philosophy—is failure to understand the nature of industrial strain; and in this they are at least as ignorant as company directors. Bitterness in nationalized industries is not merely the result of past history, though that must long remain as a millstone round the neck of management. Nor is it simply the question of size and impersonality; though that adds to the difficulty of handling labour. It is the fact that 'handling labour' means that the organization is necessarily divided into 'we' and 'they'. It does not matter that work-people are working for the public good in coal, or power, or telegraphs. The fact remains that there are organizers and organized, the first-named being 'they' and the latter, of course, 'we'. It is perfectly possible to get people to understand that they must be organized; and it is true that people want to be organized. It is also a normal perversity of human nature that this nevertheless means that 'we' are often against 'them'. Joint consultation, formally or informally, and good communications are, of course, sheet anchors of management, nationalized or not, in 'labour relations'; and they must remain so. The constant effort to bridge the gap between management and workers must go on; but it is not a problem that can be solved permanently, for it is a permanent problem like growing-up or dying. It produces strikes and every trouble known to management short of strikes (and there are many) even in the most enlightened firms—for a completely harmonious and democratic organization is impossible just as a paternalistic one is obsolete.*

> 'You think you're a democrat, Robert,' says a consultant to a managing director, in a recent study of a strike, 'just because you're prepared to let your chaps talk back while you listen—but you're not, for the simple reason that democracy can only be practised among one's peers. Your council is really a family council . . . everyone's entitled to speak, but old Daddy Dawlish makes the laws.'[11]

He who gets rid of the business man, thinking to get rid of the friction which comes from organization itself, is indeed a dreamer. Doing so may get rid of the entrepreneur, the profits, the new ideas, and the dynamism; but it does not get rid of industrial society, which must continue to be run by the power-loving, infinitely committee-minded 'organization man'. He, of course, could very well be a socialist. Here, indeed, through the boards of nationalized industries, is an avenue for the envious, angry outsiders to become powerful, happy insiders.

It is possible that more use in State industry might be made of the experience and traditions of the civil service. Contrary to belief, civil servants from the higher grades often make good directors of large firms. Businesses take them. Moreover, the civil service is changing. In the past its whole bent, as has been pointed out,[12] was regulative, not executive, but this is, to some extent, passing; the growing role of the State as an executive and administrative organ, in conditions of cradle-to-grave welfare, is giving to higher civil servants of the present generation a new training. They no longer distrust the telephone on the grounds that callers who can speak to them directly might prompt them to make decisions without due consideration. Certainly the arduous life of the higher civil servant in the past ten years cannot be matched by any but the most hard-working of company directors. The higher civil service is, however, small. Nor can it supply certain requirements of push-and-go, and certainly not of salesmanship, for which commerce calls. Even the civil servants' knowledge of State trading, though growing, is limited.

---

* The nearest approach to perfect management-labour relations we have seen is recorded in a case history of Henry H. Payne Ltd., in *Persuasion*, Winter, 1948–9.

The Russians, of course, seem to have produced a breed of socialist managers and directors, to whose efficiency the recent triumphs of Russian technology must in some degree be attributed. They offer one alternative model for those who want to develop efficient organizers. Their methods are, it is reported, ruthless schooling by means of self-criticism, by suppression of personal thought and feeling, and by disciplinary methods which have few counterparts elsewhere and are based on their own laboratory work on human psychology.[13]

To alternatives of this kind the trade unionists themselves may well decide to object. They may well feel that it is one thing to negotiate with British business men, educated at Eton or even at an L.C.C. secondary school, or with employers' federations composed of such men; quite another to deal with State directors and managers cast in the Russian mould. Besides, the strength of the trade unions is now very great; to erect a monolithic employing organization opposite to it would hardly seem in the trade unions' interest. It is not absurd to suggest that the erosion of capitalism will be slowed down at the point at which the trade unions feel that it is losing them their independence of action. It is far from certain that the trade union boss will not come to the rescue of the big business boss. A little more nationalization, a little more State participation in industry, may bring such an alliance perceptibly nearer.

3. HOW MUCH EQUALITY?

Though the foregoing considerations suggest that the business man will survive, partly because the anti-business idealists have no complete alternative, partly because other interests, including the trade unions, are more and more inclined to agree with Professor Hayek that an official's little finger is thicker than any business man's loins, and the road to serfdom runs over Crichel Down, a good many questions remain to be answered. To the business man, the most important of these is just how far the process of nationalization and State shareholding might go under a new Labour government: just how large the 'private sector' is to be in the end. Will he be left with any public companies at all; will radical socialist ideas set the frontier of private enterprise at the private company with its fifty shareholders.[14]

The next is what degree of freedom the business man will be given in that sector. The process of making the business man into a socially accountable agent of national policy is, after all, capable of going a great deal further, and many socialist writers have been giving this problem a lot of thought. As some of them see it, the object of policy ought to be not the abolition of the business man, but his transformation.

> What will be at issue is, in the first place, whether capitalists . . . should be allowed to retain the quite substantial portion of their privileges which still remain to them; and, in the second place, whether the society which is growing out of capitalism is to be a participant, democratic socialist society or whether it is to be a managerial society controlled by a privileged élite enjoying a standard of living substantially different from that of the mass of the population.[15]

It is, in fact, the privileges and comforts of the boardroom which worry this school of business critics.

> The essentials to be achieved are that a pattern of ownership compatible with the abolition of great fortunes should be worked out and that control over the rewards of the managers should be firmly in the hands of those whose natural interests are opposed to privilege, *except insofar as such privilege is strictly necessary to the success of the economy*. (Our italics.)[16]

This indeed is the problem. Most business men, as we have seen, consider that they would regard such 'privileges' as they have as a bare minimum. As is well known, the privileges accorded to the managers of Russian State plants are very considerable indeed, and very profoundly affect the output of the plants concerned. The basic salary, though far higher than the average, is not the whole income; premiums are also awarded based on the plant's performance and graded according to the degree of managerial responsibility. The premium is very large and adds substantially to the income of top Russian executives, and if it is badly adjusted, so that, for example, the management makes a larger income by producing too many or too few spare parts, then patriotism will not ensure that the correct quantity is made to the detriment of managerial income. Nor do they work the plant flat out, only to find that their 'norm' has been raised for the following year; but on the contrary always keep plenty in hand; a system which not only minimizes trouble with headquarters but also maximizes premiums.

In their hogging of perks—'blat and zis!'—they behave very like the capitalist of the more splenetic socialist dreams. They reveal that under socialism as under capitalism, the social goals of management are a high standard of living, prestige, power and authority; in short, privilege.[17]

The British business man's rate for the job may well be, taking like with like, rather less than the Russian's, but what that rate is nobody quite knows. Are the conservatives right when they speak of the enterprise and production lost as the result of the disincentive effects of taxation, or are the socialists right when they say that the boss gets so much that he would probably work as well, if not better, if there were more equality of reward? Business men with whom we have spoken in general declare that they would not work harder if they got more money. In private, many admit that the disincentive effects of taxation are overrated; executives work, in large part, for the other rewards—which in some respects correspond to Russian premiums—which top positions command; and indeed this is also true under the far less oppressive American tax burden.[18] They do exhibit a reluctance, apparently, to take on extra tasks at present tax levels; according to Dr Copeman, one director of many companies declared that he would only take on another directorship 'if it meant mixing with interesting people', another said he would only do so for the sake of the friendship of the chairman who offered it, a third would put out more effort only for a ballet company.[19]

It is still harder to get any clear answer to the hypothetical question, 'Would you work less hard if taxation were raised?' The whole trend of the discussion suggests, however, that if personal taxation were increased there would be a rapid further growth of other incentives, such as love of power and status symbols, which may well be socially less desirable. Mr R. H. S. Crossman has discussed[20] the need for greater equality of rewards and more parity of esteem between those receiving different rewards; but sociologists apparently find that greater equality of rewards may, with the encouragement it gives to other incentives, lead actually to less parity of esteem. As the standard of life in a community grows, access by everyone to plentiful, durable consumer goods produces one outward and visible form of social equality now quite noticeable in America; this would certainly be the British business man's solution of the problem of social equality.

Though the disincentive effects of high taxation in the boardroom may be exaggerated, it has other disadvantages. For example, it may cause enterprising young men, who might otherwise have devoted their energies to raising the British workman's living standards, to emigrate to countries where it is easier to become very rich. It also encourages people at the top to divert their energies from organizing efficient production into tax avoidance. It leads to fiddling of expense accounts and to the highly inegalitarian difference between the Haves, with scope to fiddle, and the Have-Nots who cannot fiddle, either because they have not reached a high enough grade, or because they are in the wrong department,* or because they work in a company that does not provide sufficient latitude for 'minimizing tax'.

Social philosophers may properly discuss the ideals of equality, and consider whether we should aim for greater equality of opportunity or, as Mr Crossman and others would prefer, for greater equality of rewards and parity of esteem. But even if it be decided that the levelling of incomes is desirable, in a strictly business context practical difficulties obtrude themselves. If the business man is given any freedom at all then—as all history goes to show—he will use it to make money; and *a priori* having more business sense than the rest of us, he will find ways round every barrier and therefore tend to make more money or enjoy a higher standard of life than other people.

4. IMPROVING THE BUSINESS MAN

The points made in some of the preceding chapters, moreover, may suggest that the adjustment of the business man's reward—in terms of money, perks, prestige, authority and so on—to get the best result out of him may well be almost as complex a calculation as that of adjusting the incentives of the Russian plant manager. Both carrot and stick may be used, but in what combination? A régime of high and progressive taxation and creeping inflation, for example, provides a greater carrot for entrepreneurs like Mr Charles Clore to exercise their talents, than for a young engineer to build up a great firm from the purchase of a

* Such as Research and Development.

single second-hand machine and its installation in his own backyard.*
The continual emphasis on size of organization means that the rewards
go to the men who know best the arts of top businessmanship. It is,
further, very difficult to develop a really keen sense of holiness of competition in this country, by applying the stick with an Act of Parliament,
when almost everybody, including the trade unions, is so deeply opposed
to 'breaking his neighbour's rice-bowl', in the Chinese phrase. Finally,
the point must be made that, even if by Acts of Parliament trade associations and so forth are made relatively unholy, it is difficult for the
business man to do his job enthusiastically in an atmosphere of moral
disapproval. Can Britain demand a continually higher standard of life
and at the same time denigrate those who are expected to organize the
increase? Modern psychology suggests that all human beings need a
little love if they are to give of their best—and perhaps this is true of
the boardroom, as well as of the bench. Ought not the industrial
psychologists to turn their attention towards this problem?

Business men may concede that before the war too little attention
was given to workpeople's feelings. Some now wryly declare that the
pendulum has swung too far, that they are human too, and need
encouragement. What the boss sometimes resents more than penal
taxation is the lack of recognition of the importance and difficulty of
his job. Optimism is an essential business trait; but how can the British
business man be as optimistic as business life demands (especially in
the export market) if he is discussed rather as the colonial empire is
discussed—a leftover to be liquidated according to a time-table? Such
an argument leads, of course, in the opposite direction of producing
an American system, a dynamic society in which the business man and
the business system commands immense social approval, and, enjoying
this sense of social approval, in a moderately competitive system,
delivers an extremely high standard of life to his fellow-Americans.
But for reasons which we have examined, no such whole-hearted approval for the American way of business life is likely to be accorded
here.

Instead, the problem of giving the British business man a measure
of recognition to keep him efficient, while reserving the power to chastise
him when necessary, has been explored rather along the lines of making
business a profession. As we have seen, in this attempt a great effort
has been made to take over American management techniques without

---

* Now in any case discouraged by vigilant health and planning authorities.

taking over other features of American business life. The British Productivity Council has laboured long not only to promote the application of the lessons learnt by the various productivity teams which visited America, but also to stimulate interest in management through local joint productivity committees. Certainly British boards of directors have become much more management conscious than before the war. They tell shareholders so.[21] There is plenty of worthy talk about 'professional management'. Yet it is difficult, however, hard one tries, to be enthusiastic about the achievement. It is all too plain that the British Institute of Management arouses little positive response. Useful as a clearing-house for management information, it has failed to be a spearhead for management proficiency.

The government has encouraged the development of management courses and has helped to establish the Diploma in Management Studies which is taught at the technical colleges. But not even managers take it very seriously and directors look down on all such uplift benevolently from a great height. Along with the official diploma have sprung up a variety of short management courses, which British industry likes better; these have been painstakingly indexed by the B.I.M. in an impressive handbook; but no attempt has been made—the first thing a respectable academic body would do—to assess their worth. Scepticism prevails. For purposes of public relations, the professional status of management may be vaguely promulgated, but the hard-headed view of it in British business was defined by *The Economist*:

> The majority of British top executives are not convinced that the results to date have shown that managers can be made or that management is a science which can be swotted out of books or attested in examinations. The idea of a diploma is for them, mostly selfmade men, the final absurdity. It is indeed quite possible that many of them would fail the final examinations, which range from functional factory organisation to higher cost control.[22]

Even the managerial salariat is in the profit-making game, most boards of directors feel. Besides it is certainly not in the board's interest that managers should become professionalized while directors remain 'capitalists'. Nor are all Americans, who draw so heavily upon their business schools for their executives, great believers in a status which takes the entrepreneurial sting out of business.

> ... any serious attempt to make management 'scientific' or a 'profession' is bound to lead to the attempt to eliminate those 'disturbing

261

nuisances', the unpredictabilities of business life—its risks, its ups and downs, its 'wasteful competition', the 'irrational choices' of the consumer—and, in the process, the economy's freedom and its ability to grow.[23]

British boardrooms in fact are full of amateurs who still dislike the idea of management becoming a profession. Would—or will—a highly professionalized, and perhaps trade unionized, cadre of managers operating both State and private industry and trade provide the exports, the annual rises in productivity, the growth of welfare, that the nation anticipates? They might be wonderful organizers, they might be respectable and non-profit-making, but would they actually *sell* things? Peter Drucker, looking at the big American firms, concludes that 'on the whole it looks very much as if "integrated" business education tends to make a man unfit to be an entrepreneur by paralysing his intellectual muscles'.[24] Looking at British industry, Professor Sargant Florence opined:

> My own belief is that flair remains an essential element in top management decisions, but that, especially in the smaller firms, reliance on flair is still too absolute where some scientific knowledge and method can be used to correct sources of inefficiency.[25]

This is perhaps the authentic note of a British compromise; not too much of the organization man at the top—but a little bit more of him at the bottom. However the balance may be struck, the conclusion is plain. The entrepreneur is a less pleasant person than the manager, but a prosperous Britain will need him as well as the smooth, mature manager, trained not only in all the 'tools of management' but also in 'human relations'. Business is often not nice, but there are not wanting economists, like Professor John Jewkes, who would like to make it a great deal nastier; who would thrust the directors even more deeply into the jungle of cut-throat competition. The further issue, which this book must leave open for wider discussion in the light of what we know about business men and their motives, is just what degree of *laisser-faire*, and what combination of incentives, privileges and discipline will induce the business man to serve the nation to the required extent.

But one thing can be said about the possibility of making business 'nicer' and more humane. So long as the fruit of dynamic progress is desired—and by desired we do *not* necessarily mean desirable in religious or philosophical terms—so long as it is *desired*, its price must indubitably be paid. It must be paid in the overturning of established positions, in the disappointment of expectations, in the uprooting of workpeople from habitual techniques, workplaces and communities, and of managers from restful routines, in the constant competitive chivying of the inefficient (by work-study standards) through every rank of production.

Any reforms aimed at evading payment of that price can succeed only by braking and strangling economic progress, and this is true whether such reforms are imposed from outside by law and counter-vailing power, or are embodied in a professional code, or prompted by individually tender consciences or sympathies. It can be otherwise, however, with reforms which accept the price; which aim not at block-ing change but at easing it, and trying more equitably to distribute its social costs. The featherbedding of workers is an example of the anti-dynamic, if humane, 'niceness' in business; generous severance pay, of the kind which British business men refused when suggested as far back as 1923, is an example of the less anti-dynamic reform. The test for social policies, for those who want dynamic change in a dynamic world—business men who certainly do, trade unionists who vaguely do, legislators who feel that Britain must export or die—should always be the effect on dynamic progress.

5. DATE WITH DESTINY

This may be a general conclusion with which to leave the general reader. But is it enough for the business man? It is hardly to be expected that he will be particularly satisfied with the prospect as we have indicated it. It promises at most a grudging acceptance, the status of necessary nuisance. A little more thought, however, may suggest that in the very ambiguity of the public's and the politicians' attitude to the business man, in the uncertainty whether he is to be turned into a State nominee or told to take more leaves out of the Americans' book, in the equivocal position he holds, there is opportunity. There is something in it for every type of business man, even the entrepreneur in the old sense.

Clearly substantial pickings await the man climbing to the top in all forms of enterprise; and the growth of nationalized industry, the gradual march of arteriosclerosis in their boards, promise safe billets at the top for the self-important mediocrities.* 'The last stage of capitalism', as some socialists describe the present state of affairs,[26] may, after all, prove to be extremely prolonged. Indeed, it may well prove very convenient for Labour governments of the future to prolong it indefinitely. Business men may be with confidence recommended to study this phrase, and all the possibilities inherent in it for making the world safe for business men. For one thing, it is a wonderful face-saver for socialists who have doubts about the milk-of-the-word doctrine of nationalization; to their supporters they can say, 'We are in the last stages of capitalism; don't rush; everything is now evolving naturally into socialism without loss of efficiency or unnatural breaks which might impair the export trade or endanger our small reserves of sterling and gold.' To the Russians (and to idealistic left-wingers in Asia and elsewhere) they can equally say, 'Stop calling us rude names; we are in the last stage of capitalism, and we are ahead of you in evolving a new and happier society.' Coming from the Foreign Office this should be very effective, and particularly helpful to the boards of large companies involved in oil and mining developments overseas.

Among business men there are very real advantages in being able to dodge to and from professional status. Since the public is in two minds about business, at one moment emphasis on the scientific approach of management as a 'service' is likely to be right; at another time it will be best placed on 'enterprise'. Moreover, when the discreditable side of entrepreneurship gets publicity it will be possible to say that such things belong to the dying capitalistic past. The failings of large firms can be the occasion for homilies on the need for old-fashioned 'flair', and the misdeeds of small firms for reassurances about the steady march of professional management. In this way, reasonable scope will be preserved for business. So, too, will be a reasonable amount of competition. The importance of competition can be urged when the State shows signs of taking over too much of the private sector; on the other hand, the growth of State shareholding should enable business men to prevent further legislation on the lines of the Monopolies and Restrictive Practices Act. State directors are to a man likely to be against this sort of thing, and readily to join hands with the National Union of Manufacturers in opposing it. Their advent, the ordinary business man may be expected to realize presently, would be by no means

* Management consultants are beginning to talk of the 'Law of Maximum Mediocrity' akin to the second law of thermodynamics which operates in very large organizations, nationalized or not.

an unmitigated disaster. On the contrary, his job is to assimilate the State director into the genial atmosphere of top business circles. All in all, the last stage of capitalism, properly managed, could be a great deal pleasanter for the individual capitalist than was the first.

The translation of all this into some sort of generally agreed big business policy will need thought. The hand must not be overplayed, nor must too much be expected. It would be unwise for company directors to think that under a Labour government, for example, any further concessions on surtax are to be anticipated; on the contrary, some sort of *démarche* against expense accounts must probably be faced as a necessary matter of political window-dressing. But in general it is to this kind of atmosphere that public relations policy should be attuned, and the shaping of individual business careers should be adjusted. The concluding portion of this essay will glance at the problem thus posed for the individual and for the boardroom as a whole.

The boards of big business, and the executives of trade associations and bodies like the Institute of Directors, the Iron and Steel Federation or the F.B.I. have to decide just how far to resist further political interference in business, considered as a national institution. They have little, obviously, to fear from further nationalization for some years. But their own experiences should have indicated that they cannot make or oppose government policies. It is not just the history of the past fifteen years, but of the past 150,[27] that should teach the business man that if a political party is determined to pass legislation of which he disapproves, it will be passed—however many memorials he sends to Downing Street, however many times he takes politicians out to champagne lunches, and however many acres of newspaper space he purchases. In the 1959 election campaign, the business campaigns in favour of free enterprise proved useful auxiliaries to the professional big battalions of the Conservative party, and the fact that they were regarded as allowable trade expenses will always permit industrialists to indulge in them to the tune of £1,400,000. But they would have failed if the electorate had decided to vote the government out of office on any other set of grievances (as it looked like doing only 18 months previously). They were rowing with the tide. If the 'Mr Cube' and 'Mr Ingot' type of business public relations campaign is to make democracy safe for business men it will have to develop beyond its present penny-farthing stage; and the techniques adopted in the 1959 election campaign suggests that it might. [28]

The whole range of techniques by which American business puts over its basic message—that competitive business is the fundamental institution in a free, dynamic and democratic American way of life—is almost unknown in Europe. This is not merely because British and continental business men are backward in advertising techniques. When a European régime wants to put over a propaganda line it usually proves at least as efficient as Madison Avenue; both Dr Goebbels and British psychological warfare in two world wars can, in their different ways, be cited as evidence. When the aim is clear and the will exists the methods are to hand; but the lack of a clear aim is debilitating. What European business needs is (however much directors may deride it in their clubs) the American sense of mission. They need to think greatly of their function before they can hope to persuade others to do so too. At present British business men have often not got much beyond thinking of it pompously.

The European business man also needs to take a more careful look at what the American business man has already done to ingratiate himself with the public and to live down a not entirely savoury past. The Germans come nearest to this. The British business man, though he clearly now has the advantage that the country has been inocculated against state control, suffers from an almost pathological distaste for criticism. It is charitable to think of him as a man who has gone through one serious operation and dreads going to the doctors lest he be told he is in for another. His case is that of the neurotic individual who because he is not loved is hypersensitive to criticism from which he protects himself; and yet so long as he does this, he presents an unattractive, unlovable façade.

The British business man has got to look a little deeper for his security. He could try to convince the public that there should be no further diminution of the private sector on grounds of democratic policy. One argument is that under capitalism you can always change your job, just as under democracy you can always change your government—but then, it must be made possible to change your job, and Britain must not slide into a permanent Conservative one-party state. The trouble is that the public ascribes its freedom to full employment which it is not yet convinced the bosses like. A similar argument is that in capitalism if you don't like your boss you can go it alone. The weakness of this appeal is that only a minority react so sturdily to the day-to-day tyrannies of office or factory life, and it is further diminished by heavy taxation on those who do. Consumers' choice is another argument: under capitalism you can have the goods you want, even if they are bad for you (unless, of course, they are horror-comics or benzedrine), not what the planners think you should have. In the market-place the individual does count; in the planning and statistics bureau he does not. Again, the weakness here is that the public cannot dream that freedom of consumers' choice is endangered; and in any event it is all too evident that in the welfare state small groups of well-organized fanatics will always be able to remove specific 'evils' from the shopping-list.

The Aims of Industry campaign in favour of private enterprise failed to get very far. Yet the arguments for freedom to choose, whether of goods or of jobs, are strong. They will be strongest, perhaps, when there is a balance between public and private enterprise; the best antidote to nationalization of everything is nationalization of some things. As we have suggested, business men should take advantage of this. The thought that there will be an ever-contracting area of private enterprise, forced by stringent legislation to ever more cut-throat competition, set over against an ever-widening area of public ownership forced by its inefficiency continually to put prices up against private industry, is a formidable one for business men; but there seems reason to think the last stage of capitalism will not be allowed to come to this. Business men rail against nationalized industry for its inefficiency, profligacy and weak concessions to wage demands, yet they should see in this very maladministration a safeguard for them. Let them keep up the shouting—but maintain the contrast. As it is, the railways have no friends. The fight of the private bus companies against nationalization in the last years of the (weakened) Labour government was a striking success just for this reason. It might happen again, even against a future Labour government. But private industry must choose the ground to stand on with great tactical skill.

There is little in this prospect to make the average business man despair in private, whatever views he finds it politic to express in public. The vast majority of business men in any case do not think about the matter at all. Some realize that the present state of affairs will last their time. Many, in any case, are not equipped by nature to think out the dilemma in which as a group they find themselves, or to understand the psychology of other people. Some who do understand, and feel deeply, remain inarticulate for the simple reason that they are inarticulate. This may be thought to place something of a burden on those who feel that the business man should demonstrate to the public, in speech, action, and behaviour, that he fully justifies his existence. Some business men get very worried about this. Why cannot they, why cannot their fellow-directors, impress the public? Why, when they talk, does nobody listen? One answer, perhaps, was given by Sir Frederic Hooper when he said:

> Never before have P.R.O.s laboured so relentlessly to 'personalize' their employers. Yet most people, even those engaged in business, would not find it easy to recall the names of a dozen prominent industrialists. Perhaps the reason is that too many managers, their horizons bounded by office or factory walls, are incapable of developing qualities of leadership to match their widening responsibilities. The most skilful P.R.O. cannot make an engaging personality out of a hermit.[29]

Another business man in similar terms calls his fellows to a positive crusade:

> Why! oh why! hide behind the walls of a factory instead of going through the land as the ambassadors of prosperity, banishing suspicion and doubt from the mind of their employees, by substituting the human and personal for the impersonal attitude and cultivating mutual confidence and respect. To arms, gentlemen! The flag of truce is not for me or you or else we shall surely die![30]

So far there has been little response. The plain fact is that business men are not natural leaders, and rarely rush to arms. They work in secret, they are intensely individualistic—as individualistic as artists—and they have a shrewd suspicion that the less the public sees and hears of them in the flesh, the better they get along. There are small and medium-size firms where the boss is the father of his people, or perhaps leader of an exciting expedition; but this is only one of many faces that the business man wears.

There are, no doubt, as writers on management insist, great opportunities for leadership in manufacturing industry today. They exist because so few top executives, on or off the board, have the insight to consider how differently their workers feel. Many are not just uninterested, but are actually afraid to know. They may be willing to let social research workers question their managers, but for these to try to find out the workers' point of view is considered too explosive. Sometimes an industrial psychologist may be called in to make an 'attitude survey' of the firm's employees, the results of which not infrequently grieve top management deeply, and on occasion have successfully caused the chairman to retire.[31] This is not to suggest that the proper attitude is to abdicate as boss. Paradoxically, the danger today is that managers and directors are afraid to be boss; if they had more self-confidence they would not be scared to know what their workpeople think. In their present unhappy midway position, they can no longer exercise autocracy successfully but lack the genius to exercise democratic bossmanship. Large rewards await the men who master this technique, along with the technique of getting on to the board itself.

Many business men, surveying the outlook, however, will not feel it necessary to put themselves to any such trouble. They will, very properly, decide that, whether the socialists greatly enlarge the area of public enterprise, or develop State holdings in the 500 largest firms, or indeed do something of both, there will always be a niche for the man of business ability with his wits about him and the right contacts. A prominent industrialist, asked what business men in an industry threatened with nationalization should do, replied, 'Get on the committee, boys.' For there is an expanding market for the skilled committee man, the man who is

> . . . well educated, intelligent and good-natured and with an instinctive understanding of people. He is trustworthy, fair, and willing to compromise. He does not seek to dominate and has never been known to insist. He leads, guides and suggests. Persuasion is his method and speech his medium.[32]

Admittedly, this is not a type which all business men like, or a type which necessarily rises to the top in private enterprise, though increasingly it does so; but State industry gives it its real chance. When nationalization impends, different types of business men take different paths. Some sell out profitably to the State, and go into a different business with the proceeds. Others emigrate. But a third group gets in on the ground floor of the new board (or, as would be the case in steel renationalization, boards). During road haulage nationalization, the executives of the firms that handed themselves over voluntarily are believed to have got the best jobs in the B.R.S. hierarchy; these were mostly the firms which were finding competition toughest. However that may be, trade unionists are now often perfectly reconciled to letting the boss continue as boss. 'You've always looked after us pretty well—don't worry, we'll see you're all right when the time comes,' said a trade union official in 1949 to the manager of a steel company who was worried about the effects of nationalization.[33]

There is, in the foreseeable future, plenty of room at the top for business men. 'The business of America is business,' remarked President

Coolidge in a striking phrase about a remarkable era in the history of the United States. Does it not perfectly describe Britain, in terms of its general national objectives today? Notwithstanding all the difficulties, the business man should be able to strike a pretty good bargain with the people who need his services in the long run. His innate abilities will show him how; he need not be recommended any course of reading, which in any case he would not follow. But if this book has indicated one or two directions in which he can advantageously turn his eyes, and put a more effective face upon his dealings with the public and the politicians, it may claim to have done him some modest service.

NOTES

1. Cf. 'The Business Leader as a Daemonic Figure', *American Journal of Economics and Sociology*, Vol. 12, January, 1953.

2. Crosland, C. A. R., *The Future of Socialism*, op. cit., p. 472.

3. Attlee, C. R., *The Will and the Way to Socialism*, Methuen, 1935, p. 110.

4. Kelf-Cohen, R., *Nationalised Industries in Britain*, London, MacMillan, 1958, p. v.

5. Mr Thorneycroft to his constituents, reported in *The Times*, 15 January 1958.

6. 'Meet Mr Smith', Harold Wincott, *Financial Times*, 6 July 1954.

7. Cf. *Future*, June–July, 1950. 'What Do Workers Think?'

8. Jenkins, Roy, 'Equality', Chap. 3, p. 72, of *New Fabian Essays*, ed. Crossman, R. H. S., London, Turnstile Press, 1952.

9. Cf. 'The Insiders' supplement to *Universities and Left Bank Review*, No. 3, Winter 1958.

10. Cf. Winshuh, *op. cit.* p. 159.

11. Clewes, W., *Men at Work*, London, Michael Joseph, 1951.

12. Cf. Kelsall, R. K., *Higher Civil Servants in Britain*, London, Routledge and Kegan Paul, 1955.

13. Cf. Wolfgang Leonhard, 'Life in the Comintern School', *The Observer*, 22 September 1957.

14. Cf. Shore, Peter, 'Capitalism and Equality', *New Statesman and Nation*, 1 and 8 October 1955.

15. Jenkins, Roy, op. cit., p. 72.

16. Ibid, p. 84.

17. Berliner, Joseph S., *Factory and Manager in the U.S.S.R.*, Harvard, 1957, pp. 321 ff.

18. Cf. Fetter, R. B. and Johnson, D. C., *Compensation and Incentives for Industrial Executives*, Indiana University Press, 1952, pp. 55 ff.

19. *The Director*, July 1952.

20. Crossman, R. H. S., ed. *New Fabian Essays*, op. cit., Chap. I, *Towards a Philosophy of Socialism*, p. 29 ff.

21. Cf. Lord Heyworth's Address to Shareholders of Unilever, 1956.

22. 'What Makes a Manager?', *The Economist*, 17 December 1955.

23. Drucker, Peter F., *The Practice of Management*, op. cit., p. 7.

24. Drucker, Peter F., 'The Graduate Business School', *Fortune*, August 1950.

25. Florence, P. Sargant, 'Knowledge, Flair and Tact', *Technology*, March 1957.

26. Cf. Strachey, John, *Contemporary Capitalism*, London, Gollancz, 1956, especially Chap. XIV.

27. Cf. Florence, P. Sargant, *Industry and the State*, London, Hutchinson, 1957, especially pp. 20–22.

28. Butler, D. E., and Rose, R. *The British General Election of 1959*. London, Macmillan, 1960, p. 253ff.

29. *The Director*, January 1957.

30. Willmott, F. B., *The Time for Decision: An Industrialist looks at Life*, London, St Catharine Press, 1953, p. 80.

31. *The Economist*, July 1955.

32. *Future*, June 1950.

33. *Future*, October, 1949.

Appendix

NOTES ON SOURCES

THE PAUCITY OF INFORMATION at present available about the lives, personality traits, psychology,* social circumstances, political, religious and other
beliefs of senior business men, as members of a distinct social and functional
group, has been emphasized in this study. The following bibliography does not
claim to be complete. It ranges over the field covered by us, and indeed more
widely. Social anthropologists and others who glance through this book, and the
list of such authorities as it can cite, will be in no doubt about the desirability for
much more thorough research. Such first-hand information as we have been
able to collect and use, however, suggests that the first problem of properly-
equipped and qualified academic investigators will be to persuade the subject to
submit to study, either in the form of honest answers to a searching questionnaire,
or to a similar probing in a private interview. It is one thing to put junior managers
on the couch; another to interrogate men who make £20,000 a year and tend to be
contemptuous of academic investigators. A further difficulty is that those business
men who will show a reasonable degree of co-operation will not necessarily be
representative either of the business community as a whole, or of their industry,
region, or size and type of firm. If it were, however, possible to put a representative
sample of business men under skilled psychological and sociological investigation,
much would be learned on the subject of their incentives and everyday motives
and ethics which is now a matter of conjecture, eked out by such reference as is
possible to business men's own written testimony, and to the other sources set out
below.

1. TESTIMONY OF BUSINESS MEN

The main sources here are autobiographies and biographies. A cursory examination of these will show how less than frank they are. The most useful on British
business men are:

SAMUEL COURTAULD

Courtauld, Samuel, *Ideals and Industry*, C.U.P., 1949 (with a memoir by
Charles Morgan). Though not an autobiography, but a collection of papers,
this book gives valuable insight into a business man's way of looking at all
subjects from politics to labour relations and the philosophy of directorship.

F. H. CRITTALL (of Crittall Windows)

Crittall, F. H. and Ellen, *Fifty Years of Work and Play*, London, Constable,
1934. This gives, in some detail, an account of a business man's early years and
attitudes.

* Motives, goals, values, attitudes; what accounts for their obsessions, neuroses, ulcers,
and other ailments.

LORD LEVERHULME

Wilson, Charles, *The History of Unilever*, 2 Vois, London, Cassell, 1954. A large part of this book deals with the company's policy rather than the personality of its founder.

LORD NUFFIELD

Andrews, P. W. S. and Brunner, Elizabeth, *The Life of Lord Nuffield—A Study in Enterprise and Benevolence*, Oxford, Blackwell, 1955. The authors are mainly concerned with the development of the company and Lord Nuffield's benefactions. Only one chapter is devoted to describing Lord Nuffield himself and that is very limited in scope.

SIR THOMAS LIPTON

Waugh, A., *Lipton Story*, New York, Doubleday, 1950. This book is interesting, both for its description of how Lipton built up his business and, even more so, for its account of his sudden social prominence and friendship with King Edward VII.

LORD MELCHETT

Bolitho, Hector, *Alfred Mond, First Lord Melchett*, London, Secker, 1933. This book does examine the business methods and attitudes of the creator of I.C.I.; it can be supplemented by reference to Mond's own writings, notably *Industry and Politics*.

GORDON SELFRIDGE

Williams, A. H., *No Name on the Door: A Memoir of Gordon Selfridge*, London, W. H. Allen, 1956. A not purely adulatory description of Mr Williams's personal impressions of Mr Selfridge, for whom he worked. It portrays, unlike many business biographies, a credible human being with strengths, weaknesses and contradictions.

Others of very varying usefulness are:

Benn, Sir Ernest, *Confessions of a Capitalist*, London, Benn, 1928. (Publishing.)

Briggs, Asa, *Friends of the People* (Lewis's), Batsford, 1956. (Retail.)

Cohen, J. M., *The Life of Ludwig Mond*, London, Methuen, 1956. (Chemicals.)

Cole, G. D. H., *Robert Owen*, London, Benn, 1925. (Philanthropy.)

Crowther, S., *J. H. Patterson, 1844–1922*, London, 1923. (Retail family business.)

Driberg, T., *Beaverbrook*, London, Weidenfeld & Nicolson, 1956. (Newspapers.)

Gresswell, Fred, *Bright Boots*, London, Hale, 1956. (Auctioneering.)

Harrison, Godfrey, *Life and Belief in the Experience of John W. Laing, C.B.E.*, London, Hodder & Stoughton, 1954. (Building contracting.)

Lambert, R. S., *The Universal Provider*, London, Harrap, 1938. (Whiteley).

Mass Observation, *Browns and Chester*, Drummond Society. (Retailing family business.)

Leaf, Charlotte M., *Walter Leaf, 1852–1927*, London, Murray, 1932. (Banking and clothing.)

Spender, J. A., *Weetman Pearson, First Viscount Cowdray, 1856–1927*, London, Cassell, 1930. (Building, contracting.)

Smallwood, R. B., *Sir Thomas Lipton*. (Retailing.)

There are a few biographical collections and studies of sects or dynasties of business men, such as:

Allen, Trevor, *Roads to Success*, Kingswood (Surrey), World's Work, 1957.

Beable, W. H., *Romance of Great Businesses*, London, Cranton, 1926.

Brown, H., *Parry's of Madras, Parry & Co.*, 1954. (Exporting.)

Emden, Paul, *Quakers in Commerce*, London, Sampson Low, 1940.

Roth, C., *Sassoon Dynasty*, London, Robert Hale, 1941.

Urwick, Col. L., *The Golden Book of Management*, London, Newman Neame, 1956.

Urwick, L. and Brech, E., *The Making of Scientific Management*, Vol. I, Thirteen Pioneers, London, Management Publications Trust, 1949.

Various Authors: *Great Industries of Great Britain*, Cassell, *circa* 1880.

The main journals in which articles by or about business men in Britain are published are:

Scope, published by Creative Journals. This ran for some years a lively series of profiles of eminent business men interviewed by Miss Olive Moore; we are indebted to these for various business opinions quoted in this book.

The Director, the journal of the Institute of Directors; this is particularly useful for the reports of proceedings at conferences of company directors, who form the greater part of the business community studied in this book.

The Manager, published by the British Institute of Management, deals mainly with the practical problems of departmental management, but occasionally produces business men's reflections on the philosophy of their profession.

The British Manufacturer, the official organ of the National Union of Manufacturers, a body mainly concerned with pressuring the government on issues important to industry, e.g. the Restrictive Practices Act.

Business, published by Business Publications Ltd, deals with general business problems, extols private enterprise, and provides occasional valuable surveys on executive remuneration. Dr Copeman, its editor, has been responsible for two pioneering studies of business men quoted earlier.

The city journals, like the *Financial Times*, *The Economist*, etc., deal impersonally with economic issues and only occasionally turn to the vicissitudes of the directorial life. An important source of business men's opinions on their own condition is, of course, the annual statements of company chairmen to their shareholders; very few indeed of these venture to do more than report on the financial fortunes of the company in question. But when nationalization or the credit squeeze or inflation threatens any particular set of interests, company chairmen speak out. They rarely, however, give each other any support. Something, but very little, is to be gleaned from the 'official histories' of business firms which are becoming a way of achieving dignified publicity at the revenue's expense. These are two numerous to list here. We have consulted two score of them or more.

2. STUDIES OF EXECUTIVES

A number of studies of the careers and attributes of business men have been made by various authors, mostly social scientists, from a variety of standpoints; these are very much more frequent in America than in Britain (or the Continent). It is, as we have confessed, necessary to supplement the offerings of British research by American findings if any complete picture of business life is to be attempted. The very titles of American studies show the consideration give to the impact the business man has on society—and this in a country where business is far more secure than it is in Britain.

A. BRITISH

(i) Books

Acton Society Trust, *Management Succession*, London, Acton Society Trust, 1956.

Clements, R. V., *Managers: A Study of Their Careers in Industry*, London, Allen & Unwin, 1958.

Copeman, Dr G. H., *Leaders of British Industry*, a study of the careers of more than a thousand public company directors. London, Gee, 1955.

Copeman, Dr George, *Promotion and Pay for Executives*, London, Business Publications, 1957.

Creedy, F., *Human Nature in Business*, London, Benn, 1927.

Ord, Lewis C., *Secrets of Industry*, London, Allen & Unwin, 1944.

Steindl, J., *Small and Big Business*, Oxford, Blackwell, 1945.

(ii) Periodicals and Lectures

Hamilton, Sir P., 'Remuneration of Executives'. Paper given to the B.I.M. 1951 conference.

Hooper, F., Dunn C., *et al.*, 'What I think of British Management', *The Manager*, 1953.

Kennedy, Dr Alexander, 'Individual Reactions to Change as seen in Senior Management in Industry', *The Lancet*, 2 February 1957.

Marsh, John, 'Realities in Human Relationships', Industrial Welfare, Sept./Oct. and Nov./Dec. 1956.

Paterson, T. T., 'The New Profession of Management', *The Listener*, 6 December 1956.

Tronchin-James, Dr Nevil, 'The Toil of Power', *The Director*, February/July, 1957.

Tronchin-James, Dr Nevil, 'The Changing Manager', *The Manager*, March 1957.

Mayer, K., 'Business Enterprise': traditional symbol of opportunity. *British Journal Sociology*, June 1953.

B. AMERICAN

(i) Books and Reports

Brandeis, Louis, *Business—a Profession*, Boston, Small, Maynard, 1914.

Copeland, Melvin, J., *The Executive at Work*, Harvard University Press, 1952.

Diamond, Sigmund, *The Reputation of the American Business Man*, Harvard University Press, 1955.

Fetter, R. B. and Johnson, D. C., *Compensation and Incentives for Industrial Executives*, Bloomington, Indiana University Press, 1952.

Fortune, the Editors, *The Executive Life*, New York, Doubleday, 1956.

Gordon, R. A., *Business Leadership in the Large Corporation*, Washington, D.C., The Brookings Institution, 1945.

Houser, J. D., *What the Employer Thinks*, Cambridge, Harvard University Press, 1927.

Lundberg, F., *America's Sixty Families*, New York, Vanguard Press, 1937.

Maurer, Herrymon, *Great Enterprise, Growth and Behaviour of the Big Corporation*, New York, Macmillan, 1955.

Michigan Business Studies: *Management Compensation*: a statistical study of Executive Compensation to Capital Employed and Earnings, 1953.

Mills, Wright C., *The Power Élite*, New York, Oxford University Press, 1956.

National Industrial Conference Board, *Compensation and Pay for Executives*, 1949.

Newcomber, Mabel, *The Big Business Executive*: the Factors that Made Him. 1900–1950. New York, Columbia University Press, 1955.

Redich, F., *History of American Business Leaders*, Michigan, Edwards Bros, 1940.

Taussig, F. W. and Joslyn, C. S., *American Business Leaders*, New York, Macmillan, 1932.

Warner, Lloyd W. and Abegglen, James C., *Big Business Leaders in America*, New York, Harper, 1955, p. 92.

Wector, Dixon, *Saga of American Society*, New York, Scribner, 1937.

(ii) Periodicals

Fortune is, of course, a major source, and its studies, in its own style, are too numerous to list.

Alderson, Wroe, 'Social Adjustment in Business Management', *Expl. Entrepr. Hist.*, October, 1953.

Buozen, Y., 'Determinants of Entrepreneurial Ability', *Social Research*, Autumn, 1954.

Culver, John E., 'Group Comparison of the Personalities of Business Executives and College Professors', *MA Thesis*, Princeton, 1954.

Cochran, T. C., 'Entrepreneurial Behaviour and Motivation', *Expl. Entrepr. Hist.* II, 5.

Fairchild, Henry P., 'Business as an Institution', *American Sociological Review*, February 1937.

Henry, William E., 'The Business Executive: The Psychodynamics of a Social Role', *Am. J. Soc.*, January 1949.

Janney, J. Elliot, 'Company Presidents Look at Themselves', *Harvard Business Review*, Vol. XXX, May/June 1952.

McCaffrey, John L., 'What Corporation Presidents think about at Night', *Fortune*, September 1953.

Mills, C. Wright, 'The American Business Élite: A Collective Portrait', *J. Ec. Hist.*, December 1945.

Redlich, Fritz, 'The Business Leader as a "Daemonic" Figure', *Am. J. Ec. and Soc.*, January 1953.

Stauss, James H., 'The Entrepreneur: The Firm', *J. Pol. Ec.*, June 1944.

Wald, Robert M. and Doty, Roy A., 'The Top Executives—a Firsthand Profile', *Harv. Bus. Rev.*, July/August 1954.

C. EUROPEAN

Berliner, Joseph S., *Factory and Manager in U.S.S.R.*, Harvard University Press, 1957.

Carlson, Sune, *Executive Behaviour*, Stockholm, Stromberg, 1951.

Landes, David S., *French Business and the Business Man* in *Modern France*, ed., E. M. Earle, Princeton, 1951.

Lauterbach, Alfred, 'Managerial Attitudes in Western Europe', *American Economic Review*, Papers and Proceedings, May 1955.

Schlamm, W. S., 'European Business is Different', *Fortune*, February, 1950.

3. PHILOSOPHY OF MANAGEMENT

This subject is still largely an American preserve; British writers on management in the broadest sense tend to deal either in terms of labour relations, scientific management, or particular industrial problems. A few have invented business Utopias, which would make a separate subject in itself. The major British contributions seem to be:

Florence, Sargant P., *The Logic of British and American Industry*, London, Routledge, 1953.

Hammersley, S. S., *Industrial Leadership*, London, Simpkin, 1925.

Hutton, Graham, *We Too can Prosper*, London, Allen & Unwin, 1953.

Ord, Lewis C., *Industrial Facts and Fallacies*, London, Mayflower, 1950.

Renold, C. G., *Joint Consultation over Thirty Years*, London, Allen & Unwin, 1950.

Rowntree, B. S., *The Human Factor in Business*, London, Longmans, 1921.

Urwick, L., *The Making of Scientific Management*, Vol. II, London Management Publications Trust.

Even a short American list on this subject shows how American business men and business professors have taken the lead in developing the thesis that business —modern capitalism—can, through the institution of scientific management and public relations, develop a new type of society, neither collectivist nor yet capitalistic and competitive in the old sense. Whether they make their own case is another matter. The seminal books of this type, of which there are no British counterparts, are:

Burnham, James, *The Managerial Revolution*, N.Y., John Day 1941.

Drucker, Peter F., *Big Business*, London, Heinemann, 1947.

Drucker, Peter F., *The Practice of Management*, London, Heinemann, 1955.

Filene, E. A., *Successful Living in this Machine Age*, 1925.

Filene, E. A., *The Way Out*: A forecast of coming changes in American Business and Industry, N.Y., Doubleday, 1924.

Filene, A. L., *A Merchant's Horizon*, New York, Houghton Mifflin, 1924.

Ford, Henry, *Moving Forward*, Heinemann, 1951.

Mooney, J. D. and Riley, A. C., *Onward Industry*, New York, Harper, 1931.

Whitehead, A. N., *Leadership in a Free Society*, Oxford University Press, 1936.

Whyte, Wm. H., *The Organization Man*, London, Cape, 1957

4. THE PROFESSIONAL ECONOMISTS' VIEWPOINT

It is very difficult to find, throughout the vast range of economic science, much indication that economists ever took a detailed interest in business men as such, though economics and political ideals profoundly affect the climate of business life and thinking, difficult as this is to trace in operation. Only a few books will be cited here, therefore:

Marshall, A., *Industry and Trade*, especially Book II Chap. X, London, Macmillan, 1932. 3rd edition.

Mises, L. Von, *Human Action*, London, Hodge, 1949 (esp. p. 300 ff).

Robertson, D. H., *The Control of Industry*, London, Nisbet, 1936.

Samuelson, P. A., *Economics an Introductory Analysis*, Chapter 4, London, McGraw Hill, 1955.

Stocking, G. and Watkins, M., 'Monopoly. Free Enterprise', New York, Twentieth Century Fund, 1951.

Schumpeter, J. A. *Capitalism, Socialism and Democracy*, London, Allen & Unwin, 4th ed., 1954.

Wiles, P. J. D., *Price, Cost and Output*, Oxford, Blackwell, 1956.

There are, of course, plenty of controversial works campaigning for and against capitalism as such—far more than in America where British economists' defence of capitalism, on historical, theoretical or political grounds, is very highly esteemed, e.g.:

Clarke, V. N., *New Times, New Methods and New Men*, London, Allen & Unwin, 1950.
Hayek, J. A., *The Road to Serfdom*, London, Routledge, 1944.
Jewkes, John, *Ordeal by Planning*, London, Macmillan, 1948.
Parkinson, Hargreaves, *The Ownership of Industry*, London, Eyre & Spottiswoode, 1949.
Withers, H., *The Case for Capitalism*, London, Methuen, 1920.

and on the other side, e.g.:

Aaronovitch, S., *Monopoly, A Study of British Monopoly Capitalism*, London, Lawrence & Wishart, 1955.
Burns, C. Delisle, *Industry and Civilization*, London, Allen & Unwin, 1925.
Crosland, C. A. R., *The Future of Socialism*, London, Cape, 1956.
1948.
Reynolds, Clifton A., *A Simple Guide to Big Business*, London, Bodley Head,
Strachey, John, *Contemporary Capitalism*, London, Gollancz, 1956.
Strachey, John, *The Coming Struggle for Power*, London, Gollancz, 1935.

5. PROFESSIONAL MANUALS

There are innumerable manuals which offer to demonstrate how a man can either (a) make a fortune (b) build up a profitable business or (c) be a successful manager. These fall outside the scope of this study, but we have consulted a few of them aimed at British business men for the insight they give into the climate of business thinking at various periods. Artless or otherwise, a selected list of these are set out in order of date, here:

Defoe, D., *Compleat English Tradesman*, London, Rivington, 1726.
Platt, J., *Business*, Simpkin Marshall, 1878.
Boyle, Sir C. E., *Hints on Business*, 1900.
Casson, H., *Ads and Sales*, London, Efficiency Exchange, 1913.
Casson, H., *Axioms of Business*, London, Efficiency Exchange, 1915.
Murrell, William, *The Toady's Handbook*, London, Cayme Press, 1929.
Beaverbrook, Lord, *Success*, London, Stanley Paul, 1935.
Beaverbrook, Lord, *Don't Trust to Luck*, London, Express Newspapers, 1954.
Spade, M., *How to Run a Bassoon Factory*, London, Hamish Hamilton, 1950.
Whitehead, H., *How to Become a Successful Manager*, Allen & Unwin, 1956.
Wright, F., *Teach Yourself Business Organisation*, English Universities Press, 1957.

It is not necessary here to set out the innumerable manuals of business administration, which take up shelves of serious-minded managers' libraries or, even more important, the many books on boardroom procedure. Some of those who fortify themselves with these navigation aids might find a glance at books in the list above not unrewarding for their lighter moments. American books in this class probably outnumber British by about twenty to one; those given here are mainly British. Probably the most-read of all books by British business men, at least of the self-made variety, is Mr Dale Carnegie's *How to Win Friends and Influence People*, which has quite displaced *Self-Help*, by S. Smiles. Among neophytes in big business, S. Potter's works have a following, and all are reading *Parkinson's Law*, by C. Northcote Parkinson.

6. HISTORY

The materials for a history of business men, as opposed to economic history as such, are also scanty; and in some respects more has been done to investigate the lives and circumstances of business men in the early stages of capitalism than in the period immediately prior to our own. Two learned journals, both American, are devoted to this type of research: *Explorations in Entrepreneurial History*, issued by the Harvard University Research Centre in Entrepreneurial History and, to a lesser extent, *the Bulletin of the Business Historical Society* published in Cambridge, Massachusetts. Most of the articles published by these relate to America. The only general history of the business man—as opposed to economic history which deals with broad economic change and the development of industrial organization is Dr Miriam Beard's *A History of the Business Man*, Macmillan, New York, 1938. This racy volume, which covers the whole field from classical times and all countries contains an extensive bibliography which may be consulted and need not be repeated here. We have found it helpful in covering the narrower field from 1800 on, besides using the biographies entered in (1) to consult the following:

Allen, G. C., *The Industrial Development of Birmingham and the Black Country*, 1860–1927, Allen & Unwin, 1939.
Ashton, T. S., *The Industrial Revolution*, 1760–1830, Oxford University Press, 1948.
Bourne, H. R. F., *English Merchants*, London, Bentley, 1866.
Clapham, Sir J., *Economic History of England*, Cambridge, 1930-2.
Hayek, F. A., ed. *Capitalism and the Historians*, London, Routledge, 1954.
Holbrook, S. H., *Age of the Moguls*, N.Y., Doubleday, 1953.
Miller, W., ed., *Men in Business*: Essays in the History of Entrepreneurship, Harvard University Press, 1952.
Redford, A., *Manchester Merchants and Foreign Trade*, Manchester University Press, 1956.
Rees, J. A., *The English Tradition:* Heritage of the Venturers, London, Muller, 1934.
Sombart, W., *The Quintessence of Capitalism*, London, Fisher Unwin, 1915.
Tawney, R. H., *Religion and the Rise of Capitalism*, Penguins, 1948.
Thrupp, S. L., *Merchant Class in Medieval London*, Chicago, 1948.
Wantoch, A., *Magnificent Moneymakers*, London, Harmsworth, 1932.

7. THROUGH THE NOVELIST'S EYE

The way in which the novelist portrays the business man is important for several reasons. Firstly, his insight into the man behind the entrepreneurial or directorial façade is of direct value. Secondly, the attitude of novels (and plays) reflect the attitude of the intellectual world towards business men's values. Thirdly, because novelists to a very great extent use the findings of contemporary schools of political, social, and psychological theory, their appraisal of the business world influences the attitude of a much wider public. The importance of this has been recognized in America; cf. Chamberlain, J., 'The Business Man in Fiction', *Fortune*, November 1948. That article contains a very extensive bibliography of the major American novels about business—the British list is much shorter, because too few British novelists have so far seen the business man as an important figure in national life, nor life in business as a useful framework for the study of human nature. The business novel, however, has been the vehicle for studies in social change, conflict and struggle for power, and for the effect of social class on character, the perennial interest of the English novelists. A selected short list is appended:

PAST:

Bennett, Arnold, *The Card* [Self-made man].
Bennett, Arnold, *Imperial Palace* [Early Hotel take-over bids].
Dickens, Charles, *Dombey and Son* [Soullessness of Counting-house ambition].
Dickens, Charles, *Hard Times* [Labour relations at their worst].
Craik, Mrs, *John Halifax Gentleman* [Early industrial revolution; restrictive practices].
Fielding, Sarah, *The Adventures of David Simple* [1744, one of the earliest novels to describe English business life].
Trollope, Anthony, *The Way we Live Today* [Society and High Finance in the 1860s].
Wells, H. G., *Tono-Bungay* [Patent medicine advertising and bucket shops before 1914].
Wells, H. G., *The World of William Clissold* ['a successful, emancipated, semi-scientific, not particularly highbrow business man'—Keynes' judgment of Clissold].
Weyman, S. J., *Ovington's Bank* [County Banking before the Bank Act of 1844].

CONTEMPORARY:

Armstrong, Thomas, *The Crowthers of Bankdam* [Family business from 1860].
Balchin, N., *Sundry Creditors* [Family business, last phase].
Barnett, C., *The Hump Organization* [Management training].
Gutteridge, Berrard, *The Angency Game* [Advertising morals].
Bentley, P., *A Modern Tragedy* [Textiles in the great depression].
Bentley, P., *The Rise of Henry Morcar* [Memoirs of a successful textile manufacturer].
Blake, G., *The Shipbuilders* [Disintegration of a firm's board in shipbuilding depression].
Clewes, W., *Men at Work* [Wild cat strike].
Connell, V., *The Peacock is a Gentleman* [How to dress properly in business].
Cronin, A. J., *The Stars Look Down* [Profiteering and management succession].
Llewellyn, R., *How Green was my Valley* [South Wales Mine Owners].
Priestley, J. B., *Daylight on Saturday* [Work Study and the Managerial Revolution].
Priestley, J. B., *Angel Pavement* [Slick city finance].
Shute, N., *The Ruined City* [Merchant banker to the rescue of the shipbuilding industry].

Index